# IS AMERICA COMMITTING SUICIDE?

# IS AMERICA COMMITTING SUICIDE?

by Austin L. Sorenson
638 W. Bay Street Villas
Winter Garden, Florida 34787

SWORD of the LORD
PUBLISHERS
P.O. BOX 1099, MURFREESBORO, TN 37133

Printed and Bound in the United States of America

*To Catherine, faithful companion*

"The fall of a nation is always a suicide."
—Arnold Toynbee


"... *thou hast destroyed thyself.* ... "
—Hosea 13:9.

# TABLE OF CONTENTS

*"I have culled a bouquet of varied flowers from men's gardens, and nothing is my own but the string that binds them."*

French writer, unknown

# 1     the Collapse of a nation

*". . . our end is near, our days are fulfilled; for our end is come."*—Lam. 4:18.

*"There is no healing of thy bruise. . . . "*—Nahum 3:19.

The glory, the epitaph, and then the memory! Is that the way it will end? Will the radiant glory be lost in a terminal gasp? Is the curtain about to come down on the last act? Is that the future of the United States of America? The weeping Prophet Jeremiah warned a sinful Edom:

*". . . O thou that dwellest in the clefts of the rock, that holdest the height of the hill: though thou shouldest make thy nest as high as the eagle, I will bring thee down from thence, saith the Lord."*—Jer. 49:16.

Will the mighty exalted eagle now feed with the lowly sparrows in fallen mediocrity?

There is no doubt about the decadence of our nation. Man's hand blights everything he touches. A Republic begun in promise can finish in shame and despair. Will our roadsides bequeath to a subdued, vanquished generation only beer cans, empty whiskey bottles and cigarette butts? "If you don't know where you are going, any road will take you there." A people can lose their sense of direction.

The late President John F. Kennedy remarked, "We happen to be living in the most dangerous time in the history of the human race."

Arthur Krock, at one time associated with the *New York Times,* three times winner of the Pulitzer Prize, wrote: "I have a visceral fear; it is that the tenure of the United States as the first world power in the world may be the briefest in history."

The noted Alexander Solzhenitsyn is very dogmatic in his analysis: "The situation is not dire, the situation is not threatening—the situation is catastrophic."

## Committing Suicide on a National Scale

Nations, like men, are mortal and die at various stages. Some nations bloom for a comparatively short period of time, while others live on to senility.

Is America dying too young? Have we already reached senility? Did we become old too fast?

Ezekiel predicted a day of doom for Israel because as a people they had reached the limit of their years. "...and thou hast caused thy days to draw near, and art come even unto thy years..." (Ezek. 22:4). A nation can reach the limit of her years by choice.

Francis Bacon remarked that "it is as natural to die as it is to be born," but it is not natural to die too young. America, chronologically, is not old; in fact, the United States is just beginning to reach maturity.

Samuel Adams declared, "There never was a democracy that did not commit suicide." Historians agree that nations, like mortals, commit suicide. Some die old; some die young; some just fade away. Webster defines *suicide* as "the act or an instance of taking one's own life voluntarily and intentionally...." Suicide is literally killing one's self. America seems intent on destroying herself.

A nation can destroy itself by greed. In the frozen Arctic, wolves are desperate for food. The scent of blood can be detected at a great distance. Knowing this, the Eskimos devise a method by which the hungry wolves are captured. Small areas of ice are melted, and hunting knives are placed in the water concealing the handle. The blade protrudes through the ice and is covered with the blood of a seal, wolves or any blood that can be obtained.

Eskimos then retire to their homes and wait. Traveling in packs, the wolves catch the scent of blood and are soon ravenously licking the extended blades. The more their tongues lick the blood, the more their own blood flows. Eventually the wolves have lost so much of their own blood that they become weakened and die. They have literally destroyed themselves. They committed suicide.

Is America, like the foolish wolves, committing suicide for the same reason?

## The Fall of Civilizations

The statements have been made: "Every civilization is only twenty years from barbarism"; "Christianity is always one generation from extinction."

The question that confronts America today is: Will our Republic become a kind of terrestrial White Dwarf—a collapsed star in the galaxy of nations? Richard W. DeHaan gives this answer:

God will not permit cruel, oppressive, and immoral empires to endure unchecked. He normally does not overthrow them by miraculous raining of fire from Heaven or some other spectacular judgment, but by natural disasters, war and internal decay.

The empires of Egypt, Assyria, Babylon, Persia, Greece, and Rome all rose to prominence through the might of arms, flourished for a season, then collapsed in defeat. In every instance a major factor leading to their downfall was their selfish greed and gross immorality, first infecting the leaders and gradually spreading to include the general population.[1]

Our bankrupt cities could be a portent of our nation. Aubrey Menom, in his book, *Cities in the Sun,* makes this pertinent comment, "Now the interest is

## "Christianity is always one generation away from extinction."

piqued by a widespread feeling that we are witnessing the beginning of the end of our own."

Will our vaunted cities ever lie in ruins? Oliver Goldsmith, writing in the year 1759, described decadent London:

> What cities, as great as this, have...promised themselves immortality! Posterity can hardly trace the situation of some. The sorrowful traveller wanders over the awful ruins of others....Here stood their citadel, but now grown over with weeds; there their senate-house, but now the haunt of every noxious reptile; temples and theatres stood here, now only an undistinguished heap of ruins.

A public official of the bankrupt City of New York commented, "The dikes are crumbling, and we're running out of fingers."

### The Point of No Return

Much has been written about "The American Dream." The politicians glorify it; some insist that it will never be; others feel that it is irretrievably lost. The president of a denomination stated, "Civilization is in jeopardy. Our nation is more like ancient Rome than anyone would like to admit." One author is more dogmatic: "The fall of the Roman Empire was child's play compared to the state of the world today."

Has America reached the point of no return? Have we so declined that human solutions are no more tenable? A United States Senator warned, "The day of reckoning is now here. Our wealth has been dissipated, our strength undermined, our prestige and leadership in the community of nations greatly reduced, and the confidence of the American people in their government made a mockery."

It has been said, "America is running on the momentum of a godly ancestry; and when the momentum is spent, God help America!"

The remark is heard these days that "a politician thinks of the next election; a statesman thinks of the next generation." But the troubling question is—will there be another generation? Are we bearing the seeds of our own destruction? Is it possible that we have reached the point of no return?

## Positive Thinking in a Negative World

Diogenes, the Greek philosopher, told his followers, "Bury me on my face, for in a little while everything will be turned upside down." And it was.

What is the reaction of America today to its perilous condition? The doomsayers are having a field day. A presidential candidate stated, "As an historian, there is no hope for America. We are done for. . . ." Is it true that "man is fallible, political theories are relative and automatic progress is a mirage"?

Author James Michener, in an interview in *U.S. News and World Report,* made this observation:

> We've learned in the last ten years that we're not an immortal society. We're like every nation that's ever existed on earth. We have powers, we have strengths, we have weaknesses, and unless we keep them in balance, we—like every other great nation in world history—will go down.

The "positive thinkers" insist that everything is going to turn out all right. No calamities can befall a nation that is "positive" in its outlook. Our nation is still here and will be for a long time. In his book, *America,* Alistair Cooke comments, "Yet the original institutions of this country still have great vitality: the Republic can be kept, but only if we care to keep it."[2] It cannot be denied that "positive thinking" has much in its favor.

A church bulletin from a liberal Protestant church announced the sermon title: "Do Not Believe Doomsayers." No doubt the well-intentioned pastor told his congregation not to believe the prophets of doom. Their predictions were not to be taken seriously.

Today ministers are to "accentuate the positive." The negative aspects of the biblical message are to be minimized.

Robert Browning is often quoted: "God's in His Heaven—all's right with the world!" It is granted that "God's in His Heaven," but only a fool would say that "all's right with the world." While it is true that "optimism in the present day is reserved for Christians," one must be a realist. Is it being realistic to glow with a holy optimism in the face of Armageddon and the possible suicide of a nation? It is utter folly to conclude that "positive thinking" can keep back the judgment of God if a nation has sinned away its day of grace.

Every student of the Bible is aware that "the future is as bright as the promises of God," but also that "The wicked shall be turned into hell, and all the nations that forget God" (Ps. 9:17).

The prophets were not "positive thinkers." Their warning of coming judgment was very negative. Consider Micaiah and the passage in II Chronicles 18:12-16:

*"And the messenger that went to call Micaiah spake to him, saying, Behold, the words of the prophets declare good to the king with one assent; let thy word therefore, I pray thee, be like one of their's, and speak thou good.*

*"And Micaiah said, As the Lord liveth, even what my God saith, that will I speak.*

*"And when he was come to the king, the king said unto him, Micaiah, shall we go to Ramoth-gilead to battle, or shall I forbear? And he said, Go ye up, and prosper, and they shall be delivered into your hand.*

*"And the king said to him, How many times shall I adjure thee that thou say nothing but the truth to me in the name of the Lord?*

*"Then he said, I did see all Israel scattered upon the mountains, as sheep that have no shepherd. . . . "*

Note the fate of God's servant who was true to his calling:

*". . . Thus saith the king, Put this fellow in the prison, and feed him with bread of affliction and with water of affliction, until I return in peace.*

*"And Micaiah said, If thou certainly return in peace, then hath not the Lord spoken by me. . . . "*—Vss. 26, 27.

The man of God who declares "the whole counsel of God" will not be the most popular preacher in town. John the Baptist lost his head because of his "negative" preaching. Will today's prophets fare much better?

"Positive thinkers" fail to take into account the divine plan of the ages outlined in biblical prophecy. Armageddon precedes the millennium. It is going to get darker before it becomes brighter. "History shows too many times where the majority led a society over the abyss and where the truth was to be found in a minority report."

Eventually nations like individuals bow to the sovereignty of God. "The Lord hath prepared his throne in the heavens; and his kingdom ruleth over all" (Ps. 103:19).

The future of America is not found in a political party nor in the reasonings of men but in the hands of an Almighty God. The saintly F. B. Meyer expressed it this way:

> True, the sky before us may be dark with storm clouds. The weather prophets say that the world is shedding its old sanctions without replacing them with better ones, that seven civilizations have already passed and we are to see the death of the eighth.
>
> Be it so, but they forget that God holds the stormy waters in the hollow of His hand, that Jesus walked the threatening billows to succor His friends. They forget that, when the earth was without form and void, the Spirit of God brooded in the chaos and darkness, creating the heavens and earth. They cannot detect the voice of the Creator, saying, "Behold, I make all things new!"
>
> Out of chaos is born the cosmos. Each age ends in travail, out of which a new age is born.[3]

## God's Laws Don't Bend

**He who holds no laws in awe,
He must perish by the law.**
—Byron

Since the laws of God are immutable, the day of reckoning for America cannot be too far away. F. B. Meyer stated it well: "God's ways are the great principles on which He acts, the mighty thoroughfare of creation, providence, revelation, human history and final judgment."

Note the Second Law of Thermodynamics: "That all organized systems tend to slide slowly into chaos and disorder. Energy tends to run down. The universe itself heads inevitably toward darkness and stasis."

According to Oswald Spengler, the prescribed stages of culture are "spring, summer, autumn and winter, and then fade away. World history is the sum of such cultures."

The historians Oswald Spengler and Arnold Toynbee believe that nations rise and fall in cycles. This cyclical process involves birth, maturity and death. A Christian believes that God in His sovereignty controls the periods. The fading and disappearance of nations is in the hands of Deity.

Is this the final cycle for America? It has often been stated that a progressive cycle is experienced by the nations as follows:

"From bondage to spiritual faith; from spiritual faith to great courage; from courage to liberty; from liberty to abundance; from abundance to selfishness; from selfishness to complacency; from complacency to apathy; from apathy to dependence; from dependence to bondage."

There is no doubt where we are in this cycle.

Hyman Appelman informs us of the two major laws of history—the "law of periodics" and the "law of progressions": The "law of periodics" manifests itself when

> a barbarian, semi-civilized, vigorous nation, almost always lower in the stage of culture and civilization, is used by the hand of God to bring to time, even to punish the more refined people. . . . The "law of progressions" is simply this. In the history of every nation, with the exception of one, there have been four consecutive, well-defined periods: The Period of Discovery and Colonization, the Period of Expansion and Cultivation, the Period of Leisure and Luxury, the Period of Deterioration and Destruction. The periods well nigh define themselves.[4]

## Is the Period of Destruction at Hand?

Moral laws cannot be broken without impunity. France is an example. "What tragic words were in that requiem which Marshal Pétain pronounced over fallen France: 'Our spirit of enjoyment was stronger than our spirit of sacrifice. We wanted to have more than we wanted to give. We tried to spare effort and met disaster.'"

France should have learned from Napoleon. Marshal Foch wrote of him: ". . . in my view the deep reason for the disaster that overwhelmed him must be sought elsewhere. He forgot that a man cannot be God; that above the individual there is the nation; that above man there is moral law."[5]

The law of the harvest is immutable. The destruction of a nation follows the rejection of the principles of God's Word. Back in 1893 J. C. Ryle, a distinguished clergyman, warned his congregation thus:

> God's sorest judgments, the ancients said, are like millstones; they grind very slowly, but they grind very fine. The thing that I fear most for my country is gradual insensible dry-rot and decay.
>
> But of one thing I am sure. The state that begins by sowing the seed of national neglect of God will, sooner or later, reap a national disaster and national ruin.

Is America about to reap what she has sown?

## Until There Was No Remedy

The Holy Scriptures are replete with warnings to the disobedient nations of the earth. Consider Israel:

*"But they mocked the messengers of God, and despised his words, and*

*misused his prophets, until the wrath of the Lord arose against his people, till there was no remedy."*—II Chron. 36:16.

*"Therefore will I also deal in fury: mine eye shall not spare, neither will I have pity: and though they cry in mine ears with a loud voice, yet will I not hear them."*—Ezek. 8:18.

*"This is the rejoicing city that dwelt carelessly, that said in her heart, I am, and there is none beside me: how is she become a desolation, a place for beasts to lie down in! every one that passeth by her shall hiss, and wag his hand."*—Zeph. 2:15.

America has had her prophets. America has been blessed with an abundance of light.

Individuals commit suicide because they lose the will to live. Death appears to be the only avenue of escape. Thus it is with nations. It is possible for the

---

## "Our spirit of enjoyment was stronger than our spirit of sacrifice. We wanted to have more than we wanted to give. We tried to spare effort and met disaster."

—Marshal Pétain over fallen France

---

spirit of apathy to eventually strangle a nation. The "we-don't-care" syndrome results in spiritual lethargy causing a terminal condition.

Emma Lazarus wrote in her inscription on the Statue of Liberty:

> ...Give me your tired,
> your poor,
> Your huddled masses yearning
> to breathe free....

The "huddled masses" have become indifferent. Freedom has become a tarnished word. "The lamp beside the golden door" no longer glows with pristine glory.

Have we lost our will to live? Do we no longer possess the instinct of self-preservation? When the first dynasty was falling into ruins on an Egyptian tomb, someone inscribed the words, "And no one is angry enough to speak out." "Future historians, when writing on the decline and fall of the American Republic, will wonder most at the indifference of the people who had the most to lose."

William Howard Taft declared, "Too many people don't care what happens as long as it doesn't happen to them."

John Greenleaf Whittier aptly penned these words in his day:

> Where's the manly spirit of the truehearted and the unshackled gone? Sons of old freemen, do we but inherit their names alone? Is the old pilgrim spirit quench'd within us? Stoops the proud manhood of our souls so low that mammon's lure or party's wile can win us to silence now?
>
> Now, when our land to ruin's brink is verging, in God's name let us speak while there is time; now, when the padlock for our lips is forging, silence is a crime.

Walter A. Maier, noted radio preacher of the past generation, made these remarks on one of his broadcasts:

> We stand aghast at the unconcern of human leaders in the pivotal moments of history. When Rome was besieged by Alaric and his Goths, Emperor Honorius was more concerned about the safety of his prize poultry than the destiny of the imperial city. After a panting messenger brought the news, "Rome is lost," he sighed in relief when he learned that it was not his favorite pullet named "Rome," but that it was the capitol that had been destroyed!
>
> There have always been those who toyed and dallied when they should have led the forces of righteousness and truth.
>
> —Copyright 1980 by *Christian Herald*. Used by permission.

Will America heed the warning? Who is so deaf as he who will not hear nor so blind as he who will not see? Someone has penned, "If free men lost their freedom, it was because they were too apathetic to take note while the precious waters of God-given freedom slipped, drop by drop, down the drain." A clergyman commented, "The blackest part of the picture is the inaction of America." "A friend is one who warns you."

A student in Chicago had a room next to the fire station. He did not sleep for the first few nights because of the blare of the fire alarms. However, he soon got used to it. In fact, one night the building next to him burned completely to the ground, and he slept right through the entire fire.

Are we sleeping through the fire? Who pays any attention to those sounding out the warnings of coming judgment? Who is listening to God's prophets?

One might ask, Where are the prophets? The manager of a ten-story office building was informed that a man was trapped in an elevator between the second and third floors. He rushed to the grillwork under the stalled elevator and called to the passenger, "Keep cool, sir. We'll have you out soon. I've phoned for the elevator mechanic." There was a brief pause; then a tense voice answered, "I am the mechanic."

*"Physician, heal thyself."*—Luke 4:23.

"Due to lack of interest, tomorrow has been canceled." The question is, will there be a tomorrow? The weeping Prophet Jeremiah declared, ". . . her sun is gone down while it was yet day. . ." (Jer. 15:9). The glory departed too quickly.

If there is a future, are we ready for it? "Hell is truth seen too late." "The future of the future is in the present."

The Scripture warns: "Boast not thyself of to morrow; for thou knowest not what a day may bring forth" (Prov. 27:1).

---

# "It must be of the spirit if we are to save the flesh."

*—General Douglas MacArthur*

---

Is there an answer to our perilous predicament, a solution to our sordid problems? Will evil triumph over good? The psalmist gave this explanation: "Until I went into the sanctuary of God; then understood I their end" (73:17).

These words were seen on a bumper sticker, **GOD BLESS AMERICA— AND PLEASE HURRY!**

The urgency of the hour demands that we look beyond ourselves for divine directions. The wise Solomon in the Old Testament penned the abiding truth: "Righteousness exalteth a nation: but sin is a reproach to any people" (Prov. 14:34). Jeremiah wrote: "Thus saith the Lord, Stand ye in the ways, and see, and ask for the old paths, where is the good way, and walk therein, and ye shall find rest for your souls. [Note the sad response of the nation:] But they said, We will not walk therein" (Jer. 6:16). Toward the close of his life, Herbert Hoover spoke these significant words:

> The principal thing we can do if we really want to make the world over again is to try the word *old* for awhile. There are some *old* things that made this country. . . .
> There is the *old virtue* of religious faith. . . . But some of these things are slipping badly in American life. And if they slip too far, the lights will go out of America, even if we win these cold and hot wars. Think about it.[6]

George Sweeting reminds us, "Dying civilizations are the sum total of dying individuals." Savonarola, fiery prophet of his day, warned, "The time of singing and dancing is at an end; now is the time to shed tears for thy sins."

Standing on the battleship *U.S. Missouri* in Tokyo harbor September 2, 1945, General Douglas MacArthur uttered these profound, memorable statements:

> We have had our last chance. If we do not now devise some greater and more equitable system, Armageddon will be at our door. The problem is basically theological and involves a spiritual recrudescence. . . . It must be of the spirit if we are to save the flesh.

America does not have time for a comfortable decay. America is Sodom and Gomorrah ripening for the kill. Walter J. Chantry gives this vivid description:

> Once there was a great society. It was the envy of its neighbors. The citizens of this region were quite proud that they had excelled all known civilizations. No one could criticize the land without great resentment arising from community pride.
>
> The land was situated in the most productive area of the world. Natural resources abounded. There was plenty of land and water. Natural beauty marked the nation's borders. The people believed that God had smiled upon them in a special manner. And indeed He had.
>
> Most plentiful were the riches of this formidable nation. Almost every family was well fed. Eating held a great deal of attention, and no one can deny that the people of this region ate more than enough. Some suggested that the indulgence in food and wine was excessive. Others used the word *gluttony*. At any rate, many were fat.
>
> Prosperity began to mark the great society. So copious was the dominion's wealth that no one had to work long hours to earn a living. Everyone had many leisure hours. Entertainment and recreation began to command a larger portion of each day. Relaxation and ease were a way of life.
>
> But with the advent of luxurious ease, immorality began to increase. The crime rate was a problem. The divorce rate rose. Sexual promiscuity was rumored at all levels of society.
>
> More base forms of sexual perversion arose out of long hours of leisure. Sometimes horrible sexual orgies were reported. Homosexuality increased sharply. Men became more open in their filthy practices. It was dangerous for decent women to walk the streets. Some voices of protest were raised, but law enforcement was ineffective.
>
> The nation was not anti-religious. Increased attendance at worship was part of the great society. But people were modern. They did not feel that their actions were inconsistent with their faith. After all, a new age demands a new morality. Their church leaders pleased them by being relevant to the times.

One morning as the sun rose, all was normal. A few were about their jobs, but most were late risers. This made sense after a late night of fun, and then the day's work would not be too long.

But suddenly the land was engulfed in flame! The country was utterly destroyed in a dreadful holocaust. Only three citizens of the large population survived. The beautiful land became a barren wasteland. God had finally had His fill of impudent rebellion against His Law by His creatures.

This is a true history! The name of the society was SODOM (Gen. 13 and 19; Ezek. 16). It is rumored that she has a younger sister nation—AMERICA!

*—Puritan Publications,* used by permission.

Is the greatest nation in the world destined for the ash heap? Is it inevitable? Are we hastening that demise? Is the United States of America committing suicide?

A study of the past and a survey of the present should give us our answers.

## ENDNOTES:

[1] Richard DeHaan, *The Art of Staying Off Dead-End Streets*, 130.

[2] Alistair Cooke, *America*, 387.

[3] F. B. Meyer, *Our Daily Walk*, 270.

[4] Hyman Appelman, *Formula for Revival*, 10.

[5] Roy L. Laurin, *Life Endures*, 239-40.

[6] Eugene Lyons, *Herbert Hoover*, 426.

# history Is his Story

## The Value of History

A tour guide was eloquently describing the glories of the Greek Parthenon, declaring the marvels of the Golden Age of Greece. A bored listener yawned and remarked, "Yeah, that is some pile of rock," and wondered when the lecture would end so she could eat lunch at the hotel. A meal was more important to her than an account of one of the greatest cities of history.

It has been said, "There are three classes of people in the world today: those who make things happen, those who watch things happen, and those who don't know anything has happened"; and, "The reason history repeats itself is that most people weren't listening the first time."

Nikita Krushchev, in a rash moment, bragged, "History is on our side; we will bury you." Evidently he felt the importance of studying the past.

The ancient civilizations, particularly the historic cities, have tales to tell; and the stones cry out passionately pleading that our frivolous hurried generation take time to listen. Not only do the ghosts of the past have tales to tell; they have very important lessons to teach. It must have been a student of history who warned, "It is a dull ear that cannot hear the mutterings of the oncoming storm."

Henry Ford disdainfully remarked that "history is bunk," and others have given the same evaluation. It has been designated "the great dust heap," "the mere scum of events," "a confused heap of facts" and "facts that never happened written by ghosts."

A Welsh proverb relates, "Human history is similar to the heroic tales pigs relate to swine." Longfellow is most devastating in his remarks: "The history of the past is a mere puppet show. A little man comes out and blows a little trumpet and goes in again. You look for something new, and lo, another little man comes out and blows another little trumpet and goes in again. And it is all over."

Historians are more than "flocks of tiny bird-like old men who nest in eery piles of dirty yellow paper and brood their myths and memories into monumental Lives-and-Letters." It is my contention that there is great merit in the study of history. Cicero declared, "To be ignorant of the past is to remain a child." "The future cannot be seen clearly without the past." "An historian is a prophet turned backward" (Schlagel). Lamartine asserted, "History teaches everything, even the future." The country parson is very practical: "History is important. It tells us what we wish to go back to." In an interview, Robert Penn Warren, noted author, remarked: "But today people are interested only in now and tomorrow. They don't seem to realize that you can't see the future without the past."

Herbert J. Muller comments:

> Although the practical value of a knowledge of history is commonly exaggerated . . . men do not appear to learn readily from the mistakes of their ancestors, and historians themselves are not always conspicuous for their wisdom. . . .
>
> History has also been described as a series of messes, but only by a historical analysis can we determine how we got into the latest mess and how we might get out of it. The very idea that we are in a mess involves assumptions about the "natural" course of affairs, as do all policies for dealing with it. . . .
>
> In any event, we are forever drawing upon the past. It not only constitutes all the "experience" by which we have learned: it is the source of our major interests, our claims, our rights and our duties. It is the source of our very identity.
>
> In an eternal present, which is a specious present, the past is all we know. And as the present is forever slipping back, it reminds us that we too shall in time belong wholly to the past.[1]

Thomas Carlyle describes history as "a mighty drama, enacted upon the theatre of time, with suns for lamps and eternity for background." James Garfield exclaimed that history was an "unrolled scroll of prophecy."

The word *historia* has an informative connotation. The Latin gives the thought of "a narrative of past events," while the Greek portrays the idea of "a learning or knowing by inquiry, the knowledge so obtained, information." *The American Encyclopaedic Dictionary* gives the definition: *"The record of the most important bygone events in human history, chronologically arranged, with an inquiry into their causes and the lessons which they afford with regard to human conduct."*

## Archaeology and History

History and Archaeology are good friends, speaking the same language and giving an identical message. Archaeology may be "dry as dust," but it has substantiated history. Ancient empty cities are not empty. Their ghosts remain to haunt us; and to those who will listen, they will reveal secrets of the past. They lived and saw the glories of other years and the following sunset and bequeathed to us a priceless heritage. The ancient ground still speaks, but its message is not always pleasant.

> # The ancient civilizations, particularly the historic cities, have tales to tell; and the stones cry out passionately pleading that our frivolous, hurried generations take time to listen.

It has been said that, "next to the written Scriptures, the science of archaeology is the most exact interpretation of the Divine revelation within the reach of human faith and understanding."[2]

Oliver Wendell Holmes paid this tribute to the science: "The spade...has fed the tribes of mankind. It has furnished water, coal, iron and gold. And now it is giving them truth—historic truth."

John Elder in 1960 wrote *Prophets, Idols and Diggers (Scientific Proof of Bible History)*. In the concluding chapter he makes this significant statement, quoting another reputable scholar:

> There can be no conclusion to our survey of the magnificent panorama of history as it is contained in the Bible and enriched by the findings of archaeology. To a degree that once would have been deemed incredible, the careful accuracy of the Bible picture has been repeatedly confirmed.

> The scholar, Dr. Nelson Glueck, after many years of study and personal exploration of the Holy Land, has this to say: "As a matter of fact...it may be stated categorically that no archaeological discovery has ever controverted a Biblical reference. Scores of archaeological findings have been made which confirm in clear outline or in exact detail historical statements in the Bible."[3]

Bible believers are not afraid of the spade. Jesus Christ Himself declared:

"I tell you that, if these [people] should hold their peace, the stones would immediately cry out" (Luke 19:40). Karl Sabiers makes this observation:

> Today, there is a certain sense in which Jesus' statement is literally fulfilled. At the present time it seems that we actually have "stones crying out"—stones witnessing and testifying to the glory of God.
>
> You may ask, "How can this be?" "In what way?" The amazing story of archaeology will show us how certain stones have voices and witness and testify to the glory of God by proving that His Word, the Bible, is true—true even in every minute detail....
>
> The stone tablets, the stone and bricks and pottery of ancient cities, have cried out with strong voices to witness and testify to the glory of God—to prove that His Word is true and that the critics are wrong.
>
> When men ridicule God's Word and refuse to glorify Him, then God causes stones to cry out instead. We are living in such a day—a day in which archaeological discoveries, discoveries of stones, clay tablets, pottery, etc., prove that the Bible accounts are true....
>
> The archaeological discoveries in Bible lands are one of God's answers to modernism and unbelief. Is it not remarkable that archaeologists made their discoveries so soon after the critics began their destructive work of unbelief? We thank God for archaeology and the way in which it proves that His Word is true.[4]

We can trust God's Word to interpret history. Events do not just happen. There is a divine purpose in history. Lowell wrote:

**Truth forever on the scaffold, Wrong forever on the throne;**
**Yet that scaffold sways the future; and behind the dim unknown**
**Standeth God within the shadow, keeping watch above His own.**

## The Inexorable Facts of History

Arnold Toynbee remarked: "When we try to repudiate the past, it has, as Horace knew, a sly way of coming back on us in a thinly disguised form."

Declining cities and eventually decaying nations submit to history. A study of the past discloses that history has a destination with a beginning and an end. Oliver Wendell Holmes, Jr., declared, "A page of history is worth a volume of logic."

History has something to teach us. In the book of Ezra we read, "That search may be made in the book of the records of thy fathers..." (4:15). A noted theologian said, "Our destiny is bound up with the rediscovery of our heritage; and the road to Tomorrow leads through Yesterday." The venerable Patrick Henry exclaimed, "I know of no way of judging the future but by the past."

The Almighty has a definite role in the affairs of nations. "All history is but the goings of God if a man rise high enough to see it." Defeated in battle, the crestfallen Napoleon confessed, "God Almighty has been too much for me." J. Lanahan declared, "God is in the facts of history as truly as He is in the march of the seasons, the revolutions of the planets, or the architecture of the worlds." In his classic, *Romans Verse by Verse,* William R. Newell gives the divine analysis of the "All-seeing Historian" as he comments on Romans 3:16: "Destruction and misery are in their ways":

> What an epitome of human history. It is said that the ancient Troy of which Homer sang was built upon the ruins of an earlier Troy—and that seven other Troys, each constructed upon the ruins of a former, have been found! As Meyer vividly renders: "Where they go is desolations (fragments) and misery (which they produce)."
>
> Those who so loudly proclaim that the human race is "improving," "progressing," are blind deceivers—blind to history, blind to present-day facts, blind to the rising tide of human violence.[5]

"The highways of history are strewn with the wreckage of the nations that forgot God." "It is when the conflict is over history comes to a right understanding of the strife, and he is ready to exclaim, 'Lo, God is here, and we know it not!' " (Bancroft).

## The Lessons of History

Is it not true that "history is recorded so that we may avoid the errors of the past"? History has lessons to teach, and it would be good for her pupils to pay attention.

Aristotle (then followed by Santayana and others) made the famous statement, "Those who don't know history are doomed to repeat it."

In front of the National Archives Building in Washington, D.C., are written the words, THE PAST IS PROLOGUE; STUDY THE PAST. An antique shop window displayed this inscription, "There's no present like the past." Patrick Henry was more specific: "I have no light to illuminate the pathway of the future save that which falls over my shoulder from the past."

Hegel wrote: "What history teaches is that men have never learned anything from it, or at least their knowledge has not availed against the ancient enemy." Pearl Buck, noted author, declared: "If you want to understand today, you must search yesterday." Madame Chiang Kai-shek gave this good advice: "We live in the present, we dream of the future, but we learn eternal truths from the past."

When the famed historian, Charles A. Beard, was asked if he could summarize the great lessons of history, he replied in four short sentences: "(1) Whom the gods would destroy, they first make mad with power. (2) The mills of the gods grind slowly, but they grind exceedingly fine. (3) The bee fertilizes the flower it robs. (4) When it is dark enough, you can see the stars."

Why are we so slow to comprehend the lessons of the past? Coleridge wrote, "If men could learn from history, what lessons it might teach us! But passion and party blind our eyes, and the light which experience gives is a lantern on the stern which shines only on the waves behind us." It appears obvious: "History teaches everything, even the future." And, "In today walks tomorrow."

## Divine Sovereignty in History

Someone noted, "Without divine direction, history becomes a tale told by an idiot." Winston Churchill was cognizant of this fact as he addressed the United States Congress on December 26, 1941, with these dramatic words: "He must indeed have a blind soul who cannot see that some great purpose and design is being worked out here below...." Years before, Benjamin Franklin, speaking at the Constitutional Convention in Philadelphia, testified

> # We can trust God's Word to interpret history. Events do not just happen. There is a divine purpose....

in June, 1787: "The longer I live the more convincing proofs I see that God governs in the affairs of men; and if a sparrow cannot fall to the ground without His notice, is it probable that an empire can rise without His aid?" Closer to our era of time, D. L. Moody spoke the truth: "A Christian on his knees sees more than the philosopher on tiptoe."

Arnold Toynbee is considered by some to be "the greatest historian of the twentieth century." In his voluminous book, *Cities of Destiny,* he relates how certain famous cities became "cities of doom." Although he would not be classified as a student of the Scriptures, he does make some significant statements. Herbert Muller quotes him as follows:

> Our one hope of salvation, Toynbee asserts, is a return to the "One True God" from whom we have fallen away: "We may and must pray" that God will grant our society a reprieve if we ask for it "in a contrite spirit and with a broken heart." In effect, he seems to be saying that only a miracle can save us. I think he may be right.[6]

Does history repeat itself? The Preacher in the book of Ecclesiastes gives this answer:

*"The thing that hath been, it is that which shall be; and that which is done is that which shall be done: and there is no new thing under the sun. Is there any thing whereof it may be said, See, this is new? it hath been already of old time, which was before us."*—Eccles. 1:9,10.

Cowper spoke a great truth in his statement, "God works in mysterious ways His wonders to perform." A Christian cannot always trace His hand, but he acknowledges the presence of Deity. Winston Churchill put it this way:

The human story does not always unfold like a mathematical calculation on the principle that two and two make four. Sometimes in life they make five or minus three; and sometimes the blackboard topples down. . . and leaves the class in disorder and the pedagogue with a black eye.

## The Vengeance of History

There is a vengeance to history—the Almighty always gets the last word. Joseph Parker declared, "We lose hold of history when we lose hold of God." Trotsky, the brilliant, misled communist, wrote before his death: "Nero, too, was a product of an epoch. But after he perished, his statues were smashed and his name scraped off everything. The vengeance of history is more terrible than the vengeance of the most powerful Secretary General."

There is a glory and a horror to history.

It is assuring to know that the sovereign God controls the universe and governs the affairs of finite men. The Prophet Isaiah uttered a great truth when he asserted, "I have even from the beginning declared it to thee; before it came to pass I shewed it thee. . . " (Isa. 48:5). Jesus Christ Himself warned, "But take ye heed: behold, I have foretold you all things" (Mark 13:23).

The Lord Jesus Christ is the ultimate end of all history. "For of him, and through him, and to him, are all things: to whom be glory for ever" (Rom. 11:36). The Son of God, "the Alpha and Omega," is the One who divides what men call time.

It is thus that we study history. The ancient Aristotle was correct when he said, "In most respects the future will be like the past has been." A famous French writer once remarked: "If one neglects history in favor of current affairs, first, one does not know history, and second, one does not understand current affairs."

The late C. S. Lewis wrote, "Those who do not know history will be the victims of recent bad history." Voltaire concluded: "History is the sound of soft, silken slippers coming down the stairs and the thunder of hobnail boots going up." Wrote John B. Crozier: "The present is ever a mystery to us until it is irradiated by the knowledge of the past."

Christopher Lasch in his book gives this evaluation: "Our culture's indifference to the past—which easily shades over into active hostility and rejection—furnishes the most telling proof of that culture's bankruptcy."[7]

Looking backward, we move forward. Disraeli made a profound statement when he remarked, "Men moralize among ruins." It seems they are trying to tell us something. The ancient civilizations, and particularly their cities, have a tale to tell; and when it is finished, the discerning will agree that history is His story.

Do we have time to listen?

## ENDNOTES:

[1]Herbert J. Muller, *The Uses of the Past*, 30, 31.

[2]Harold M. DuBose, "Archaeology and the Bible," *Gospel Herald* January 27, 1945: 139.

[3]John Elder, *Prophets, Idols and Diggers: Scientific Proof of Bible History*, 231.

[4]Karl Sabiers, "How Archaeology Proves the Bible," *The Evangel* January, 1974: 10, 11.

[5]William R. Newell, *Romans Verse by Verse*, 84.

[6]Muller, x.

[7]Christopher Lasch, *The Culture of Narcissism*, 25.

# 3    the handwriting on the Wall

---

## Babylon the Great

---

*"Is not this great Babylon?"*—Dan. 4:30.

"Thou art this head of gold" (Dan. 2:38). So declared the inspired Daniel to the mighty monarch Nebuchadnezzar by divine revelation, and so the historians confirm.[1]

Babylon was "the greatest and richest city of the ancient East."[2] Between the Euphrates and Tigris Rivers is one of the most important geographical sites in the world. History began in the Garden of Eden. There are those who believe that the Garden of Eden was located in Mesopotamia. Genesis 2:8-15 gives us the following facts:

*"And the Lord God planted a garden eastward in Eden; and there he put the man whom he had formed.*

*"And out of the ground made the Lord God to grow every tree that is pleasant to the sight, and good for food; the tree of life also in the midst of the garden, and the tree of knowledge of good and evil.*

*"And a river went out of Eden to water the garden; and from thence it was parted, and became into four heads.*

*"The name of the first is Pison: that is it which compasseth the whole land of Havilah, where there is gold;*

*"And the gold of that land is good: there is bdellium and the onyx stone.*

*"And the name of the second river is Gihon: the same is it that compasseth the whole land of Ethiopia.*

*"And the name of the third river is Hiddekel: that is it which goeth toward the east of Assyria. And the fourth river is Euphrates.*

*"And the Lord God took the man, and put him into the garden of Eden to dress it and to keep it."*

It was also in this historic region that the splendor and majesty of ancient Babylon appeared on the pages of history. The "center of government, law, art, religion, science and culture"—its importance is matched only by its historical significance. This is confirmed in the volume, *Cradle of Civilization*, by Samuel Noah Kramer (and the editors of *Time-Life* books):

> But unprepossessing though this region appears today, no other place on earth holds deeper significance for the history of human progress. In this land cradled by the rivers man first became civilized. Here some 5,000 years ago, a people known as the Sumerians developed the world's earliest true civilization from roots extending far back into the dimness of prehistory.
>
> It was Mesopotamia that saw the rise of man's first urban centers with their rich, complex and varied life, where political loyalty was no longer to the tribe or clan but to the community as a whole; where lofty ziggurats, or temple-towers, rose skyward, filling the citizen's heart with awe, wonder and pride; where art and technological ingenuity, industrial specialization and commercial enterprise found room to grow and expand.[3]

Ancient Babylon plays a prominent role in ancient history:

> *Civilization* is a many-splendored word that to some people means big cities and technological progress; to others, lofty moral, ethical ideas and major achievements in the arts. By any of these criteria, Mesopotamia was the birthplace of civilization, for it was the first place in which man created and sustained—for more than 3,000 years—an urban, literate, technologically sophisticated society, one whose people shared common values and a common view of the origins and order of the world.[4]

Robert Silverberg writes concerning this region:

> The area was called, in the Old Testament, Aram-naharaim—"The Land Between the Two Rivers." The Greek word meaning the same thing is *Mesopotamia*, and it is by that name that the ancient region is called today.
>
> As time passed Mesopotamia by, the great kingdoms crumbled and were destroyed. Only legends remained of the once mighty empires of the Tigris-Euphrates region. They told of fierce kings, of wise priests, of cities with incredibly lovely gardens, of towers that nearly reached the heavens.[5]

Historians have noted that, when the West was still a wilderness and wild animals roamed on the future sites of Athens and Rome, ancient Babylon was laying the foundation for arts and sciences, law and literature that characterized the great civilizations yet to come.

*Unger's Bible Dictionary* informs us that Babylon was

> an ancient city-state in the plain of Shinar derived from Accadian "bibilu" ("the gate of God"). The name is derived from the root "balal" ("to

confound"), and has reference to the confusion of tongues and the Tower (Gen. 11:9). Thus the biblical writer refutes any God-honoring connotation of the name.[6]

Babylon is replete with the names of famous places and personalities—the Garden of Eden, the Tower of Babel, the Hanging Gardens, Nimrod, Hammurabi, Nebuchadnezzar, Belshazzar, Daniel, Alexander the Great, Napoleon.

The city of Babylon goes back to antiquity. Nimrod is considered its founder and builder. He was known as "a mighty hunter before the Lord...and the beginning of his kingdom was Babel" (Gen. 10:9, 10).

> Hammurabi was one of the great lawgivers of history. He set down a legal code of 300 paragraphs, "in order that the strong should not oppress the weak, and the widows and orphans should be rightly dealt with." Under this wise and good ruler, Babylon extended its power to every city of the South. The region became known as Babylonia, after its most important city.[7]

The Code of Hammurabi still has an influence on law and justice in our day. Archaeologists have uncovered the greatness of ancient Babylon under Nebuchadnezzar who reigned from 605–561 B.C. It was during his rule that Babylon reached the zenith of her glory. It was Nebuchadnezzar who made this capital city one of the greatest in the world.

The metropolitan area, located on both sides of the Euphrates River, covered two hundred miles. The city was noted for its public buildup. The German archaeologist, Robert Koldeway, spent fifteen years working "with a force of three hundred diggers to reveal the ruins." John Elder informs us of Koldeway's remarkable discoveries:

> ...Thousands of tons of rubble had to be removed, in some instances as much as 77 feet in depth. Koldeway discovered that an area of 12 square miles had been enclosed by double walls, the outer more than 22 feet thick and the inner 25 feet, built over 38 feet apart. The space between the walls was filled in so that on top of the walls there was a broad highway sufficient for four pairs of horses to drive abreast.
> Regularly spaced watchtowers gave the guards a still higher vantage point from which to view the countryside. The watchtowers were about 160 feet apart, there being 360 of them on the inner walls and 250 on the outer walls.[8]

The famous Procession Street passed under the majestic Ishtar Gate. South of the Ishtar Gate on the west side of the avenue were the awe-inspiring Hanging Gardens and the spectacular Tower of Babel. Annually the procession of their gods and goddesses paraded on this prominent street. Silverberg gives us the following description:

. . . This titanic street, 73 feet wide, is perhaps the most majestic ever built in any city of the ancient or the modern world. It was bordered by massive walls, 23 feet high, decorated with brilliantly colored enameled bricks. Every 64 feet along the walls, lions were sculptured, red and yellow against a blue background.

The road was built of brick, covered with asphalt, then great slabs of white limestone. Lining the sides of the road were slabs of breccia, a form of soft stone colored red and white. . . .

The Sacred Way led up to the Gate of Ishtar. Ishtar was the chief goddess of Babylon, and her gate was magnificent. Even today the gateway stands almost 40 feet high, and it must have been far taller in Nebuchadnezzar's day. It was a double gateway, adorned by hundreds of brightly colored bulls and dragons.

Today the grand sweep of the Sacred Way leading to Ishtar Gate is breathtaking. In 600 B.C., when all was new and untouched by the harshness of time, it must have been a sight to make the traveler drop to his knees in wonder.[9]

Clarence Larkin has written a revealing chapter on "Babylon the Great." He supplies us with these details of that remarkable city:

Twenty-five magnificent avenues 150 feet wide ran across the city from North to South, and the same number crossed them at right angles from East to West, making 676 great squares, each nearly three-fifths of a mile on a side, and the city was divided into two equal parts by the River Euphrates that flowed diagonally through it and whose banks within the city were walled up and pierced with brazen gates, with steps leading down to the river.

At the ends of the main avenues on each side of the city were gates whose leaves were of brass and that shone as they were opened or closed in the rising or setting sun, like "leaves of flame."

The Euphrates within the city was spanned by a bridge, at each end of which was a palace; and these palaces were connected by a subterranean passageway, or tube, underneath the bed of the river, in which at different points were located sumptuous banqueting rooms constructed entirely of brass.[10]

The Hanging Gardens were one of the "Seven Ancient Wonders of the World." They must have excited the admiration of all who beheld them. In his book, Leonard Cottrell gives this description:

. . . The Gardens were built in a series of wide, sweeping terraces, rising like a flight of stairs to a height of nearly 400 feet. These terraces, supported by heavy arches, held thick layers of soil, sufficient to maintain the growth, not only of grass and flowers, but quite large fruit-bearing trees.

The Gardens were irrigated by hydraulic pumps, which would have had to be worked by hand or perhaps by oxen—we do not know. The platforms would be ablaze with the color of flowers brought from the remotest parts of Asia and shaded from the too-hot sun by trees, laden in season with fruits. The air would be heavy with the scent of flowers, wafted through screens of cooling water into the sumptuous inner chambers where the Median queen held her splendid court.[11]

The famous Tower of Babel is associated with ancient Babylon. The figures vary as to its dimensions, but the structure must have been of mammoth proportions. Elder remarks, "No less than fifty-eight million blocks went into it, the vast work being completed by slaves."[12] Silverberg gives these figures:

> The Tower was the most sacred zone of the city. It was set in a great courtyard and surrounded by lesser temples. Each side of the Tower was 288 feet long, and the overall height of the edifice was also 288 feet.
>
> The Tower rose in set-back steps, like a modern skyscraper; the first stage was 106 feet high, the second 58 feet. Then there were four stages of about 19 feet each, topped by a 48-foot-high temple dedicated to the god Marduk.
>
> The temple's walls were plated with gold and inlaid with blue enameled bricks so that the sun, striking the top of the Tower, illuminated the entire city with a blaze of reflected light.
>
> Within the temple, a gold statue of Marduk and golden furniture were kept—according to Herodotus, 26 tons of gold altogether, an unbelievable fortune.[13]

The biblical account is given in Genesis 11:1-9:

*"And the whole earth was of one language, and of one speech.*

*"And it came to pass, as they journeyed from the east, that they found a plain in the land of Shinar; and they dwelt there.*

*"And they said one to another, Go to, let us make brick, and burn them throughly. And they had brick for stone, and slime had they for morter.*

*"And they said, Go to, let us build us a city and a tower, whose top may reach unto heaven; and let us make us a name, lest we be scattered abroad upon the face of the whole earth.*

*"And the Lord came down to see the city and the tower, which the children of men builded.*

*"And the Lord said, Behold, the people is one, and they have all one language; and this they begin to do: and now nothing will be restrained from them, which they have imagined to do.*

*"Go to, let us go down, and there confound their language, that they may not understand one another's speech.*

*"So the Lord scattered them abroad from thence upon the face of all the earth: and they left off to build the city.*

*"Therefore is the name of it called Babel; because the Lord did there confound the language of all the earth: and from thence did the Lord scatter them abroad upon the face of all the earth."*

An interesting article entitled "From Iraq—Excavations at Babylon" appeared in the publication, *Bible and Spade,* in the winter edition 1973, pages 13 and 14. These quotations are from that article:

> Beginning with the Tower of Babel in Genesis 11, Babylon is mentioned throughout the Bible in both a literal and figurative sense. The ruins of the ancient metropolis are located in Iraq about 60 miles south of Baghdad. Archaeological explorations have been going on there since the end of the 18th century.
>
> Writing in the latest issue of *Sumer,* the official publication of the Iraqi Directorate General of Antiquities, Dr. Isa Salman of that department described the archaeological work that has been done at Babylon in recent years: ( . . . )
>
> Dr. Salman's comment on the mortar used by the ancient Babylonians is interesting in light of Genesis 11:3. There it describes the building materials for the Tower of Babel. "And they said one to another, Go to, let us make brick, and burn them throughly. And they had brick for stone, and slime had they for morter."
>
> The word translated as *slime* in Genesis 11:3 is the Hebrew word *hamar,* which actually means bitumen or asphalt. It was evidently naturally occurring, for it is recorded in Genesis 14:10 that "the vale of Siddim was full of slimepits" (pits of *hamar*). One of the challenges of modern-day science is to match this mortar from antiquity in restoring Nebuchadnezzar's palace at Babylon (*Sumer,* Vol. XXV—Nos. 1 and 2, 1969).

What do the words, "whose top may reach unto heaven" (Gen. 11:4), mean? *The International Standard Bible Encyclopedia* remarks, "an expression which is regarded as meaning 'a very high tower.' "[14] *Unger's Bible Dictionary* states, "This phrase is not hyperbole, but an expression of pride and rebellion manifest by the Babel builders."[15] Donald Grey Barnhouse makes this observation:

> In the Plain of Shinar was the first assembly of united mankind. It should give us pause when we note the United Nations Building in New York, and recall the shell of buildings by Lake Geneva, marking the grave of the League of Nations.
>
> But New York is not the second attempt to unite all mankind; it is the third. The first took place beside the River Euphrates, and the ruins of the Tower of Babel mark the grave of all human efforts to bring peace and order. It is not within the capacity of man to organize himself or his fellow man.

The Tower of Babel was a ziggurat. Remains of several such have been discovered. They were high mounds, on top of which were placed flat, carved stones on which were engraved the constellations of the zodiac. There the priests of astrology cast horoscopes in order to discern the future and to get guidance from above and beyond man, but not from the great Jehovah God, whom they hated with all the animosity of the carnal mind which desires to run its own affairs.[16]

The origin of astronomy is debatable. There are some who claim that Belus, the son of Nimrod, was the first astronomer. Some assert that the Tower of Babel was the first astronomical observatory. In the Babylonian religion we

---

### "Babylon was probably the most magnificent city the world has ever seen, and its fall reveals what a city may become when it forsakes God and He sends judgment upon it."

—*Clarence Larkin*

---

discover the roots of astrology. The Babylonians saw a message in the stars. Their towers were used as observatories by which they could behold the forms of beasts and humans in the constellations. They assiduously adhered to the signs of the Zodiac.[17] The Hebrews denounced these practices: "Thou art wearied in the multitude of thy counsels. Let now the astrologers, the stargazers, the monthly prognosticators, stand up, and save thee from these things that shall come upon thee" (Isa. 47:13).

## Religion of Babylon

What did these ancient people believe?

The religion of Mesopotamia is the oldest of which we have written records. Based on Sumerian beliefs, it provided spiritual and ethical guidance for the affairs of men, offered an acceptable explanation for the ultimate mysteries of life and death, and bequeathed a heritage of colorful mythology that strongly influenced later religions.[18]

Such a religious composite would not be acceptable to Christianity.

The ancient Babylonian religion was dominated by an enormous number of gods, devils and evil spirits with which it had to reckon. Hence there existed an elaborate system of ritual in which the temple played a prominent role. Fear of the spirits haunted the average Babylonian.

*The International Standard Bible Encyclopaedia* gives us the following information:

> Next in importance to the gods in the Bab religion are the demons who had the power to afflict men with manifold diseases of body or mind. A large part of the religion seems to have been given up to an agonized struggle against these demons, and the gods were everywhere approached by prayer to assist men against these demons.
>
> An immense mass of incantations, supposed to have the power of driving the demons out, has come down to us.

In regard to life after death:

> In Babylonia, the great question of all the ages—"If a man die, shall he live again?"—was asked and an attempt made to answer it.
>
> The answer was usually sad and depressing. After death the souls of men were supposed to continue in existence. It can hardly be called life. The place to which they have gone is called the "land of no return." There they lived in dark rooms amid the dust and the bats covered with a garment of feathers, and under the dominion of Nergal and Ereshkigal.
>
> When the soul arrived among the dead, he had to pass judgment before the judges of the dead, the Annunaki; but little has been preserved for us concerning the manner of this judgment.
>
> There seems to have been at times an idea that it might be possible for the dead to return again to life, for in this underworld there was the water of life, which was used when the god Tammus returned again to earth.
>
> The Babylonians seem not to have attached so much importance to this after-existence as did the Egyptians, but they did practice burial and not cremation, and placed often with the dead articles which might be used in the future existence.[19]

Evangelical Bible scholars seem to agree that idolatry began on the plains of Shinar. The first chapter of Romans describes in detail the idolatry which is the result of man's total depravity. John Phillips comments:

> The next step from atheism is idolatry....Idolatry is said to have commenced in ancient Babylon. From there it spread around the world, entrenched itself in most pagan religions and is with us this day. It maintains its hold on even the most cultured of modern men.[20]

He then adds this explanatory note:

> The founder of Bab-el ("the gate of God") was Nimrod. This city was

to be a center for all those wishing to rebel against God. When God judged and overthrew the city, its name was changed to Babel ("confusion").

It is claimed that the wife of Nimrod, the infamous Semiramis, led men into idolatry and that from Babylon this false system of worship spread eventually to the ends of the earth. Babylon remained the recognized center of idolatry and of a mystery religion which rejected divine revelation.

Upon the final fall of Babylon, the mysteries were transferred to Pergamos and later to Rome. The reigning Caesar claimed to be the Pontifex Maximus of the pagan religious systems and, from the time of Constantine, this title acknowledged the Caesar to be both the head of the church and the high priest of heathendom. Afterward the title was conferred on the bishops of Rome, and the pope retains the title as the "Sovereign Pontiff" to this day.[21]

In his exposition of *The Book of Revelation,* William R. Newell writes in Appendix III these words:

From "beyond the river" (Euphrates)—that is, from Mesopotamia, more particularly from Babel (later Babylon), and still more definitely from the daring acts of Nimrod, the "mighty destroyer" whose wife, Semiramis (one of the most able and wicked women of the human race), was, upon her death deified as "queen of heaven"—do we trace the beginnings of idolatry, which eventuates in Satan-worship by means of "the image of the Beast," seen in Revelation 13.

From Babylon, idolatry extended to every land, for Babylon became "a land of graven images...mad over idols." "Babylon hath been a golden cup in Jehovah's [ed.: the Lord's] hand, that made all the earth drunken: the nations have drunk [ed.: drunken] of her wine; therefore the nations are mad" (Jer. 50:38; 51:7). Idolatry spread thence to every nation, and God was blotted out from man's knowledge.[22]

*The Two Babylons* is the title of a much-quoted source book on idolatry by the late Reverend Alexander Hislop. In the book he traces idolatry back to Nimrod. Note these significant statements:

...We have only to bring the ancient Babylonian Mysteries to bear on the whole system of Rome, and then it will be seen how immensely the one has borrowed from the other....Now, as the language of Jeremiah...would indicate that Babylon was the primal source from which all these systems of idolatry flowed, so the deductions of the most learned historians, on mere historical grounds, have led to the same conclusion.[23]

In these circumstances, then, began, there can hardly be a doubt, that system of "Mystery," which, having Babylon for the center, has spread over the world. In these Mysteries, under the seal of secrecy and the sanction of an oath, and by means of all the fertile resources of magic, men were gradually led back to all the idolatry that had been publicly suppressed, while new features were added to that idolatry that made it still more blasphemous than before.[24]

It has been said that the oldest religious symbol in the world is the worship of mother and son. Herbert J. Muller[25] and Will Durant trace the worship of mother and son back to pagan origins. Durant notes that the Christian Fathers were shocked at the similarities.[26] W. A. Criswell gives this interesting background:

> . . .Nimrod's wife. . .was named Semiramis. In Assyria and Nineveh she was called Ishtar. In the Phoenician pantheon she was called Ashteroth or Astarte. In Egypt she was called Isis. Among the Greeks, she was called Aphrodite. Among the Latins, the Romans, she was called Venus.
>
> She became the first high priestess of an idolatrous system. In answer to the promise made to Eve that the seed of the woman would deliver the race, Semiramis, when she gave birth to a son, said he was miraculously conceived by a sunbeam, and she offered her son as the promised deliverer of the earth. His name was Tammuz.
>
> When he was grown, a wild boar slew him; but after forty days of the mother's weeping, he was raised from the dead.
>
> In this story of Semiramis and Tammuz began the cult of worship of the mother and child that spread throughout the whole world. . . .
>
> As we have observed, that cult of the worship of mother and child spread throughout the whole world, from Babylon to Assyria, to Phoenicia, to Pergamos, and finally, to Rome, itself. There the Roman Emperor was elected Pontifex Maximus, the high priest of all of the idolatrous systems of the Roman Empire. And when the Roman Emperor passed away, that title of high priest of the rites and mysteries of the cult of mother and child, the Babylonian mystery of idolatry, was assumed by the Bishop of Rome.[27]

Idolatry began on the plains of Shinar and will end in the worship of a man—the Antichrist. The Tower of Babel has been called the site of the first ecumenical council in history. Its consummation will be the ecclesiastical Babylon of Revelation 17.

A. W. Pink comments:

> In Nimrod and his schemes we see Satan's initial attempt to raise up a universal ruler of men. In his inordinate desire for fame, in the mighty power which he wielded, in his ruthless and brutal methods—suggested by the word "hunter"; in his blatant defiance of the Creator (seen in his utter disregard for His command to replenish the earth), by determining to prevent his subjects from being scattered abroad; in his founding of the kingdom of Babylon—the Gate of God—thus arrogating to himself Divine

honors; inasmuch as the Holy Spirit has placed the record of these things immediately before the inspired account of God's bringing Abram into Canaan—pointing forward to the regathering of Israel in Palestine immediately after the overthrow of the Lawless One; and finally, in the fact that the destruction of his kingdom is described in the words, "Let us go down, and there confound their language" (11:7—foreshadowing so marvelously the descent of Christ from Heaven to vanquish His impious Rival, we cannot fail to see that there is here, beneath the historical narrative, something deeper than that which appears on the surface; yes, that there is here a complete typical picture of the person, work and destruction of the Antichrist).[28]

---

## The Book of Daniel and Babylon

---

*"In the third year of the reign of Jehoiakim king of Judah came Nebuchadnezzar king of Babylon unto Jerusalem, and besieged it.*

*"And the Lord gave Jehoiakim king of Judah into his hand, with part of the vessels of the house of God: which he carried into the land of Shinar to the house of his god; and he brought the vessels into the treasure house of his god."*—Dan. 1:1, 2.

Babylon plays a major role not only in ancient history but in Bible prophecy. The statement has been made that "all history is connected with Israel in some form." While Bible scholars agree that the book of Daniel itself primarily has to do with "the times of the Gentiles" (Luke 21:24), Israel is in the background. Daniel was a Hebrew captive when Babylon was at the zenith of her power.

The Babylonian captivity was a humbling experience. The psalmist lamented: "By the rivers of Babylon, there we sat down, yea, we wept, when we remembered Zion" (Ps. 137:1). W. A. Criswell enumerates the blessings that flowed from the captivity. Note two of them:

> The nation was never again idolatrous. In the tragedies of the Babylonian exile, the Jews were forever purged from their hankering after the cheap gods of wood, silver, stone and gold.
>
> Can you imagine a Jew bowing down and worshipping before a graven image? There are three vast religious groups who refuse to make unto themselves idols of worship: the Jew, the Mohammedan and the New Testament Christian. These three have that in common: they refuse to worship before a graven image, whether the image be named Jupiter or Joseph, Mercury or Mary....
>
> The canon of the Holy Scriptures was born in the Captivity. As the people wept in their despair, they sought the comfort and the promises of God's Word. This made the scrolls of the prophets of God doubly precious. Ezra

and the men of God in the Great Synagogue gathered these scrolls together, and the Old Testament Scriptures became the holy possessions of the people.[29]

It is to be remembered that in the great image of Daniel 2, Babylon is designated as the "head of gold" (vs. 38). Gold is a most precious metal, and hence ancient Babylon is depicted in all of its glory.

Nebuchadnezzar ruled as an absolute sovereign over his vast empire. Alexander Whyte describes him thus:

> Nebuchadnezzar was by far the most famous of all the kings of the East. In his early years, and before he came to his great throne, Nebuchadnezzar had won victory after victory over all the surrounding nations. Jerusalem fell before his army after eighteen months' siege, and Tyre, the proudest of ancient cities, succumbed to him after an investiture of thirteen years. . . .
>
> But the fame of this magnificent monarch has rested even more on his unparalleled works of peace than on his great successes in war. Great as Nebuchadnezzar was as a warrior, he was still greater as a statesman and an administrator. The vast public works that he planned and executed for his capital and his kingdom in walls and in water-works: in parks and in gardens: in palaces and in temples—all these things, in their vastness, in their usefulness, in their beauty, and in their immense cost make Nebuchadnezzar to stand out absolutely unapproached among the great builder-kings of the ancient East.[30]

Nebuchadnezzar could look back with pride at his accomplishments. Lehman Strauss makes this comment:

> Every student should read a good history and a reliable encyclopedia on the city of Babylon, and he will be convinced that this ancient city surpassed anything that man has built on earth in its military fortifications, its beauty and wealth, its religious pomp and extravagance. Nebuchadnezzar indeed had been an ambitious builder, and his own words fit well his accomplishments when he said, "Is not this great Babylon, that I have built. . . ." (Dan. 4:30)?[31]

The last we hear of Nebuchadnezzar after his humbling experience is in Daniel 4:37: "Now I Nebuchadnezzar praise and extol and honour the King of heaven, all whose works are truth, and his ways judgment: and those that walk in pride he is able to abase."

Chapter 5 of Daniel is one of the most dramatic portions of the Bible. It has been the inspiration for many sermons. The chapter has been entitled: "A Thousand and One on a Drunk," "The Fatal Night," "The Handwriting on the Wall," "Belshazzar's Doom," etc.

Belshazzar, the son of Nabonidus and grandson of Nebuchadnezzar, and the Babylonian kingdom are the subjects of the narrative. Never did a city seem more secure. They evidently had confidence in their pagan gods. The Babylonians boasted that they had stocked provisions plus arable and pasture land within the walls to last for a twenty-year siege. Alexander Whyte gives this description:

> Never did a military commander attempt a more impossible task than Cyrus attempted when he sat down before Babylon to blockade it. For Babylon was indeed "Babylon the Great." Babylon was great in size, in fortified strength, in wide dominion, in wealth, in every kind of resource, and in her proud defiance of all her enemies.
>
> But then, to set over against all that, Cyrus was a soldier of the foremost military genius: and, besides that, Almighty God was with Cyrus, and was against Belshazzar.
>
> That was an high day in all the temples and palaces of Babylon. It was the day that Bel had made, and all Babylon was in public worship before Bel their god. And as an evening sacrifice to Bel, a great feast was to be held in Belshazzar's palace that night.
>
> But before the sunset, and to prepare his proud heart for his great banquet, Belshazzar rode out in his royal chariot that afternoon on that splendid chariot-drive that his famous father, Nebuchadnezzar, had built round about Babylon.
>
> The wall of Babylon was the wonder of the world. The wall of Babylon reached unto heaven; and such a mighty rampart was that wall round the city that no less than four royal chariots were driven abreast on the top of the wall that afternoon, and all in the sight of Cyrus lying below. And as Belshazzar saw Cyrus and his thin red line lying round the mighty fortress, he mocked at Cyrus, and all Belshazzar's princes laughed with him at that spider's thread laid round a sleeping lion.
>
> It was a dazzling spectacle at Belshazzar's supper-table that night. All the grandeur, all the wealth, all the princely blood, and all the beauty of Babylon, drank wine at the king's table, and praised the gods of Babylon.[32]

The wall around the city seemed impregnable. Strauss adds these details:

> Outside the huge wall was a large ditch, or moat, which surrounded the city and was kept filled with water from the Euphrates River. The large ditch was meant to serve as an additional protection against attacking enemies, for any attacking army would have to cross this body of water first before approaching the great wall.
>
> The cost of constructing this military defense was estimated to be in excess of one billion dollars. When we consider the value of a billion dollars in those days, plus the fact that it was all built with slave labor, one can

imagine something of the wonder and magnificence of this famous city.[33]

*"Belshazzar the king made a great feast to a thousand of his lords, and drank wine before the thousand."*—Dan. 5:1.

In their excavations, archaeologists have uncovered some of the magnificence and grandeur of Belshazzar's day, including a mammoth throne room 56 feet wide and 173 feet long.[34] Babylonian monarchs were known to have dined with a great number of guests. Some historians estimate the number at 10,000 or more.[35]

The feast turned into a saturnalia of "wine, women and song":

*"Belshazzar, whiles he tasted the wine, commanded to bring the golden and silver vessels which his father Nebuchadnezzar had taken out of the temple which was in Jerusalem; that the king, and his princes, his wives, and his concubines, might drink therein.*

*"Then they brought the golden vessels that were taken out of the temple of the house of God which was at Jerusalem; and the king, and his princes, his wives, and his concubines, drank in them.*

*"They drank wine, and praised the gods of gold, and of silver, of brass, of iron, of wood, and of stone."*—Dan. 5:2-4.

Belshazzar was without moral principles. To command the sacred vessels from the Temple was considered a blasphemous act. To seek the favor of the Babylonian pantheon was to desecrate the holy vessels of Israel. These utensils of gold and silver came from Solomon's Temple, and their spiritual significance looked forward to the sacrifice of Christ on the cross. Paganism was thus exalted over the Messiah which was to come. Belshazzar defiantly had not taken to heart the lesson Nebuchadnezzar had so grievously learned. Such an act was more than the Almighty would tolerate.

The handwriting then appeared upon the wall, and Belshazzar was petrified. He sensed that he had gone too far and that which was sacred he had profaned. His call to the astrologers of the Chaldeans brought no explanation. The wisdom of this world cannot comprehend the acts of Deity. The discerning queen recommended the counsel of the aged and godly Daniel:

*"There is a man in thy kingdom, in whom is the spirit of the holy gods; and in the days of thy father light and understanding and wisdom, like the wisdom of the gods, was found in him; whom the king Nebuchadnezzar thy father, the king, I say, thy father, made master of the magicians, astrologers, Chaldeans, and soothsayers;*

*"Forasmuch as an excellent spirit, and knowledge, and understanding, interpreting of dreams, and shewing of hard sentences, and dissolving of doubts,*

*were found in the same Daniel, whom the king named Belteshazzar: now let Daniel be called, and he will shew the interpretation.*

*"Then was Daniel brought in before the king. And the king spake and said unto Daniel, Art thou that Daniel, which art of the children of the captivity of Judah, whom the king my father brought out of Jewry?*

*"I have even heard of thee, that the spirit of the gods is in thee, and that light and understanding and excellent wisdom is found in thee."*—Dan. 5:11-14.

Dr. Joseph Parker eloquently makes this comforting application to ministers of the Word of God:

> Preachers of the Word, you will be wanted someday by Belshazzar; you were not at the beginning of the feast, but you will be there before the banqueting hall is closed; the king will not ask you to drink wine, but he will ask you to tell the secret of his pain and heal the malady of his heart.
>
> Abide your time. You are nobody now. Who cares for preachers, teachers, seers and men of insight, while the wine goes round and the feast is unfolding its tempting luxuries? Midway down the programme, to mention pulpit, or preacher, or Bible, would be to violate the harmony of the occasion.
>
> But the preacher, as we have often had occasion to say, will have his opportunity. They will send for him when all other friends have failed; may he then come fearlessly, independently, asking only to be made a medium through which divine communications can be addressed to the listening trouble of the world.
>
> Daniel will take the scarlet and the chain by and by, but not as a bribe; he will take the poor baubles of this dying Babylon and will use them to the advantage of the world through actions that shall become historical, but he will not first fill his hands with bribes, and then read the king's riddles. The prophet is self-sustained by being divinely inspired. He needs no promise to enable him to speak the truth, the whole truth, and nothing but the truth. Indeed, he has nothing to say of himself.
>
> Every man, in proportion as he is a Daniel, has nothing to invent, nothing to conceive in his own intellect; he has no warrant or credential from the empty court of his own genius; he bears letters from Heaven; he expresses the claims of God.
>
> O Daniel, preacher, speaker, teacher, thunder out God's Word, if it be a case of judgment and doom; or whisper it, or rain in gracious tears, if it be a message of sympathy and love and welcome.[36]

After the severe denunciation of Belshazzar's act of desecration, Daniel pronounced the awful verdict of history.

*"And this is the writing that was written, MENE, MENE, TEKEL, UPHARSIN.*

*"This is the interpretation of the thing: MENE; God hath numbered thy kingdom, and finished it.*

*"TEKEL; Thou art weighed in the balances, and art found wanting.*

*"PERES; Thy kingdom is divided, and given to the Medes and Persians."*—Dan. 5:25-28.

W. C. Stevens gives us this explanation:

> These pregnant words (for the interpretation only is in sentences) read: NUMBERED; WEIGHED; DIVIDED; while the word PERES alludes to the similar word *Persia.*
>
> The interpretation presents the full import of the decree in its threefold compass: God hath numbered the years of the Babylonian Empire and terminated it; thou art weighed in the balances of divine authority and found wanting in obedience and service to God; thy kingdom is cut off and divided between the Medes and the Persians.[37]

Note the dramatic application of these words by Alexander Whyte:

> O my soul, what a day that will be for thee when the God of truth, and not any more of lies, brings forth His great balances! His balances, so awful in their burning truth and holiness! What a reversal of reputations! What a stain and overthrow of great names! What a dreadful trumpet-blowing upon the house-tops! What nakedness! What shame! What everlasting contempt! Rocks, fall on us and hide us.
>
> O ministers! O people! But O ministers, above all, on that day! Your people will gnash their teeth at you on that day unless you preach to them now the terrible balances of that day. Be sure you preach for one whole sermon every Sabbath the terrors of the Lord. To have even one of your people saved as by fire on that terrible day will be your salvation. For your God is a God of knowledge, and by Him every minister's motives and aims and ends will be weighed before the whole assembled world that day. Rock of Ages, cleft for me![38]

There was no extension of time. God had decreed the doom of Belshazzar and his kingdom. Cyrus attempted an impossible task in the attempted overthrow of this famous fortified city. The sovereign hand of God was behind the scenes.

Two traitors from within helped to bring down Babylon, the "head of gold," the mightiest kingdom of its day. These terse lines explain it all:

*"In that night was Belshazzar the king of the Chaldeans slain.*

*"And Darius the Median took the kingdom, being about threescore and two years old."*—Dan. 5:30,31.

Philip R. Newell gives this account of that eventful night:

The historian Xenophon abundantly confirms the scriptural account of Babylon's fall and describes the method by which it was subsequently accomplished. The River Euphrates flowed under the walls to divide the city into two parts, and since the river itself was barred at its entrance and exit from the city by impassable gates, the plan was conceived of digging a channel to divert the river's course and thus permit the Persian army to enter the city by means of the river bed.

There is no more intensely melodramatic scene in history than that which is therefore here before us, for it was in the very night that this feast of Belshazzar's was held that the Persians completed their diversion of the Euphrates and brought to pass their entrance into the city, and through the otherwise supposedly impregnable gates. Indeed, God had plainly stipulated long before through the prophet Isaiah (45:1,2) that He would open to Cyrus the Persian "the two leaved gates; and the gates shall not be shut; I will go before thee, and make the crooked places straight: I will break in pieces the gates of brass, and cut in sunder the bars of iron."[39]

The rest is history. W. C. Stevens notes the fulfillment of the Prophet Isaiah:

History agrees with the prophecies in recording that the city of Babylon was taken at night when a great revelry was going on, without the opportunity for a single blow of resistance. Cyrus, the captain of the combined forces of the Medes and Persians, diverted the water of the Euphrates, which flowed through the city, to another channel; and, guided by two deserters, he marched into the city through the dry river-bed, gaining access into the city proper through the great brazen gates along the river channel, which were found carelessly left open and unguarded.

The sudden, paralyzing announcement of the city's capture was issued by the prophet Isaiah nearly two centuries in advance: "And, behold, here cometh a chariot of men, with a couple of horsemen. And he answered and said, Babylon is fallen, is fallen; and all the graven images of her gods he hath broken unto the ground" (21:9).[40]

The mighty Belshazzar discovered when it was too late that "pride goeth before destruction, and an haughty spirit before a fall" (Prov. 16:18). The fall of what some consider "the greatest world city of antiquity" is recorded in the historic verses of Daniel 5:30,31: "In that night was Belshazzar the king of the Chaldeans slain. And Darius the Median took the kingdom. . . ."

It was not only "night" in the soul of the arrogant Belshazzar, but the "long night" settled on the doomed city. The decay of the empire was evident.

Clarence Larkin makes this significant statement: "Babylon was probably the most magnificent city the world has ever seen, and its fall reveals what a city may become when it forsakes God and He sends judgment upon it."[41]

The Scriptures are very specific in proclaiming the doom of Babylon. The psalmist declared: "O daughter of Babylon, who art to be destroyed. . ." (Ps. 137:8). Isaiah wrote by inspiration:

*"And Babylon, the glory of kingdoms, the beauty of the Chaldees' excellency, shall be as when God overthrew Sodom and Gomorrah.*

*"It shall never be inhabited, neither shall it be dwelt in from generation to generation: neither shall the Arabian pitch tent there; neither shall the shepherds make their fold there.*

*"But wild beasts of the desert shall lie there; and their houses shall be full of doleful creatures; and owls shall dwell there, and satyrs shall dance there.*

*"And the wild beasts of the islands shall cry in their desolate houses, and dragons in their pleasant palaces: and her time is near to come, and her days shall not be prolonged."*—Isa. 13:19-22.

In Jeremiah 50 and 51 "the weeping prophet" describes the fall of Babylon:

*"A sound of battle is in the land, and of great destruction.*

*"How is the hammer of the whole earth cut asunder and broken! how is Babylon become a desolation among the nations!. . .*

*"Therefore the wild beasts of the desert with the wild beasts of the islands shall dwell there, and the owls shall dwell therein: and it shall be no more inhabited for ever; neither shall it be dwelt in from generation to generation.*

*"As God overthrew Sodom and Gomorrah and the neighbour cities thereof, saith the Lord; so shall no man abide there, neither shall any son of man dwell therein. . . .*

*"And Babylon shall become heaps, a dwellingplace for dragons, an astonishment, and an hissing, without an inhabitant. . . .*

*"So Jeremiah wrote in a book all the evil that should come upon Babylon, even all these words that are written against Babylon.*

*"And Jeremiah said to Seraiah, When thou comest to Babylon, and shalt see, and shalt read all these words;*

*"Then shalt thou say, O Lord, thou hast spoken against this place, to cut it off, that none shall remain in it, neither man nor beast, but that it shall be desolate for ever.*

*"And it shall be, when thou hast made an end of reading this book, that thou shalt bind a stone to it, and cast it into the midst of Euphrates:*

*"And thou shalt say, Thus shall Babylon sink, and shall not rise from the evil that I will bring upon her: and they shall be weary. Thus far are the words of Jeremiah."*—Jer. 50:22,23,39,40; 51:37,60-64.

The decline of ancient Babylon was steady. The walls and great palaces became utter ruins. The infamous city plodded on into the Roman Empire, but by the thirteenth century it had gasped its last breath. The desert sands buried its grandeur.

Gray's "Elegy Written in a Country Churchyard" is an appropriate epitaph
to the departed glory of Babylon:

> **The boast of heraldry, the pomp of power,**
> **All that beauty, all that wealth e'er gave**
> **Await alike the inevitable hour:**
> **The paths of glory lead but to the grave.**

Leonard Cottrell's comment is worthy of note:

> Nebuchadnezzar is only a name in the Old Testament. His beautiful Me-
> dian queen is a legend. Their frescoed halls of state, bright with candelabra,
> the gold-inlaid furniture, the wine goblets, the slaves and dancing girls,
> the flower-filled, tree-shaded terraces and the water which fed them, all
> are gone. All that remains is a cellar and the empty well where slaves
> and animals toiled endlessly in the darkness.[42]

Where once the Hanging Gardens stood, "where kings and nobles feasted
in bejeweled robes," where once the sacred vessels of Israel were desecrated—
there is nothing but desolation.

Although the Babylonian Empire was not completely destroyed at this time,
this was the beginning of the end. The handwriting on the wall was but a portent of ultimate destruction.

Will this mighty empire ever be restored? Will the ancient city of Babylon
be rebuilt? Theologians still argue over the possibility. It is not the purpose
of this book to enter into that debate (although the pros and cons have been
evaluated). Needless to say, Babylon does have a major role in Bible prophecy.

## Babylon Tomorrow

*"And upon her forehead was a name written, MYSTERY, BABYLON THE
GREAT, THE MOTHER OF HARLOTS AND ABOMINATIONS OF THE
EARTH."*— Rev. 17:5.

"Thou art this head of gold" (Dan. 2:38) was not only the designation of the
great Babylonian kingdom by Daniel himself, but it also has a future reference
to what it will someday become in a spiritual sense. Babylon will again be
the head dominating the affairs of the world.

In Daniel's day, Babylon was the greatest city in the world. In the future,
Babylon will be the site of the greatest apostasy (the evil reaping of the ages).
Idolatry began on the plains of Shinar; it will culminate in the worship of a
man—the Antichrist.

The world is getting ready for such an event. Babylon will play a leading role. It has been said that Babylon is more frequently mentioned in the
Bible than any other city except Jerusalem. In fact, Babylon and Jerusalem

play an important role in the end-time.

The Antichrist will be brought into power through the agency of the false church. The world is being conditioned for the worship of a man—the false Christ. Revelation 13:8 declares, "And all that dwell upon the earth shall worship him." Today Christ is forming His body, and Satan is building his church.

Some expositors believe the city mentioned in Revelation 17 and 18 is Rome (ecclesiastic and political Rome). Others contend it is rebuilt Babylon. Both will play a promanent role in Bible prophecy.

Two chapters are needed to announce the fall of this noted city. Seiss makes this significant statement:

> The fall of Babylon is one of the most marvelous events of time. More is said about it in the Scriptures than perhaps any one great secular occurrence.[43]

Criswell comments:

> Chapter 17 of the Revelation is one of the most astounding of all the prophecies to be found in the Word of God. It is one that cannot only be verified in history but can also be followed closely in the daily newspapers of this present hour.[44]

The venerable John on the Island of Patmos envisions a system enmeshed within a city. Consider the description given in Revelation 17:1-7:

*"And there came one of the seven angels which had the seven vials, and talked with me, saying unto me, Come hither; I will shew unto thee the judgment of the great whore that sitteth upon many waters:*

*"With whom the kings of the earth have committed fornication, and the inhabitants of the earth have been made drunk with the wine of her fornication.*

*"So he carried me away in the spirit into the wilderness: and I saw a woman sit upon a scarlet coloured beast, full of names of blasphemy, having seven heads and ten horns.*

*"And the woman was arrayed in purple and scarlet colour, and decked with gold and precious stones and pearls, having a golden cup in her hand full of abominations and filthiness of her fornication:*

*"And upon her forehead was a name written, MYSTERY, BABYLON THE GREAT, THE MOTHER OF HARLOTS AND ABOMINATIONS OF THE EARTH.*

*"And I saw the woman drunken with the blood of the saints, and with the blood of the martyrs of Jesus: and when I saw her, I wondered with great admiration.*

*"And the angel said unto me, Wherefore didst thou marvel? I will tell thee the mystery of the woman, and of the beast that carrieth her, which hath the seven heads and ten horns."*

This noted woman possesses several striking characteristics. She is sitting upon waters, immoral, astride a beast, magnificently clothed and intoxicated. Someone has depicted her as the source of great power, wealth and pleasure. John portrays this prominent personage as "the great whore." This is in contradistinction to the bride of Christ, "a chaste virgin" (II Cor. 11:2). Lehman Strauss makes a helpful observation:

> This false church which dominates the world scene in these climactic hours immediately preceding the second coming of Christ to earth, is shown first as a woman, a filthy and dissolute harlot. She is seen "[sitting] upon many waters" (17:1). The symbolic phrase "many waters" is interpreted in the chapter, and it means "peoples, and multitudes, and nations, and tongues" (17:15).
>
> This shows the scope of the seducing harlot's influence. She sways the surging masses of humanity throughout the whole earth in an ecclesiastical rule.[45]

Ford C. Ottman begins his exposition of Revelation 17 with these words:

> The woman of this chapter is, beyond all possibility of successful contradiction, an apostate ecclesiastical system. Whether she represents the papal church—as many contend—or the entire mass of professing Christendom after the true Church has been taken from the earth, is an open question. But that she stands for one or the other of these is absolutely certain.
>
> By no possibility can she be identified with the woman of the twelfth chapter; for that woman, as has been shown, represents Israel, the mother of Christ after the flesh, and can represent no other.
>
> The woman of this chapter, however false, is in bridal, not maternal, relation to Christ. Claiming to be His bride, she has fallen from her pure condition and become a harlot. Such a condition shall assuredly be manifest in the apostate church just prior to the return of our Lord with the true Church.[46]

H. A. Ironside is very dogmatic in his identification of Rome:

> There is no mistaking her identity. Pagan Rome was the lineal successor of Babylon. Papal Rome absorbed the Babylonian mysteries; and the Rome of the Beast in the last days will be the seat of the revived satanic system that began with Nimrod and his infamous consort Semiramis, which has from that day to this been opposed to everything that is of God; and which changed the truth of God into a lie, worshiping and serving the creature more than the Creator.[47]

Tim LaHaye makes this comment:

> The only answer is the one system before which all kings, dictators and nations have been forced to bow down throughout history—that is, the

Babylonish religion of idolatry. One cannot go anyplace in the world without being confronted with some semblance of the Babylonish religion of idolatry.[48]

Spiritual fornication is the result of apostasy. This conveys the thought of "prostituting religion to obtain power." This is the unholy union spoken of in verse 2.

I. M. Haldeman exposes the "fake church" thus:

But this woman and this city stand in terrific contrast to the woman and city which set forth the church of Christ.
They contrast and contradict each other.
The church is represented by a chaste virgin.
This woman is a bedizened harlot, and is called in plain speech, "the whore."
The church is espoused to one husband.
This woman holds promiscuous commerce with the kings of the earth.
The church is the mystery of godliness.
This woman is "MYSTERY, BABYLON."
The church is called "the pillar and ground of the truth."
This woman is called "Babylon," signifies "confusion," and recalls an unfinished tower.
The church offers the cup of salvation and stands for holiness.
This woman holds in her hand a golden cup full of abominations and filthiness.
The church is the mother of the saints.
This woman is "THE MOTHER OF HARLOTS."
The church is the bride of Christ.
This woman, by the law of symbolism, is a professed church of Christ, and therefore a would-be bride of Christ; but, as she is a harlot, she cannot be the true bride of Christ, she cannot be the true church of Christ. If she is not the true church of Christ but a corrupt and corrupting harlot, then she is a false and corrupt church professing the name of Christ.[49]

The arena of activities is described as "the wilderness" (Rev. 17:3). This represents a "vast expanse" of apostasy—apostasy in Protestantism, apostasy in Roman Catholicism, apostasy in the Greek Orthodox church and liturgical churches, apostasy in the cults and the world religions. This is the conglomerate of false doctrine. Here is the climax of man's deliberately rejecting revealed truth and hence incurring the inevitable anathema of God.

Note the false church rides the beast into power. Blasphemy results from a departure from the Faith. The blasphemy in pulpits in our day and in the secular world is but a portent of the coming Tribulation.

This woman is "gilded" in gorgeous apparel. In his commentary on Revelation, Walvoord gives this description:

> The description of the woman as arrayed in purple and scarlet and decked with gold, precious stones and pearls is all too familiar to one acquainted with the trappings of ecclesiastical pomp today and especially of high officials in the Roman Catholic and Greek Orthodox churches.
>
> Purple and scarlet, symbolically so rich in their meaning when connected with true spiritual values, are here prostituted to this false religious system and designed to glorify it with religious garb in contrast to the simplicity of pious adornment (cf. I Tim. 2:9-10). . . . The most striking aspect of her presentation, however, is that she has a golden cup in her hand described as "full of abomination and filthiness of her fornication."
>
> The Word of God does not spare words in describing the utter filthiness of this adulterous relationship in the sight of God. Few crimes in Scripture are spoken of in more unsparing terms than the crime of spiritual adultery of which this woman is the epitome. As alliance with the world and showy pomp increase, so spiritual truth and purity decline.[50]

Strauss, in writing of the folly of Belshazzar in Daniel 5, makes this pertinent application to our day:

> Such description of the vessels of the Most High God is typical of Babylonianism. The holy things of God, consecrated by God for His own praise and glory, are being desecrated on a larger scale today than ever before. Such desecration will increase until the man of sin stretches forth his hand to touch God's holy Temple and His covenant people, Israel.
>
> Babylon the great, the mother of harlots, will show herself glamorously in the last days, "arrayed in purple and scarlet colour, and decked with gold and precious stones and pearls, having a golden cup in her hand full of abominations and filthiness of her fornication" (Rev. 17:4).
>
> The climax of the age will be marked by an amalgamated federation of religious groups set forth in Revelation 17 and 18 under the figure of a drunken harlot. This apostate religio-political machine, the largest organized church in world history, will bear the name of Christ; but in reality it will be the masterpiece of Satan.
>
> Babylon, the mother of harlots, will come to certain doom. All of this is foreshadowed in Daniel 5.[51]

It seems that the Holy Spirit wanted to give us a clear identification of the false church. Note the words, "upon her forehead" (Rev. 17:5). This means an intellectual system. Hislop makes the reference to ecclesiastical Rome:

> What means the writing of that name "on the forehead"? Does it not naturally indicate that, just before judgment overtakes her, her real character was to be so thoroughly developed that everyone who has eyes

to see, who has the least spiritual discernment, would be compelled, as it were, on ocular demonstration, to recognize the wonderful fitness of the title which the Spirit of God had affixed to her?

Her judgment is now evidently hastening on; and just as it approaches, the Providence of God, conspiring with the Word of God, by light pouring in from all quarters, makes it more and more evident that Rome is in very deed the Babylon of the Apocalypse; that the essential character of her system, the grand objects of her worship, her festivals, her doctrine and discipline, her rites and ceremonies, her priesthood and their orders have all been derived from ancient Babylon.[52]

John on Patmos wrote "MYSTERY, BABYLON THE GREAT" (Rev. 17:5). The word *mystery* does not mean something that is veiled or hidden but a revelation of truth that should be known. Bullinger gives this explanation: "The English word *mystery* is a transliteration of the Greek word *musterion,* which means a sacred secret—hence something concealed that can be revealed."[53]

The word *Babylon* immediately refers us back to Genesis 11 and the Tower of Babel. Here is the zenith of all idolatry. What was begun with "Nimrod the mighty hunter" (Gen. 10:9) culminates in the eventual worship of the Antichrist.

Someone has said that in the building of the Tower of Babel there was congregation, concentration, centralization and consolidation. Note these words from *The Companion Bible*:

> Babylon is the fountainhead of all idolatry and systems of fake worship. This is the "mystery of iniquity" (II Thess. 2:7) seen in all the great "religions" of the world. All alike substitute another god for the God of the Bible, a god made either with the hands or with the imagination, but equally made; a religion consisting of human merit and endeavor.[54]

Babylon represents "confusion." Ottman remarks: "The word *confusion,* and, therefore, *Babylon,* is nothing but 'confusion the great.' "[55]

Gaebelein adds these words:

> And she is "Babylon the Great." Babylon means confusion; it is great confusion, all the evils and perversions of the truth of God brought into one powerful organization. And she is the mother of all harlots and abominations on the earth.
>
> Every religious system which aims at worldly power and grandeur and which shares more or less her assumptions and false doctrines is an offspring of her. These systems, after the restraining power of the Holy Spirit is gone, will naturally unite with "mother church" and form the great Babylon.[56]

This is religion at its worst. This is the Devil's millennium (although confined to a few short years). Again, let it be noted this is not just apostate Rome but all the false religions of the world combined. Seiss emphasizes this as he writes:

> And it is only when we understand this mystic Harlot as the whole body of organized alienation from God, as in heathenism, false religion and spiritual prostitution, that we find an abject co-extensive in time and territory with the "peoples, and multitudes, and nations, and tongues," which make up the seat, dependence and support of this great Harlot.[57]

"And I saw the woman drunken with the blood of the saints, and with the blood of the martyrs of Jesus" (Rev. 17:6). I quote this lengthy commentary of Dr. I. M. Haldeman, published in 1913:

> Read history, not the history written by one author, but by all, and in their pages you will learn how men and women were led into torture chambers or buried in dismal dungeons. You will read how beautiful women were stripped before black-masked judges gloating over unprotected shame, and were led away to racks and stretched till their delicate limbs were snapped and their tender flesh torn into shreds.
>
> You will read how men and women were broken on the wheel, or flayed alive, their eyes put out, their tongues plucked forth by the roots, their feet placed in boots filled with boiling oil, bags thrust down their throats, and then filled with water till they agonized with slow and calculated strangulation, legs placed between boards and the boards driven together by wedges till the bones were crushed little by little to a pulp, nails wrenched from the fingers, bodies sawn asunder as you might saw a log in two, members of the body cut off one at a time—now a hand, then an arm, first one leg, then another—till the victim was a mere quivering, though still living, trunk; men and women taken to the stake and burned alive, the wood dampened, or green wood used, that the fire might burn slowly and the agony and torture of the victim be lengthened.
>
> Try and count, if you can, the men and women driven from their homes, their houses burned, their property confiscated, and themselves hunted on the mountains and pursued through the valleys like beasts of prey.
>
> Look at the blood flowing like water from the martyred bodies of men and women, whose only crime was that they loved the Lord Jesus Christ, believed in His finished redemption on the cross, refused to buy their salvation by penance or good works, rejected the intercession of a human priest, or a woman, no matter how good, claimed the Lord Jesus Christ as their sin-bearer and Saviour at the right hand of the Father, owned Him as their only high-priest and intercessor and would not, even at the price of their own life, deny Him who died for them and rose again.[58]

The writer of Revelation, the Apostle John, is amazed at what he saw. Criswell gives the reason:

> John could not believe his eyes, for in his day it was pagan Rome that was persecuting the Christians. When the Christian in John's day was martyred with the sword or was crucified or was thrown into a boiling cauldron of oil or was fed to the wild beasts, it was pagan Rome that crucified him or slew him or fed him to the wild and ferocious animals.
>
> But in this vision that God gave to John, the blood of the saints and the blood of the martyrs of Jesus is shed by that rich and scarlet idolatrous church. John "ethaumasa thauma mega"—he wondered with a great wonder.[59]

It is imperative that we note God's admonition concerning Babylon. The message is loud and clear: "And I heard another voice from heaven, saying, Come out of her, my people, that ye be not partakers of her sins, and that ye receive not of her plagues" (Rev. 18:4). Theodore Epp comments: "As Lot had to come out of Sodom, so God's people will have to come out of Babylon before He destroys the wicked city...."[60]

In studying Revelation 18, one is aware of the fact that, "as Babylon is great, so her fall is great." From the zenith of worldly acclaim, Babylon is soon lost in abject dissolution. John writes:

*"And after these things I saw another angel come down from heaven, having great power; and the earth was lightened with his glory.*

*"And he cried mightily with a strong voice, saying, Babylon the great is fallen, is fallen, and is become the habitation of devils, and the hold of every foul spirit, and a cage of every unclean and hateful bird....*

*"Standing afar off for the fear of her torment, saying, Alas, alas, that great city Babylon, that mighty city! for in one hour is thy judgment come....*

*"And saying, Alas, alas that great city, that was clothed in fine linen, and purple, and scarlet, and decked with gold, and precious stones, and pearls!...*

*"And they cast dust on their heads, and cried, weeping and wailing, saying, Alas, alas that great city, wherein were made rich all that had ships in the sea by reason of her costliness! for in one hour is she made desolate....*

*"And a mighty angel took up a stone like a great millstone, and cast it into the sea, saying, Thus with violence shall that great city Babylon be thrown down, and shall be found no more at all."*—Rev. 18:1,2,10,16,19,21.

A study of this chapter reveals the suddenness and devastation of God's judgment (vs. 19). The reasons for God's judgment are found in verses 20 to 24.

In his commentary, Charles Caldwell Ryrie quotes Walter Scott thus:

> Joyless, dark and silent, Babylon stands out as a monument to the utmost vengeance of God....At last, when she had filled to the full her

cup of iniquity, God rises in His fierce anger, His indignation burns, and Babylon falls to rise no more. Her destruction is irremediable.

The chapter closes with a reiteration of the bloody character of the system.[61]

Clarence Larkin gives this description of Babylon at the height of her glory and just before her ignominious fall:

Babylon the Great will be an immense city, the greatest in every respect the world has ever seen. It will be a typical city—the London, the Paris, the Berlin, the Petrograd, the New York, the Chicago—of its day. It will be the greatest commercial city of the world.

Its merchandise will be of gold and silver, and precious stones and pearls, of purple, and silk, and scarlet and costly wools. Its fashionable society will be clothed in the most costly raiment and decked with the most costly jewels. Their homes will be filled with the most costly furniture of precious woods, brass, iron and marble, with the richest of draperies, mats and rugs.

They will use the most costly of perfumes, cinnamon, fragrant odors, ointments and frankincense. Their banquets will be supplied with the sweetest of wines, the richest of pastry, and the most delicious of meats.

They will have horses and chariots and the swiftest of fast moving vehicles on earth and in the air. They will have their slaves, and they will traffic in the "souls of men." That is, women will sell their bodies and men their souls to gratify their lusts.

The markets will be crowded with cattle, sheep and horses. The wharves will be piled with goods from all climes. The manufactories will turn out the richest of fabrics, and all that genius can invent for the comfort and convenience of men will be found on the market.

It will be a city given over to pleasure and business. Business men and promoters will give their days and nights to scheming how to make money fast, and the pleasure-loving will be constantly planning new pleasures.

There will be riotous joy and ceaseless feasting. As it was in the days of Noah and of Lot, they will be marrying and giving in marriage, buying and selling, building and planting.[62]

In passing, it is revealing to discover that, since we live in a day of drug addiction, the word *sorceries* found in Revelation 9:21 is *pharmakia*, from which we derive the word *pharmacy* or *drugs*. Dean Henry Alford interprets *sorceries* and *witchcraft* as "drugs."[63] Barnhouse suggests that thus the world will be drugged into insensibility and the masses of men controlled.[64]

The sovereign decree of the Almighty has determined the fall of Babylon. No power on earth can alter Holy Writ. The Prophet Jeremiah declared:

*"Behold, I am against thee, O destroying mountain, saith the Lord, which destroyest all the earth: and I will stretch out mine hand upon thee, and roll thee down from the rocks, and will make thee a burnt mountain.*

*"And they shall not take of thee a stone for a corner, nor a stone for foundations; but thou shalt be desolate for ever, saith the Lord."*—Jer. 51:25, 26.

## Ecclesiastical Babylon

*"So he carried me away in the spirit into the wilderness: and I saw a woman sit upon a scarlet coloured beast. . . ."*—Rev. 17:3.

The modern ecumenical movement will be the reason why all roads will eventually lead back again to Rome. Ecclesiastical Rome will once again be a dominant force in the world.

J. Marcellus Kik remarks, "Enthusiasm for ecumenicity has taken hold of the ecclesiastical world." It has been said, "The ecumenical movement is probably the greatest religious surge since the Protestant Reformation"; "We live in an age of unprecedented ecumenical acceleration."

James DeForest Murch has remarked, "Christian unity is in the air. The chief concern of Christendom today is the movement to unite all churches in one universal Christian church 'throughout the whole inhabited world.'"

Pope Paul VI expressed the desire, "We hope we will soon see the day when all religions will unite their efforts concretely in the service of man, his freedom, and his dignity" (*Observator Romano*, June 15, 1972, p. 5). The Vatican is engaged in a global enterprise to bring all faiths into a union with the Roman Catholic church. A leading Anglican clergyman has put it bluntly, "Christian denominations ultimately will join as one church under the vicar of Rome—the Pope."

To millions of people on the earth, such a move is commendable in that "the real distinction between Catholicism and Protestantism means very little in the minds of most people." A great number of Protestants seem willing to accept the Pope as their spiritual leader.

The ultimate purpose of the ecumenical movement is the unification of all mankind exemplified in the doctrine of "the fatherhood of God and the brotherhood of man." This is considered by many to be the wave of the future.

René Pasche in his booklet, *The Ecumenical Movement,* gives this explanation:

> The expressions, "ecumenical" and "ecumenical movement," are heard repeatedly in religious circles today. Many are asking just what these terms mean and whether they represent fields of truth and action which merit serious study.

The Greek word *oikoumene* means "the inhabited earth" (cf. Luke 2:1); thus the adjective *ecumenical* means that which has to do with the whole earth, that which is universal. So the title "ecumenical movement" has been given to that organization which seeks to unite all Christian denominations and confessions in order that the church may be visibly one, thereby showing her universal character.

There is no doubt that we live in "ecumenical" times. Everything is tending to become universal. In the political world, the nations are speaking more and more of the necessity for a single world government to save humanity from complete annihilation. From an economic standpoint, the interdependence of all lands is more and more apparent. In the same way, a growing tendency toward unification is appearing in religious circles.

The World Council of Churches is the leader in this movement. "The emblem of the World Council of Churches shows an ancient representation of the church in the form of a ship, with the mast signifying Christ. *Oikoumene* is Greek for 'the inhabited world' and is the root of 'ecumenical.'"

The danger of following such a movement is that the great doctrines of the church are set aside for the sake of unity.

Bible believers contend that unity cannot be achieved at the cost of truth. They want no part in "Bridge Building for Unity." To those who adhere to the Word, there is no "mandate for unity." The Scripture is very plain, "Thou shalt not follow a multitude to do evil" (Exod. 23:2).

Note this definition of ecumenicity: "[Ecumenism] is not an authentic manifestation of the Holy Spirit but merely the cultural drift among nominal Christians who are without convictions. It is a sickness of our time, or a symptom of it" (*How to Get Along Without God*, C. Stanley Lowell).

The modern ecumenical movement is the master plan of Satan in preparation for the reign of the Antichrist.

The ecumenical leaders insist that the unity of all faiths is in answer to Christ's prayer in John 17:21, "That they all may be one." These blind leaders fail to realize that unity is spiritual, not organizational, and true unity is inseparable from truth.

There is a vast difference between "unity" and "union." Christ's prayer in John 17 is for a "unity" of believers, not a "union" of churches. Theodore Epp gives this evaluation:

Our present-day ecumenical movement is a manmade program which can only produce a manmade unity....It is an amazing counterfeit of truth from the time of Semiramis down to the present day....Babylonianism is not dead in our day. The ecumenical movement with its dream of a one-world church has been thoroughly infiltrated by the rites and practices of Babylonianism.[65]

Ecumenism will reach its zenith during the first part of the Tribulation. What was once a dream of apostate ecclesiastical leaders will become a reality. The counterfeit Christ will offer a troubled world peace and unity. The deceived world will accept him with open arms. It will be the Devil's millennium.

---

**These blind [ecumenical] leaders fail to realize that unity is spiritual, not organizational, and true unity is inseparable from truth.**

---

Rome today is leading the way in preparation for the ultimate worship of the Antichrist. She is willing to dialogue with the various religions of the world. The Vatican is engaged in a worldwide endeavor to make Catholicism attractive to those outside her fold. The "positive values" of a reunited church are stressed. Setting aside the Word of God, Rome is stressing "religious experience" and "mysticism," thus proving a common ground for the gullible.

The biblical injunction concerning the modern ecumenical movement is very plain: "And I heard another voice from heaven, saying, Come out of her, my people, that ye be not partakers of her sins, and that ye receive not of her plagues" (Rev. 18:4).

To enter into dialogue with apostate Christendom is "the old Garden of Eden" reenacted.

It is reported that a certain high church dignitary asserted, "Let's forget history." Another prominent ecclesiastical leader called the Reformation a "mere lovers' quarrel." It would be tragic for Protestants to forget the bloodshed and the awful price paid in defense of the historic doctrines of Christianity.

Today tolerance is the word, but the true church can never be subordinate to the claims of error. As someone has remarked, "Beware when the shepherds speak well of the wolves." It has been said, and rightfully, "Tolerance is good, but tolerance which sells our convictions is treason." The Apostle Paul warned the church at Ephesus, "And have no fellowship with the unfruitful works of darkness, but rather reprove them" (Eph. 5:11).

Dr. H. A. Ironside writes these pertinent words:

We hear a great deal about the possibility of church federation at the present time; but men seem to forget, or never have known, that it is God Himself who has rent Christendom asunder because of her unfaithfulness and apostasy.[66]

The Bible clearly teaches separation from apostasy:

*"Be ye not unequally yoked together with unbelievers: for what fellowship hath righteousness with unrighteousness? and what communion hath light with darkness?*

*"And what concord hath Christ with Belial? or what part hath he that believeth with an infidel?*

*"And what agreement hath the temple of God with idols? for ye are the temple of the living God; as God hath said, I will dwell in them, and walk in them; and I will be their God, and they shall be my people.*

*"Wherefore come out from among them, and be ye separate, saith the Lord, and touch not the unclean thing; and I will receive you,*

*"And will be a Father unto you, and ye shall be my sons and daughters, saith the Lord Almighty."*—II Cor. 6:14-18.

*"For such are false apostles, deceitful workers, transforming themselves into the apostles of Christ.*

*"And no marvel; for Satan himself is transformed into an angel of light.*

*"Therefore it is no great thing if his ministers also be transformed as the ministers of righteousness; whose end shall be according to their works."*—II Cor. 11:13-15.

*"I marvel that ye are so soon removed from him that called you into the grace of Christ unto another gospel:*

*"Which is not another; but there be some that trouble you, and would pervert the gospel of Christ.*

*"But though we, or an angel from heaven, preach any other gospel unto you than that which we have preached unto you, let him be accursed.*

*"As we said before, so say I now again, If any man preach any other gospel unto you than that ye have received, let him be accursed."*—Gal. 1:6-9.

*"If there come any unto you, and bring not this doctrine, receive him not into your house, neither bid him God speed:*

*"For he that biddeth him God speed is partaker of his evil deeds."*—II John 10,11.

Men of God are needed in these last days to warn of the perils of the ecumenical movement and Babylonian apostasy. These days call for prophets of discernment like "the children of Issachar, which were men that had understanding of the times" (I Chron. 12:32). Our example should be the Daniel of ancient Babylon. The words of Vance Havner are appropriate here: "Thank God, at the original feast of Belshazzar, the queen could say, 'There is a man,' a man who knows what time it is and who can read what God is writing."

## Babylon—America

It is imperative that America learn the lessons of ancient Babylon before it is too late. Belshazzar followed the same pathway as his grandfather Nebuchadnezzar. America does not have forever to repent. Babylon had a false security. Nothing could happen to her. That America could ever perish is far removed from the thinking of the average citizen.

Babylon did not fall from without but from within. Traitors from within betrayed their country. The Persians were able to enter mighty Babylon because certain Babylonians helped the enemy.

Abraham Lincoln said, "If this nation is destroyed, it will be from within and not from without." There are insidious forces that are committed to the destruction of America.

God is sovereign. Not only does He reign in Heaven, but He has a divine plan for the nations of the earth. Finite man must submit to the sovereignty of the Almighty.

Daniel 4:35 declares: "And all the inhabitants of the earth are reputed as nothing: and he doeth according to his will in the army of heaven, and among the inhabitants of the earth: and none can stay his hand, or say unto him, What doest thou?" The politics of men will eventually be resigned to the policy of God. Writing on "Belshazzar's Feast and Fall," W. C. Stevens concludes:

> The political lesson of this chapter emphasizes that the Son of God is the supreme Sovereign of the earth. Not only are private individuals accountable to Christ for their conduct according to light and opportunity, but so also are great monarchs, yea, even dynasties and empires. All human authority and rule is ordained and stands in direct responsibility to Him.
> Abraham Lincoln, in proclaiming in 1863 "a day of national humiliation, fasting and prayer," embraced in this preamble the words, "devoutly recognizing the supreme authority and just government of Almighty God in all the affairs of men and nations." With the Senate, he saw in that hour of national travail a call to prayer, not for "success to our arms"—righteous indeed as seemed to be the cause—but for "clemency and forgiveness"; a call to "national humiliation" "before the offended Power" under a felt "necessity of redeeming and preserving grace."
> The devout Bible student must feel the lack of this disposition in warring Christendom. And whoever remembers that solemn day has doubtless

long prayed that we might hear from Washington again the voice of 1863.[67]

A nation is only as strong as those who govern it. "The graveyards of civilizations are filled with nations whose leaders made wrong decisions in times of international crisis." Jenkin Lloyd Jones makes this observation:

> Things were very hunky-dory at Belshazzar's feast until the mysterious hand wrote "MENE, MENE, TEKEL, UPHARSIN" upon the wall. And Daniel spoiled the festivities when he said it meant the days of the kingdom were numbered, that its leaders had been weighed and found wanting, and that the realm was about to be taken over by the Medes and the Persians. Sure enough, that night Belshazzar was slain. Darius moved in. And the ancients marveled at how fast it happened.

> ## "Not only are private individuals accountable to Christ for their conduct according to light and opportunity, but so also are great monarchs, yea, even dynasties and empires."
> —W. C. Stevens

It has been said, "Once we roared like lions for liberty; now we bleat like sheep for security! The solution of America's problem is not in terms of big government, but it is in big men over whom nobody stands in control but God."

The Almighty always warns before He sends judgment. There is always a Noah to warn of a coming flood, a Moses to warn of the consequences of unbelief, and a Daniel to warn of the fall of Babylon.

Lehman Strauss' is worthy of consideration:

> While Daniel was giving the interpretation, the Medes and the Persians were already on Babylonian soil, and the inebriated Babylonians were helpless to stop their advance. The Most High God was ruling in the kingdom of men. The head of gold was about to be removed from the body of Gentile world power.
>
> "In that night" (5:30) judgment struck very swiftly. Certainly Belshazzar could not have expected the end to come so soon and suddenly. But even while Daniel was interpreting the writing, God had already given the kingdom to the Medes and Persians, "in that night."
>
> Empires do not stand by human might, manmade machines and missiles.

There is not a wall high enough nor thick enough to prevent a nation from falling when God pronounces that nation's doom.[68]

No nation can survive apostasy. The Bible clearly teaches that there is no remedy for apostasy. That America has deliberately departed from God's truth there can be little doubt. Like Israel and Babylon, we have become idolatrous.

America's hope is in a return to spiritual values—the principles of God's Word. There must be a fervent militancy and holy boldness for the fundamentals of the Bible. Alexander Hislop concludes his masterful book with these words:

> . . . The commandments of God, to our corrupt and perverse minds, may sometimes seem to be hard. They may require us to do what is painful, they may require us to forego what is pleasing to flesh and blood. But, whether we know the reason of these commandments or no, if we only know that they come from "the only wise God, our Saviour," we may be sure that in the keeping of them there is great reward; we may go blindfold wherever the Word of God may lead us, and rest in the firm conviction that, in so doing, we are pursuing the very path of safety and peace.
>
> Human wisdom at the best is but a blind guide; human policy is a meteor that dazzles and leads astray; and they who follow it walk in darkness, and know not whither they are going; but he "that walketh uprightly," that walks by the rule of God's infallible Word, will ever find that "he walketh surely," and that whatever duty he has to perform, whatever danger he has to face, "great peace have they which love thy law: and nothing shall offend them."[69]

The head of gold has become badly tarnished with age of the centuries until today archaeologists seek her remnants in the dust of ancient Babylon. Gone is Nimrod; gone is the Tower of Babel; gone is Nebuchadnezzar; gone is Belshazzar; gone are the Hanging Gardens; and gone is the splendor of a glorious civilization—but the God of Daniel lives on!

Need we repeat that the handwriting is on the wall for America? Do we have eyes to see and intelligent discernment to comprehend the warning? We bow before history and Holy Writ to acknowledge, "for strong is the Lord God who judgeth her" (Rev. 18:8).

A few years ago in the ancient ruins of Babylon, a traveler picked up a little delicate flower, probably the only living thing in that vast waste. As he looked at its lovely delicacy, he said, "How is it, little flower, that you, so frail that I could crush you between my fingers, have survived, and this vast empire founded on military might has perished?"

The flower seemed to smile back at him and say, "I obeyed the laws of God written in myself. I lived. They disobeyed those laws of God written in themselves. They perished."

Nations commit suicide.

## ENDNOTES:

[1]James Orr, *The International Standard Bible Encyclopedia*, Vol. I, 352.

[2]Leonard Cottrell, *Wonders of the World*, 50.

[3]Samuel Noah Kramer, *Cradle of Civilization*, 11.

[4]*Ibid.*, 257.

[5]Robert Silverberg, *Lost Cities and Vanished Civilizations*, 93.

[6]Merrill F. Unger, *Unger's Bible Dictionary*, 115.

[7]Silverberg, 116, 117.

[8]John Elder, *Prophets, Idols and Diggers: Scientific Proof of Bible History*, 102.

[9]Silverberg, 107, 108.

[10]Clarence Larkin, *Dispensational Truth*, 141.

[11]Cottrell, 54.

[12]Elder, 104.

[13]Silverberg, 109.

[14]Orr, 355.

[15]Unger, 115.

[16]Donald Grey Barnhouse, *God's Grace*, Vol. 5, 41, 42.

[17]National Geographic Society, *Everyday Life in Bible Times*, 278.

[18]Kramer, 99.

[19]Orr, 373.

[20]John Phillips, *Exploring Romans*, 29.

[21]Phillips, 30.

[22]William R. Newell, *The Book of Revelation*, 375, 376.

[23]Alexander Hislop, *The Two Babylons*, 12.

[24]*Ibid.*, 66, 67.

[25]Herbert J. Muller, *The Loom of History*, 33.

[26]Will Durant, *Caesar and Christ*, 33.

[27]W. A. Criswell, *Expository Sermons on the Book of Revelation*, Vol. 4, 183, 184.

[28]Arthur W. Pink, *Gleanings in Genesis,*, 135.

[29]W. A. Criswell, *Expository Sermons on the Book of Daniel,* Vol. 1, 99, 100.

[30]Alexander Whyte, *Bible Characters*, Third Series, 173, 174.

[31]Lehman Strauss, *The Prophecies of Daniel*, 149.

[32]Whyte, 185, 186.

[33]Strauss, 147, 148.

[34]John F. Walvoord, *Daniel*, 120.

[35]*Ibid.*, 117.

[36]Wilbur M. Smith, *Therefore Stand,* 490.

[37]W. C. Stevens, *The Book of Daniel,* 73.

[38]Whyte, 190, 191.

[39]Philip R. Newell, *Daniel the Man Greatly Beloved and His Prophecies,* 61, 62.

[40]Stevens, 74, 75.

[41]Larkin, 142.

[42]Cottrell, 56.

[43]Joseph A. Seiss, *The Apocalypse,* Vol. 3, 190.

[44]Criswell, *Expository Sermons on the Book of Revelation,* Vol. 4, 180.

[45]Lehman Strauss, *The Book of Revelation,* 296.

[46]Ford C. Ottman, *The Unfolding of the Ages,* 378.

[47]H. A. Ironside, *Lectures on Revelation,* 299.

[48]Tim LaHaye, *Revelation Illustrated and Made Plain,* 316.

[49]I. M. Haldeman, *The Signs of the Times,* 367, 368.

[50]John F. Walvoord, *The Revelation of Jesus Christ,* 245.

[51]Strauss, *The Prophecies of Daniel,* 153.

[52]Hislop, 3.

[53]*The Companion Bible, Acts to Revelation,* Part 6, Appendix, 211.

[54]*Ibid.,* 1905.

[55]Ottman, 379.

[56]A. C. Gaebelein, *Revelation,* 101.

[57]Seiss, 124, 125.

[58]Haldeman, 374, 375.

[59]Criswell, *Expository Sermons on the Book of Revelation,* Vol. 4, 186.

[60]Theodore H. Epp, *Practical Studies in Revelation,* Vol. 2, 321.

[61]Charles Caldwell Ryrie, *Revelation,* 109.

[62]Larkin, 143.

[63]Henry Alford, *The New Testament for English Readers,* 1860.

[64]Donald Grey Barnhouse, *Revelation,* 346.

[65]Epp, 285, 287, 290.

[66]Ironside, 295.

[67]Stevens, 76.

[68]Strauss, *The Prophecies of Daniel,* 168, 169.

[69]Hislop, 290.

# 4    the Glory Is Departed

The ruins on the Acropolis of Athens are awesome. Perhaps in no other country in the world do the stones cry out so painfully and yet so eloquently, "We had it, we had it all; but we lost it!" The glory is gone. *Ichabod.* What remains is a faded glory.

There is no doubt about it—the ancient Greeks had it all. Will Durant, in the Preface of his volume *The Life of Greece,* acknowledges that practically everything we have in our western culture today came from the Greeks.[1]

The philhellene, Edith Hamilton, with deep admiration writes:

> ...In a sense it was a miracle and remains a miracle; the anthropologists and archaeologists have been unable to explain how the passion for truth, beauty, simplicity and freedom developed in a rocky little seaport in the midst of barbarian superstition, despotism and splendor.
>
> There [is] a light...that has indeed never been matched in the centuries since. For in those brief centuries, which reached their summit in the few years of the Great Age of Pericles, literature, science, philosophy, art, democracy, religion—the main achievements of the modern world— developed almost overnight, full-blown in many cases and as perfect as they could ever be.[2]

Considered an authority on Greek culture, she also made the observation that "a light was lit that can never go out"; and yet with due respect to this gifted scholar, it must be conceded that the light has dimmed and is now but a faint glow. Athens today is a mere memory of another day.

The ancient Greeks have been described as "the most remarkable people in history." Historians state that "humanity reached its highest degree of civilization of which it is capable under purely natural conditions." Sir Henry Moore was more explicit: "Except the blind forces of nature, nothing moves in this world which is not Greek in origin."[3] John Pentland Mahaffey makes this observation:

The Greeks were as supreme in science as in other departments, and, though they did not discover the powers of steam or electricity, they nevertheless carried out in mechanics works that no modern builder, with all his vaunted control of nature, has yet equalled, and so in other pursuits, not only Greek form, but Greek thought, has been the greatest and the clearest that the world has yet seen.[4]

The Golden Age of Greece was the zenith of history. Said one, "The soil of Greece might well be termed the literacy sanctuary of the human race." Wilbur M. Smith makes these pertinent remarks:

It is doubtful if we may expect to ever see again such genius as was revealed among the Greeks, especially during the fifth century B.C. . . .

As Rome's system of government and her legal codes have stamped themselves upon Western civilization forever, so Greek culture, art, philosophy and science, literature, ethics, and political theory, have given to Europe its ideals in these realms, its vocabulary, and its greatest masterpieces.

In almost every major department of life, and certainly of the inner life, with the single exception of religion, Greece has given us the noblest achievements of the race. Ancient Greek culture is that which has forever been looked up to as almost perfect, and, at the same time, almost incapable of being repeated, except in inferior copies.

Of the entire period of Greek history, it was the age of Pericles in which the greatest concentration of human genius ever appeared, in one locality, at one time.[5]

The Apostle Paul declared, "I am debtor . . . to the Greeks" (Rom. 1:14). John Gunther enumerates their achievements:

No people in history ever gave so much to the human race in so short a time as the ancient Greeks. They produced architectural monuments as noble as the Parthenon. They produced in rapid succession four of the greatest dramatists who ever lived—Sophocles, Euripides, Aeschylus and Aristophanes. They produced one of the most brilliant statesmen who ever lived—Pericles, and two of the greatest historians—Thucydides and Herodotus.

They produced scientists of the first rank, and three philosophers whose thought has done so much to arouse good for the world that they are household words today—Socrates, Plato and Aristotle.[6]

Athens was the university capital of the world. Frederic W. Farrar gives this detailed description:

Athens! With what a thrill of delight has many a modern traveller been filled as, for the first time, he stepped upon that classic land! With what an eager gaze has he scanned the scenery and outline of that city!. . .

As he approached the Acropolis, what a throng of brilliant scenes has passed across his memory; what processions of grand and heroic and beautiful figures have swept across the stage of his imagination! As he treads upon Attic ground, he is in "the Holy Land of the Ideal"; he has reached the most sacred shrine of the "fair humanities" of Paganism.

It was at Athens that the human form, sedulously trained, attained its most exquisite and winning beauty; there that human freedom put forth its most splendid power; there that human intellect displayed its utmost subtlety and grace; there that Art reached to its most consummate perfection; there that Poetry uttered alike its sweetest and its sublimest strains; there that Philosophy attuned to the most perfect music of human expression its loftiest and deepest thoughts.

Had it been possible for the world by its own wisdom to know God; had it been in the power of man to turn into bread the stones of the wilderness; had permanent happiness lain with the grasp of sense, or been among the rewards of culture; had it been granted to man's unaided power to win salvation by the gifts and qualities of his own nature and to make for himself a new Paradise in lieu of that lost Eden, before whose gate still waves the fiery sword of the Cherubim—then such ends would have been achieved at Athens in the day of her glory. No one who has been nurtured in the glorious lore of that gay and radiant city and has owed some of his best training to the hours spent in reading the history and mastering the literature of its many noble sons, can ever visit it without deep emotions of gratitude, interest, and love.[7]

"The Greeks were the first intellectualists," and nowhere was that fact more evident than on the Acropolis and its environs. Everywhere Athens was acclaimed as "the most cultivated city of the old world." She proudly held the title, "the mother of arts and eloquence." "Here the human mind had blazed forth with a splendor it has never exhibited elsewhere. In the Golden Age of its history, Athens possessed more men of the very highest genius than have ever lived in any other city. To this day their names invest her with glory."[8]

Athens thus became the teacher of the world and the seat of learning. Her famous teachers taught the love of knowledge, the love of beauty, the love of truth. It is an historical fact that Rome conquered Greece, but Greece became the teacher of Rome and hence the world.

It is worth noting that the Apostle Paul challenged the prevailing philosophies of his day. Paul's ministry was carried on in influential cities. Someone has remarked, "Christianity germinated in what is called the corruption of the big cities." Here was the center of the political, commercial, intellectual and religious world. Paul was where the action was.

The true character of the ancient Athenians was revealed in Paul's address on Mars' Hill. Both the message and the reaction to it give us an insight into their spiritual dearth. Note that the apostle "stood in the midst of Mars' hill" (Acts 17:22). The great metropolis was located on a plain in Attica, surrounded by hills and mountains. In the center of the city was the Acropolis (the citadel crowning the hill), "260 ft. high with a flat oval top 500 ft. wide and 1,150 ft. long" (*The Columbia Encyclopedia,* Third Edition, p. 13).

On the summit of Mars' Hill Paul could behold the magnificent Parthenon, built on the Acropolis. This "marbled glory of absolute perfection" is considered one of the most majestic buildings of all history. Wilbur M. Smith is more succinct in his comment: "One can say that the Parthenon was the most beautiful building ever built by man and let it go at that...."[9]

Professor Mahaffey is profuse in his praise of this historic building. Note his words: "There is, in fact, no building on earth which can sustain the burden of its greatness" (*Rambles and Studies in Greece,* p. 309).

Pericles was right when he boasted, "We shall be the marvel of the present day and of ages yet to come."

H. V. Morton seems to be carried away as he gives this description:

> As I passed through Propylaea, I saw before me a great space of rough rock rising upward, and on the summit of this rock the Parthenon stood against the blue sky.
>
> I thought that never in my life I had seen anything so beautiful. Lifted high above Athens, with nothing behind it but the blue summer sky, far larger than I had imagined it to be, yet looking queerly weightless, the Parthenon, even in ruin, looks as if it had just lighted from Heaven upon this summit of the Acropolis.
>
> As I drew near to this inspired building, I said to myself: "I have seen the Pyramids and a hundred other remains of the ancient world, but you are the most lovely thing I have ever seen: you are the only ruin on earth that a man would come to see again, again, and again; and I would like to climb this hill to see you every year until the end of life!"[10]

Athens specialized in religion. One wit remarked that there were more gods in the city than human beings. Paul observed the altar "To the Unknown God." This great ambassador of the cross realized that Athens was suffering from an overdose of religion. His indictment was, "Ye men of Athens, I perceive that in all things ye are [very religious]" (Acts 17:22). Here was paganism at its best and religion at its worst.

Wilbur M. Smith makes this evaluation:

> In fact, the very passions and shame of men were actually deified in the religion of these Greeks, which some in our modern time try to tell us was the most beautiful religion that the earth has ever seen....

Smith then quotes Gerhard Uhlhorn:

> "Each man's fearful passion becomes his god. A Greek wishes to be drunk, Dionysus was his patron; to be vicious, and he turned to Aphrodite Pandemos. He was a thief, and could rely on the help of Hermes...."

Smith adds:

> Above everything else in considering ancient Greek religion, we must remember—and this none can deny—that no matter how much we try to idealize the life of these ancient people, Greek religion was emphatically mythical, not historical; its gods had no real existence, they were the creations of men and of finite sinful men, without divine inspiration of any kind....[11]

This was a nation influenced by worthless gods. Ironside remarks, "Practically every false deity worshipped on earth could be found in Athens, yet this was the educational center of the world." William Arnot writes: "Idols, idols everywhere, and living men boasted themselves to be God's offspring, bowing down before images of wood and stone, graven by art and man's device."[12]

The Apostle Paul was a Christian and a Jew and therefore horrified at the gaudy display of idolatry on every hand. J. Patterson Smyth explains:

> We would be enthusiastic over Athens. Paul would not. His Hebrew ideal was not beauty and art, but righteousness. He would value more a sweating slave boy who loved the Lord than a whole university of artists and philosophers....
>
> To a cultured tourist, Athens of that day would be a dream of beauty and delight. But Paul was not enjoying it. "His spirit was stirred within him as he saw the city crowded with idols." "The ugly little Jew," says Renan, "had no taste for beauty." That may be. But that is not the explanation. That ugly little Jew stood on a higher plane. His eyes were on God, and righteousness, and the love of Christ, and the strength to conquer sin, and the glory of eternal life. So he looked on these proud people, not with envy or admiration, but with heartfelt pity.
>
> Vanity of vanities. They had missed the Highest.[13]

Paul was angry; in fact, furious. Like his Master, he was filled with righteous indignation. "A paroxysm [for that is the literal word] seizes his heart. His soul is stirred within him; a paroxysm of agony seizes his whole nature when he sees such a sight as he had never beheld before—a city wholly given to idolatry."[14] Conybeare and Howson in their classic work, *The Life and Epistles of St. Paul,* make this observation:

> He burned with zeal for that God whom, "as he went through the city,"

he saw dishonoured on every side. He was melted with pity for those who, notwithstanding their intellectual greatness, were "wholly given to idolatry."

His eye was not blinded to the reality of things, by the appearances either of art or philosophy. Forms of earthly beauty and words of human wisdom were valueless in his judgment, and far worse than valueless, if they deified vice and made falsehood attractive. He saw and heard with an earnestness of conviction which no Epicurean could have understood, as his tenderness of affection was morally far above the highest point of the Stoic's impassive dignity.[15]

To the great apostle "the aesthetic glory of Greece was but a gorgeous covering which genius had woven and spread over a vast cemetery of corruption." Here was a malignant cancer, and no physician present was able to use the surgeon's scalpel. What a feeling of utter helplessness must have descended upon him, yet he had the answer for all their sordid ills.

Ancient Athens was deceiving. With all of her intellectual attainments, she was the queen of the world; yet her garments were tainted, and her soul reeked of decay.

The beautiful gods of Olympus were but heroes of fable. Their worship was but a screen for lust and rottenness. Life was beautiful, bright, sparkling, on the surface. But it was utterly hollow. The human soul, made in the likeness of God, could not get satisfaction out of beauty alone.

The day of sorrow came to them, and there was no comfort. The day of death came, and they had no hope.

In art and culture, they were first of the nations. If it were possible for human wisdom alone to find out God, Athens must have found Him. But, alas, as Paul writes later to the Corinthians, "the world by wisdom knew not God." For it is through spiritual aspiration, not through intellectual knowledge, that men find the Father.[16]

The Golden Age of Greece was an age of philosophy. Athens was a philosopher's paradise. Their craze then (as now) was for something new ["(For all the Athenians...spent their time in nothing else, but either to tell, or to hear some new thing)" (Acts 17:21).] Said one, "The period between the birth of Pericles and the death of Aristotle has been proclaimed the most memorable in the history of the world." Pericles boasted, "We love the things of the mind without being soft."

Professor R. W. Livingstone asserted, "The only thinking civilization in the world before our own was that of Greece." The ancient Xenophanes of Colophon declared, "Truly the gods have not from the beginning revealed all things to mortals, but by long seeking mortals make progress in discovery." Thus W. C. Guthrie concludes that the origin of philosophy as we know it today was by "sheer force of intellect."[17] Yet John Calvin dogmatically asserts, "The city, which was the mansion-house of wisdom, the fountain of all arts, the mother of humanity, did exceed all others in blindness and madness."[18]

---

**They knew philosophy, but they did not possess the divine revelation; they knew science, but they did not know the Creator; they knew literature, but they did not know "the sweetest love story ever told."**

---

In the marketplace Paul confronted the philosophers [the university professors of his day]. "Then certain philosophers of the Epicureans, and of the Stoics, encountered him" (Acts 17:18).

The Epicureans were the followers of Epicurus who taught that pleasure was the chief end of life—the highest human pursuit. Over the entrance to the garden of Epicurus were inscribed the words:

**GUEST, THOU SHALT BE HAPPY HERE, FOR HERE HAPPINESS IS ESTEEMED THE HIGHEST GOOD.**

The soul was matter and did not survive the dissolution of the body. Eventually the followers of Epicurus contended that death ends all and hence the philosophy of "eat, drink and be merry" [the glorification of self].

"The essential principle of the Epicurean philosopher was that there was nothing to alarm him, nothing to disturb him."[19] In other words, "You will be a short time alive, and a long time dead." This was not the total of Epicureanism; but in essence, their philosophy was revealed in personified pleasure.

While the Epicureans enjoyed pleasure, the Stoics were the epitome of pride. This school of thought, founded by Zeno, derived its name from the founder who taught in a porch [stoa]. Their philosophy represented man's quest for a refuge and escape from the impact of troubled times. According to Coneybeare and Howson:

> The Stoics condemned the worship of images and the use of temples, regarding them as nothing better than the ornaments of art. But they justified the popular polytheism and, in fact, considered the gods of

mythology as minor developments of the Great World-God, which summed up their belief concerning the origin and existence of the world.[20]

They believed that the highest good was virtue (however, their belief and practice were often different). Their philosophy was in conflict with Christianity in that they were Pantheists.

The physical theory underlining Stoicism is materialistic. All that has reality is material. Force, which is the shaping principle, is joined with matter. This universal working force, God, pervades all and becomes the reason and soul in the animate creation (*The Columbia Encyclopedia,* Third Edition, p. 2047).

A resurrection from the dead was considered irrational. Everything was judged according to reason, hence the rejection of a future punishment. Like Henley's poem, "Invictus," they could boast:

**I am the master of my fate;**
**I am the captain of my soul.**

Theirs was the pride of face, place and race.

No wonder the great apostle was branded a "babbler" (Acts 17:18). He was referred to as a "spermologos"—a seed picker. Ramsey interprets the designation as living at the expense of another. The connotation is that of absolute vulgarity and inability to rise above the most contemptible standard of life and conduct.[21]

The ultimate conclusion of these vain philosophers was that God cannot be personally known. The altar "TO THE UNKNOWN GOD" (Acts 17:23) was but the void felt in their own hearts. Thus they admitted that the true God was unknown to them.

Their famous city was filled with gods, but they had not discovered the God of Christianity. They knew architecture, but they did not know the Architect of the Ages; they knew philosophy, but they did not possess divine revelation; they knew science, but they did not know the Creator; they knew literature, but they did not know "the sweetest love story ever told."

To this unbelieving group of intellectual snobs Paul preached repentance, the fact of the coming judgment and the resurrection (Acts 17:30,31). And what were the results of this masterful message? Derision—"some mocked" (Acts 17:32), literally, "to throw out the lip, to jeer at." Paul's message was too much for the pleasure-loving Epicureans or the pharisaical Stoics. "They rudely shut the preacher's mouth, and so shut the door of mercy against themselves."

Joseph Parker comments, "We mock the preacher's manner and think that that excuses us from attending to the preacher's doctrine." It is possible to make a jest of life; but those who make a jest of life will find that that which began as a comedy must end in tragedy.

There was not only derision but also delay—procrastination ["and others said, We will hear thee again of this matter" (Acts 17:32)]; in other words, at a more convenient time.

> They did not venture to say never, but they went the length of saying not now. . . . They are willing to possess a religion; but not willing that a religion should possess them. They will wear it as a becoming ornament; but they will not flee to hide it as their life.[22]

Farrar suggests that "they were too busy to spare time from the important occupation of gossiping."[23]

The most dangerous of all days is when a man discovers how easy it is to talk about tomorrow. "We will hear thee again of this matter" (Acts 17:32), but they never did. A more convenient season never came. Athens never again heard the greatest preacher of history.

Derision, delay; but there were also decisions. Although not spectacular, they were significant (Acts 17:34). His audience has been described as "a butterfly nature, loving sunshine, sipping honey, without a thought of the grave, and a solicitude as to what was beyond it."

The names of the university professors at that august gathering are forgotten, but the names of Dionysius and Damaris will be remembered for their confessed faith, for their names were inscribed in the Lamb's Book of Life.

Acts 18:1 records, "After these things Paul departed from Athens. . ." for good. He wrote no epistle to them. He never mentioned the church or converts in his epistles. On his next voyage he completely avoided the city. Athens had received her day of "visitation."

> And men do not judge Paul with the sneering judgment of that day by their failure to know the greatness of the hero and saint who now left their gates forever. Of all the men who ever spoke in Athens, the greatest were Socrates and Paul. Athens slew Socrates by poison; it froze Paul out with a laugh.[24]

Renan confesses, "Paul belonged to another world; his Holy Land was elsewhere."[25]

Some believe that the Apostle Paul failed in Athens. Others like Henry T. Sell conclude: "Paul did not fail. The trouble with the Athenians was that they possessed only intellectual curiosity; they had no appetite for the truth."[26]

In his book, William M. Taylor shows remarkable discernment:

> Such, then, was the first conflict between human philosophy and the gospel of Christ. It looks almost, on the first blush of the matter, as if it had been a defeat for Christianity. But no; in these converts, few though

they were, its power was made manifest; and before three centuries had passed away, it was discovered that the only way in which philosophy could flourish was by grafting itself in some form or other on the gospel.

It was defeated in its own high places. Then it sought to enter the church, and there it did more damage by its alliance than it had done before by its enmity.[27]

And what about Athens and Greece today? Lord Byron, who died fighting for the cause of freedom in that land, wrote:

> **The isles of Greece, the isles of Greece!**
> **Where grew the arts of war and peace;**
> **Eternal summer gilds them yet,**
> **But all, except their sun, is set.**

Herodotus, the famous Greek historian, made this solemn prediction:

> **Greece will be strong and a match for the invader;**
> **But if some of us betray and stand aside**
> **And the loyal are few,**
> **Then there is reason to fear that all Greece may fall!**

Historians write of "the glory that was Greece," but today it is a faded glory. An ambassador to Greece remarked: "With the longest history of any country in Europe, Greece has had as many lives as the proverbial cat, and has died as many deaths."

What is witnessed today by the tourist is just a memory of the past. The pristine glory is gone. Today the Acropolis is but a haven for pilgrims and sightseers. Only the stones cry out of a departed majesty.

It has been noted that "every great nation which has risen to power has declined." Pericles' statement, "We love the things of the mind," gives us a clue as to the demise of ancient Greece.

Man was endowed by his Creator with more than a mind. Man possesses a soul. The book of Proverbs asserts, "The fear of the Lord is the beginning of knowledge" (1:7). It is admitted that the citizens of Athens "were the most intelligent and knowledgeable people who ever lived," but they were spiritually ignorant. They were victims of gross superstition.

In his book, Leonard Cottrell comments:

> Yet these same brilliant people respected oracles, and could base vital decisions—such as whether or not they should resist the invading Persians [and therefore, whether Western civilization should survive]—on the babblings of an old woman squatting in a cave at Delphi, chewing laurel leaves.[28]

The ancient Greeks were void of spiritual foundations. Their philosophies were built on sinking sand. Time has ravaged much of their pagan bulwarks away. What the contemporary world sees today is but a shadow of a sparkling civilization. A post mortem of the corpse reveals basic deficiencies.

Note the following words from Herbert J. Muller:

> The Greeks accordingly had no idea of growth and development, no clear perspective on their heritage. Homer was their Bible; his half-amused, ironic portraits of the immoral gods became the model for respectable piety; and when the more thoughtful became distressed by their "lies" about the gods, they could not understand him as the product of an earlier culture....[29]

The glowing glory of Athens did not last. Cottrell explains one of the reasons:

> Art, intelligence, beauty, courage—all the finest qualities and achievements of the human heart and mind—seemed concentrated, for a brief period, in that little Greek city-state, two thousand four hundred years ago. In a way it might be regarded as the creaming-off of the all that was best in the collective experience of mankind over three thousand years.
>
> It did not last, of course. But when the bright light of Hellenic culture was dimmed (though never extinguished), the tragedy was brought about, not by the hand of a foreign invader, but through that spirit of jealous independence which had been the strength of the Greeks; but which, when turned inward, weakened and almost destroyed them.[30]

It is ironic that a city which boasted of so much knowledge should be a victim of spiritual ignorance. Her basic problem was a theological one. Muller comments:

> While recognizing the guilt and folly of man, the Greeks had little sense of sin—of inherent unworthiness before their Creator, or of their short-comings as crimes against their Creator. The mystics aside, they lived neither in fear nor in love of God but went about their own business of making the most of life on earth. Granted a decent piety, their primary duties were to the city-state and to themselves.[31]

The higher the mountain, the longer the shadow. The Greeks in their thinking represented man's highest achievement without divine revelation. Wilbur M. Smith makes this pertinent statement, "The gods of Greece were myths, and this is what doomed Greek religion."[32] The Apostle Paul declared a momentous truth when he wrote to the intellectuals at Corinth, "the world by wisdom knew not God" (I Cor. 1:21). The Athenians needed Christ, not culture; they needed spiritual realities, not the caprices of men.

> Men tell us that the world is to be elevated by culture, and turn away from the gospel as a vulgar thing; but let them look below the surface of the Athens which Paul visited... and they will find that art, literature,

philosophy, aesthetics, may all be cultivated to the highest extent, while morally the heart is a cage of unclean beasts, and socially the community is reeking with rottenness. So true it is that 'the world by wisdom knows not God.'[33]

The ancient Athenians were guilty of "the betrayal of the mind." They missed God's highest, hence their future was bleak. A nation that turns its back on

---

## The Athenians needed Christ, not culture; they needed spiritual realities, not the caprices of men. . . . Nothing is so hopeless as unbelief.

---

divine revelation and direction is soon wallowing in the quagmire of paganism. Nothing is so hopeless as unbelief.

From a spiritual point of view, Athens left a legacy of sheer paganism. Frederic W. Farrar describes Athens as "the corruptress of the world." He supports that view with these graphic words:

> . . . Our regret for the extinguished brilliancy of Athens will be less keen when we bear in mind that, more than any other city, she has been the corruptress of the world. She kindled the altars of her genius with unhallowed incense, and fed them with strange fires. Better by far the sacred Philistinism—if Philistinism it were—for which this beautiful harlot had no interest and no charm, than the veiled apostasy which longs to recall her witchcraft and to replenish the cup of her abomination. Better the uncompromising Hebraism which asks what concord hath Christ with Belial and the Temple of God with idols, than the corrupt Hellenism which, under pretense of artistic sensibility or archaeological information, has left its deep taint on modern literature, and seems to be never happy unless it is raking amid the embers of forgotten lusts.
>
> . . . [Greece] was but trading on the memory of achievements not her own; she was but repeating with dead lips the echo of old philosophies which had never been sufficient to satisfy the yearnings of the world. Her splendour was no longer an innate effulgence, but a lingering reflex.[34]

The bards continue down through the centuries to lament the fate of ancient Hellas:

> **Fair Greece! sad relic of departed worth!**
> **Immortal, though no more; though fallen, great!**

**Who now shall lead thy scattered children forth,
And long-accustomed bondage uncreate?**

*—Childe Harold's Pilgrimage*

The tormented history of Greece has something to teach our troubled generation. Toynbee writes of a close parallel between Hellenic civilization and our own and that the problems which confront us today are analogous to many of those faced by the Greek world.[35]

Demosthenes warned, "The time for extracting a lesson from history is ever at hand for them who are wise." Edith Hamilton, in an article entitled, "The Lessons of the Past," acknowledges that Greece fell because she lost her spiritual strength.[36]

Idolatry has always been the curse of the nations. "Thou shalt have no other gods before me" (Exod. 20:3) is still God's standard for individuals and nations. "The old Greeks worshipped with bended knee the idols that were made of gold: we worship in our hearts the gold of which their idols were made."[37] The Greeks, like the ancient Israelites, had to learn the lesson that idolatry ends with the judgment of the Almighty.

The chief cities at the beginning of the fifth century were Athens, Sparta and Corinth. All reigned supreme in their particular area of achievement. Athens was noted for intellect; Sparta, the development of the body (via the military); Corinth emphasized beauty and commerce.

However, they all had one fallacy—they forgot that man has a soul. Their fatal philosophy was "Man is the measure of all things. Man, not the gods, the relative, not the absolute." Jesus Christ declared, "For what shall it profit a man [a city or a nation], if he shall gain the whole world, and lose his own soul?" (Mark 8:36).

Cities and nations are mortal. Some live longer than others, but eventually they go the way of all flesh. Some commit suicide.

Hendrik William van Loon comments:

> Emperor Justinian...discontinued the role of philosophy at Athens which had been founded by Plato.
>
> That was the end of the old Greek world, in which man had been allowed to think his own thoughts and dream his own dreams according to his desires. The somewhat vague rules of conduct of the philosophers had proved a poor compass by which to steer the ship of life after a deluge of savagery and ignorance had swept away the established order of things. There was more need of something more positive and more definite. This the Church provided.[38]

"The night of paganism had its stars to light it, but that they called to the morning-star which stood over Bethlehem."[39]

> **But mourn [fair Greece], mourn that the sacred band**
> **Which made thee once so famous by thy songs,**
> **Forced by outrageous fate, have left thy land,**
> **And left thee scarce a voice to plain thy wrongs.**
>
> —William Drummond
> *Sonnet before a poem of Irene*

The glory of Athens and Greece is gone, not by "outrageous fate," but by the hand of the sovereign God ["Behold, the nations are as a drop of the bucket" (Isa. 40:15)]. And to our frenzied generation, the ruins of the once mighty Acropolis plaintively mourn, "We had it; we had it all; but we lost it!"

The passing of time teaches that today will be yesterday, tomorrow. Yesterdays can only speak of the past. Will America have a tomorrow? Will we learn before it is too late? Has the glory departed?

Is America committing suicide?

## ENDNOTES:

[1] Will Durant, *The Life of Greece*, vii.

[2] Edith Hamilton, *The Greek Way*, Frontispiece.

[3] Durant, 667.

[4] John Pentland Mahaffey, *What Have the Greeks Done for Civilization?*, v.

[5] Wilbur M. Smith, *Therefore Stand*, 204, 205.

[6] John Gunther, *Alexander the Great*, 17, 18.

[7] Frederic W. Farrar, *The Life and Works of St. Paul*, 295, 296.

[8] Henry T. Sell, *Bible Studies in the Life of Paul*, 47.

[9] Smith, 212.

[10] H. V. Morton, *In the Steps of St. Paul*, 268.

[11] Smith, 230.

[12] William Arnot, *The Church in the House*, 377.

[13] J. Patterson Smyth, *The Story of St. Paul's Life and Letters*, 103, 105.

[14] Joseph Parker, *The People's Bible*, "Acts of the Apostles," Vol. 23, 43.

[15] W. J. Conybeare and J. S. Howson, *The Life and Epistles of St. Paul*, 279.

[16] Smyth, 104.

[17] Michael Grant, *The Birth of Western Civilization*, 108.

[18] Smith, 252.

[19] Conybeare and Howson, 285.

[20] *Ibid.*, 283.

[21] W. M. Ramsay, *St. Paul the Traveller*, 242.

[22] Arnot, 395.

[23] Farrar, 311.

[24] Basil Matthews, *Paul the Dauntless*, 223.

[25]Farrar, 296.

[26]Sell, 47.

[27]William M. Taylor, *Paul the Missionary*, 275.

[28]Leonard Cottrell, *The Anvil of Civilization*, 180.

[29]Herbert J. Muller, *The Uses of the Past*, 113.

[30]Cottrell, 228.

[31]Muller, 138.

[32]Smith, 231.

[33]Taylor, 262.

[34]Farrar, 230.

[35]Arnold J. Toynbee, *Greek Civilization*, Frontispiece.

[36]Richard Thruelson and John Kobler, *Adventures of the Mind*, 70.

[37]Arnot, 380.

[38]Hendrik William van Loon, *The Story of Mankind*, 125.

[39]B. F. Crocker, *Christianity and Greek Philosophy*, 524.

# 5     all Roads lead to Rome

## The Grandeur of Rome

If Greece reflected glory to the ancient world, Rome dazzled the world for over a millennium with grandeur. Poets and historians have exhausted themselves in an attempt to portray "the grandeur that was Rome." If the Greeks were smug in their achievements, the Romans were vocal in their aggrandizement.

"A thousand roads lead men forever to Rome" because this city on the Tiber has been praised as the greatest empire of all history.[1] What was the attraction of this famous city? Rome in all her majesty has been referred to as "the greatest phenomenon in history."[2] All roads led to Rome because Rome was "The Capital of the World." A contemporary has characterized the ancient metropolis as "First among cities, and the home of the gods...."

> It was in October 1764 that Edward Gibbon first walked "with a lofty step" among the ruins of the Roman Forum, and not until several days later could he properly collect his thoughts. Then he reported his feelings to his father at home. He was "almost in a dream," he wrote; the city had far surpassed his expectations.
>
> During the whole course of history, Gibbon believed, there had never, never arisen such another people as the Romans; and "for the happiness of mankind," he hoped there never would again.[3]

What Cicero declared of Athens is certainly true of Rome: "On whatever spot we tread, we awake a memory." A Latin poet, at the end of the eleventh century, lamented, "Rome, there is nothing like thee, although thou art almost wholly ruined."

The ruins of Rome speak eloquently and are "silent testaments to the last days of the imperial Empire." "Of ancient world empires, none had more grandeur and power than Rome. At its peak, it reached from Spain on the east, and from Egypt on the south, to Britain on the north."

"If all roads lead to Rome, they also lead out again from Rome. For those who have learned to think beyond yesterday, Rome is the focusing point of world's history."[4] Rome has much to teach us. Professor Cesare Foligno gives this word of caution:

> There are two sources of error which must be guarded against in considering the connection of ancient with modern civilization: unreasoned worship of the past and unjustified pride in the present.
>
> It is as pernicious to overrate the value of ancient civilization and to exaggerate the amount of the heritage which the modern world has actually received, as it is foolish to ignore the great achievements of the ancients and to deny that a portion of their assets has leavened progress in later days.[5]

Ancient Rome and contemporary America are not the same in every detail. There are differences, but it is the purpose of this chapter to show the striking parallels. As Dr. Robert C. Stone has pointed out, there are distinct parallels in the political, moral and religious areas.

The sordid problems of our day were also the problems of the Roman senate. Their predicament is our predicament today. The Caesars failed to give a solution to their dilemma. Our modern-day Caesars are also finding solutions difficult.

Rome was the toast of the ancient world until she was forced to drink the bitter dregs of her degeneracy, perversity and hence mediocrity and eventual obscurity. Our Rome is burning. Do we care?

## The Glories of Rome

Let us, first of all, consider Rome in her glory. It has been said, "To count up the glories of Rome is like counting the stars of the sky." Rome in all of her glory must have been something to behold. Historians are most lavish in their praise. Most noted of all, Edward Gibbon, describes his first visit to the city in 1764:

> ...I have already found such a fund of entertainment for mind, somewhat prepared for it by an acquaintance with the Romans, that I am almost in a dream. Whatever ideas books may have given us of the greatness of that people, their accounts of the most flourishing state of Rome fall infinitely short of the picture of its ruins.[6]

Called by millions "The Eternal City," Rome was the largest city of the world. It is reported that its walls extended twenty-one miles in circumference.[7]

Although this historic city has been designated "the center of the world," it was "a city of tombs," "a city of the dead."

What the Acropolis was to the ancient Greeks, the Forum was to Rome. The heart of the empire was Rome, and the heart of Rome was the Forum. Fulton Sheen gives this description:

> The Forum... is one of the most appealing ruins in the world. It is not as beautiful as the Parthenon is beautiful; you do not catch your breath in wonder when you see it first, as if some glorious white bird had suddenly alighted near you; you look at it with much the same sorrow that we of this generation have known in our cities as, turning a corner, we come upon a scene once noble and dear to us but now flattened by aerial bombardment.[8]

The Romans were tremendous builders. The city contains many impressive buildings. Someone has designated it "a city of marble."

> The creak of cranes lifting blocks of stone and the chip and twinkle of the stone mason's chisels and hammers must have been the characteristic sounds of Rome for centuries; and in a hundred distant gashes in the earth's crust an unknown and forgotten army of slaves and criminals labored and died, generation after generation, with stone dust in their hair and lungs to satisfy Rome's insatiable appetite for marble.... And most of that marble is still in Rome. It has migrated to the churches and the palaces....[9]

The Pantheon, dedicated to Mars, Venus, the deified Caesar and the other deities, is yet today a silent monument to Roman genius. It was the largest temple in Rome.

The Roman baths were very distinctive. The Baths of Caracella "surpass in luxury all the other baths of ancient Rome. There 1,600 bathers could take hot, cold, or tepid baths, enjoy a massage, converse, stand, read, or play games."[10]

Nero's Golden House was colossal. Suetonius gives this description:

> There was nothing... in which he was more ruinously prodigal than in building. He made a palace extending all the way from the Palatine to the Esquiline, which at first he called the House of Passage, but when it was burned shortly after its completion and rebuilt, the Golden House. Its size and splendor will be sufficiently indicated by the following details.
>
> Its vestibule was high enough to contain a colossal statue of the Emperor 120 feet high. So large was this house that it had a triple colonnade a mile long. There was a lake in it too, like a sea, surrounded with buildings to represent cities, besides tracts of country, varied by tilled fields,

vineyards, pastures and woods, with great numbers of wild and domestic animals.

In the rest of the house all parts were overlaid with gold and adorned with jewels and mother-of-pearl. There were dining rooms with fretted ceilings of ivory, whose panels could turn and shower down flowers and were fitted with pipes for sprinkling the guests with perfumes. The main banquet hall was circular and constantly revolved day and night, like the heavens. He had baths supplied with sea water and sulphur water.

When the edifice was finished in this style and he dedicated it, he deigned to say nothing more in the way of approval than that he was at last beginning to be housed like a human being.[11]

The glory of Athens was depicted in the Parthenon; the grandeur of Rome was revealed in the Colosseum. Both represented the zenith of their cultures. This tremendous structure, the Colosseum, was four stories (over 150 feet high) "and enclosed an oval arena 287 feet long by 180 feet wide." Peter Quennell writes:

> To the generations of tourists who have come to gaze in admiration and wonder, the vast arena has long appeared ageless—always ancient, always silent, always crumbling and ruinous.
>
> It is difficult to imagine it as it must have been when new: with sunlight striking its unblemished surfaces and flashing off the statues that decorated the arches; with hordes of people in a holiday mood dwarfed by its bulk as they approached across a broad plaza; and inside, with ring after ring of excited spectators cheering the bloody spectacles being presented for their amusement.[12]

The Colosseum was like a modern sports arena. Daniel P. Mannix gives us these interesting details:

> In addition to the problems of handling the animals, the arena might in the course of a day's show be flooded for a sea fight and then planted to represent a forest. This might be followed by the erection of an artificial mountain complete with streams, bushes and growing flowers, which then had to be cleared for chariot races and immediately afterwards a gigantic fight might be staged representing Hannibal's attack on Rome, including elephants and catapults, plus a mock city . . . .[13]

Another structure of importance (at least for its size and activity) was the Circus Maximus. "After its rebuilding by Julius Caesar [it] could hold 150,000 persons, and it was again enlarged, as in the early empire, to admit another 100,000."[14]

Besides being a city of significant buildings, ancient Rome was also a mammoth cemetery. The Appian Way has been designated "the greatest burial road in the world." "Six million Christians are in the catacombs, and if the galleries could be placed end on end, they would reach 600 miles."[15]

The dead are buried in niches four stories high. It has been estimated that there are fifty catacombs in a circle around Rome, and new ones are frequently discovered.

The Romans ruled its mighty empire with an iron hand. Julius Caesar, in triumph in Pontus, declared, "I came, I saw, I conquered."[16] According to Gibbon, this Roman Peace was proclaimed by Augustus in 27 B.C. and continued for two hundred years. Peace and prosperity were acclaimed by ancient politicians in similar fashion as politicians of our day. One historian put it thus: "All over this vast Empire, with a population and area nearly equal to that of the United States, there reigned the blessed Pax Romana."[17]

While there was Roman Peace in the empire, there was also slavery. According to Gibbon, "some landowners had 100,000 slaves." Others estimate that three out of five men were slaves.[18]

William Stearns Davis gives this description of a slave market:

> Purchasing a Slave Boy—In any large city familia, the purchase of new slaves to replace vacancies caused by death or otherwise is an everyday occurrence. Very lately a new errand boy was wanted by Calvus, who could not condescend to purchase such a menial in person; and he left the task to a competent freedman, Cleander. The latter conscientiously went through the great slave bazaars near the fora and especially along the Saepta Julia, the great porticoes lining the Via Lata.
>
> Here any quantity of human bipeds were on sale as in a regular cattle market. There were numbers of little stalls or pens with crowds of buyers or mere spectators constantly elbowing in and out, and from many of them rose a gross fleshly odor as from closely confined animals.
>
> At the entrance to these pens, notices, written on white boards with red chalk, recited the nature of the slaves inside and sometimes the hour when they would be sold at auction.
>
> Every nationality was represented among these vendable commodities—Egyptian, Moors, Arabs, Cilicians, Cappadocians, Thracians, Greeks and alleged Greeks, Celts from Gaul, Spain, and Britain, and a good many Teutons, fair-haired creatures from beyond the Rhine. They were of both sexes and of all ages, but with youths and grownup girls predominating.[19]

## Life in Rome

The ancient Romans had much in common with our generation: air pollution, crime at night, the scribbling of obscenities on walls, high taxes, excessive government and a fondness for overeating. Most of the empire emulated the women's fashions of Rome. Ovid, the Latin poet, complained, "I cannot keep track of fashion." Juvenal, another poet, remarked concerning the ladies' coiffure, "tiers and stories piled one upon another."[20]

As Rome began its decay, the mob began to control the government. Juvenal uttered a truth when he remarked, "The people who have conquered the world now have only two interests—bread and circuses."

> In a sense, the people were trapped. Rome had overextended herself. She had become, as much by accident as design, the dominant nation of the world.
>
> The cost of maintaining the "Pax Romana"—The Peace of Rome—over most of the known world was proving too great, even for the enormous resources of the mighty empire.
>
> But Rome did not dare to abandon her allies or pull back her legions who were holding the barbarian tribes in a line extending from the Rhine in Germany to the Persian Gulf. Every time a frontier post was relinquished, the wild hordes would sweep in, overrun the area and move just that much closer to the nerve centers of Roman trade.
>
> So the Roman government was constantly threatened by bankruptcy, and no statesman could find a way out of the difficulty. The cost of its gigantic military program was only one of Rome's headaches.
>
> To encourage industry in her various satellite nations, Rome attempted a policy of unrestricted trade, but the Roman working man was unable to compete with the cheap foreign labor and demanded high tariffs. When the tariffs were passed, the satellite nations were unable to sell their goods to the only nation that had any money.
>
> To break the deadlock, the government was finally forced to subsidize the Roman working class to make up the difference between their "real wages" (the actual value of what they were producing) and the wages required to keep up their relatively high standard of living. As a result, thousands of workmen lived on this subsidy and did nothing whatsoever, sacrificing their standard of living for a life of ease.[21]

In Rome one could find fabulous wealth displayed in the homes of the wealthy, while nearby wretched squalor was exhibited in the pitiful shacks of the poor.

Gluttony was common among the wealthy. Vitellius was called "the Imperial Glutton." "His senatorial friends, obliged to invite him to their houses, never dared to offer him a dinner costing less than 400,000 sesterces ($16,000)."[22] A monument is thus inscribed: "Eat, drink, enjoy yourself—the rest is nothing." Nero's Golden House contained a vomitarian which was used by those who wished to gorge themselves. "Seneca denounced the numerous gluttons who 'vomit that they may eat, and eat that they may vomit.'"[23]

The cost of food was no problem to Nero. Someone reported that a certain Crispinus "once gave 6,000 sesterces ($240.00) for a single six-pound mullet: 'More than the cost of the slave-fisherman!' indignantly exclaimed the outraged

Juvenal."[24] Suetonius reported that Nero spent $164,000.00 on a single dinner.

The morals of Rome were often shocking. Homosexuality seemed to be a way of life. According to Suetonius, Nero castrated a boy and actually tried to make a woman out of him. A marriage took place with all the usual ceremonies, including a dowry and a veil. On another occasion it is reported that he married a man and also committed incest with his mother.[25]

Sports played a major role in the life of the Romans. The most popular were the gladiatorial games and the chariot races. Davis comments, "Seemingly half of Rome exists only from one chariot or gladiator exhibition to another."[26] The men of Rome were kept busy having fun. According to some historians, seventy-six days per year were normally set aside for games, besides extra and special holidays. ". . . it is safe to say that the average Roman gains more periods of lawful vacation than the laboring classes can enjoy in other ages—another factor which tends to make the metropolis abound with idlers and parasites."[27]

The attendance at these games was phenomenal. Statistics range from 45,000 to 50,000 in the Colosseum; from 180,000 to 350,000 in the Circus Maximus. One historian noted that there were more in attendance at a given sports event than the population of some cities. The crowds chanted the names of their heroes just as in the sports arenas of the United States today.

The gladiatorial games have been described as "the wildest public massacres in the history of perverted pleasure." The following is a quotation by Daniel P. Mannix:

> "Hail, Caesar, we who are about to die salute you!"
>
> IN THE VAST MARBLE COLOSSEUM—greater than Yankee Stadium—the death struggles of the gladiators, the mangled bodies of the charioteers, whetted the people's appetite for excitement and thrills.
>
> The Empire was dying, and the Roman Games—ruthless, brutal, perverse—were the emotional outlet for the discontented mob. Feats of strength and skill no longer pleased. Men were pitted against wild beasts, professional swordsmen against unarmed prisoners. The Emperor Trajan gave one set of games that lasted 122 days during which 11,000 people and 10,000 animals were killed.
>
> Still the thirst for sadistic and perverse "novelties" mounted. Death and torture were the only spectacles that could really gratify the people's longing. Death and sex were the only emotions they could still really grasp. The sight of a lion tearing a screaming woman apart gratified both instincts. . . .
>
> Born of a corrupt and licentious age, the Roman Games were the cruelest, costliest spectacles of all time. . . .[28]

The fun-loving Romans were so actively engaged in the spectacle of sports that the games had become an integral part of the nation. The games (as these incredible spectacles were politely called) were a national institution. Millions were dependent upon them for a living. To abolish the games would have been a national calamity. The populace was conditioned to fun and games. The cost of the games was enormous.

> The games—which eventually came to cost one-third of the total income of the empire and used up thousands of animals and humans every month—started out as festivals no more bloodthirsty than the average county fair....
>
> Simply to name some figures as a rough estimate. Titus' one hundred days of games which opened the Colosseum cost about 8 million dollars, and the six days of Domitian's games...cost about $36,000 a day. In 521 A.D., Justinian spent $910,000 on the games to celebrate his rise to power.[29]

## Religion and the Martyrs

Rome had religion.

Above all other stood the great gods of the Greek and Roman Pantheon, the Olympians, acknowledged by general consent to be twelve in number...the center of Roman state religion was the cult of the Capitoline triad—Jupiter, Juno and Minerva. Jupiter in particular, invoked as Optimus Maximus, was the recognized head of the Roman state.[30]

The ancient Roman Empire tolerated every religion except Christianity. Christians at certain periods were severely persecuted. Peter wrote of "the fiery trial" (I Pet. 4:12) which was to try the new sect called Christians. Christianity was distinctive because of its message. No Christian could rightfully acknowledge the deity of the Head of the Roman State.

The followers of the lowly Nazarene paid a tremendous price for their convictions. Human life was cheap in ancient Rome. Sholem Asch relates that a life lost in a chariot race was not as valuable as a horse lost in the contest. The death agony of a poor victim was scarcely noted by "the sophisticated viewers."[31]

Mrs. Charles Rundle gives this description of the persecution of Christians:

> They were clothed in skins, driven in troops into the arena, torn by wild dogs, dragged like Dirce on the horns of bulls; crucified. Many were suspended to gibbets, covered with resin or oil; and when that day of torture and massacre, of shame and glory was over, were set on fire in the gardens of Nero on the Vatican, flashing thence across the waste spaces of Rome.
>
> Thus opened that Book of the Acts of the Martyrs called by one who saw

its grandeur without sharing its inspiration "that extraordinary poem of Christian martyrdom, that epic of the amphitheatre, which will last 250 years, and from which will spring the ennobling of women, the emancipation of the slave."

. . . But that living illumination flashed not only over the waste spaces of ancient Rome; it began an illumination for the whole world, and all the ages, never since extinguished, to be extinguished never more.[32]

It is reported that the martyr Laurence was placed on a gridiron and roasted like a pig. After a considerable period of time, he was asked if he could speak. To the chagrin of his executioners, he humorously replied, "You can turn me now!"

In a more serious vein, when St. Ignatius became the first martyr in the Colosseum, as he was thrown to the lions he proclaimed: "I am as the grain

---

# Human life was cheap in ancient Rome. . . . A life lost in a chariot race was not as valuable as a horse lost in the contest.

---

of the field, and must be ground by the teeth of lions, that I may become fit for His table." Soon afterwards, we are told 115 Christians were shot down with arrows.[33]

## The Fall of Rome

Polybius made the significant statement, "All cities. . . must, like men, meet their doom." It is incredible that Rome would fall. Gibbon declared it "the greatest, perhaps, and most awful scene in the history of mankind." Jerome lamented: "My voice is still, and sobs disturb my every utterance. The city has been conquered which had once subjugated an entire world."[34]

Someone has commented, "If we hear voices of the past and imagine what men were talking about when the stones were whole, we shall be tempted to think that it was the news from Rome that passed from mouth to mouth . . . scandals—murders. . . the fall of Empires."

Marcus Aurelius exclaimed: "What is the end of it all? Smoke and ashes and a legend—or not even a legend."[35]

R. A. Lafferty writes:

There is a term placed on everything, even the world. On the night of August 24 of the year 410 the term was finished. One account states that it was midnight; but a more trustworthy version states that it was about an hour after dark and that it began to rain.

At that time the Salarian Gate of Rome was secretly opened by Gothic slaves in the city. The troops of Alaric entered, and their entry was signaled by a giant trumpet blast such as will never be heard again until the last day.

And, on the terrible blast of the Gothic Trumpet, the world came to an end.

It had endured, in the central core of it that mattered, for 1,163 years.[36]

When Augustine heard of the fall of Rome in 410, it was "the end of the world as he had known it." He compared Rome's destruction with that of Sodom. Prudentius, a Christian poet, had proclaimed only a few years earlier that 'Rome would never fall. After all, it had the bones of Peter and Paul. Yet these relics had not prevented the sack.'

We need to be reminded that "nations, like men, are mortal." The mighty Rome became a dismal museum. Pilgrims from all over the world come to behold its relics and ruins. How did it all happen? "The question of exactly why this disaster [the fall of Rome] occurred has occupied historians ever since, and none more eloquently than Gibbon."[37]

Will Durant quotes a contemporary scholar: "The two greatest problems in history [are] how to account for the rise of Rome, and how to account for her fall."[38] Petrarch, the great Italian poet, commented: "Neither time nor the barbarian can boast of this stupendous destruction; it was perpetrated by her own citizens, by the most illustrious of her sons."

The Romans were great historians (wrote down everything); thus we have an accurate description of conditions of their day and what ultimately brought their demise.

It is not the purpose of this book to interpret the fall of Rome. One must consider the opinions of those who have made a lifelong study of the subject. Edward Gibbon spent twenty-five years writing his six volumes on *The Decline and Fall of the Roman Empire*. The opinions of the historians are varied.

Will Durant lists several reasons why Rome fell: biological factors (decline in population); pestilence; war and revolution; moral decay; rise of Christianity.[39] Muller gives this summary:

> There remains...a complex of economic, political and cultural factors in the breakdown of the empire. These cannot be reduced to a single cause. Any one of the "fatal" maladies of the empire may be found in societies that endured for many centuries, or even in Rome during its vigorous growth. Taken together, they still do not give the strict inevitability that

a scientific historian or philosopher might wish for, since the curtain did not go down on Byzantium. Yet they all point to failures in intelligence and in character that are basic enough for our purposes.[40]

Edward Gibbon, in his monumental work, *The Decline and Fall of the Roman Empire,* remarks that

> the decline of Rome was the natural and inevitable effect of immoderate greatness. Prosperity ripened the principle of decay; the causes of destruction multiplied with the extent of conquest; and, as soon as time or accident had removed the artificial supports, the stupendous fabric yielded to the pressure of its own weight.[41]

He also acknowledges that the fall of Rome was "the joint triumph of barbarians and Christianity"[42] (although this has been refuted by other historians).

Quoting Gibbon, Francis Schaeffer lists "the following five attributes" of the end of Rome:

> . . . first, a mounting love of show and luxury (that is, affluence); second, a widening gap between the very rich and the very poor (this could be among countries in the family of nations as well as in a single nation); third, an obsession with sex; fourth, freakishness in the arts, masquerading as originality, and enthusiasms pretending to be creativity; fifth, an increased desire to live off the state.
>
> It all sounds so familiar. We have come a long road since our first chapter, and we are back in Rome.[43]

The most common basic reasons for the fall of the Roman Empire attributed to Gibbon are:

> 1. The rapid increase in divorce and the undermining of the sanctity of the home.
> 2. The spiralling rise of taxes and extravagant spending.
> 3. The mounting craze for pleasure and the brutalization of sports!
> 4. The building of gigantic armaments and the failure to realize that the real enemy lay within the gates of the empire, in the moral decay of its people.
> 5. The decay of religion and the fading of faith into a mere form, leaving the people without a guide.[44]

Rome committed suicide—that is, she destroyed herself. She lost the will and the right to live. The problem was internal. Nations like men grow tired of living. Rome forgot the glory of her destiny. Gibbon admitted that "the enemies of Rome were in her bosom." One historian remarked: "It had decayed within before it was overthrown from without. Rome was old and no longer knew how to live."

Apathy is defined as "a lack of feeling or emotion; a lack of interest or concern." According to this definition, Rome was guilty of apathy. Schaeffer explains:

> ...Apathy was the chief mark of the late Empire. One of the ways the apathy showed itself was in a lack of creativity in the arts. One easily observed example of the decadence of officially sponsored art is that the fourth-century work on the Arch of Constantine in Rome stands in poor contrast to its second-century sculptures which were borrowed from monuments from the period of Emperor Trajan. The elite abandoned their intellectual pursuits for social life. Officially sponsored art was decadent, and music was increasingly bombastic. Even the portraits on the coins became of poor quality. All of life was marked by the predominant apathy.[45]

According to Gibbon, "During a period of 619 years the seat of the Empire had never been violated by the presence of a foreign enemy....The Romans were ignorant of the extent of their dangers and the number of their enemies."[46]

Rose Wilder made a profound statement when she declared, "Rome had a fine civilization and was even becoming Christian, but then it became a welfare state, declined and fell" (*The Lady and the Tycoon*).

The welfare state proved to be one of the reasons why prosperous Rome declined. The government provided cradle-to-grave protection—and it was all free. They had their cake and gagged trying to eat it, too. Welfare, social security, schools, hospitals were all provided by the ever generous state.

Who was to pay for all this largess? The government. Who was the government? The individual—the recipient of these gratuities; and thus the government eventually took control of the lives of the foolish Romans and their precious freedom was lost. With the vanishing of their freedom, the once proud nation was doomed to become an empty shell.

"Nothing but evil can come from a society bent upon coercion, the confiscation of property, and the degradation of the productive" (Professor Lawrence W. Reed).

The family is the microcosm of the nation. The demise of the family eventually means the demise of a nation. In Rome there was a breakdown of the family. Will Durant observed that marriage became only "a passing adventure."[47] When the Roman father was no longer an example to his son, it was not long before the son exceeded him in his profligacy. The decay of the family helped bring down the mighty empire.

A nation without morality cannot have morale. Rome fell through moral corruption. The barbarians merely finished the job. In its decaying condition, Rome was subject to the whims of the mobs. The government was exhausted trying to appease the clamor of the multitudes. Life was cheap. Many slaves did not possess names, only numbers. Gibbon's original thesis was that lack of morality caused the downfall of the empire (although later he changed this view).

Sexual perversion became a way of life for the ancient Romans. Homosexuality was commonplace. Mannix revealed: "...homosexuality was regarded not only as natural but as an idealized and noble relationship between an older and a younger man. In the phalanx, the young men in the front ranks each had a lover among the older men in the rear ranks."[48]

One of Cicero's correspondents "thought it a delightful joke when a homosexual pervert was prosecuted under the Lex Scantinia before a presiding judge who was himself a pervert."

Cato exclaimed that "all men rule over women, we Romans rule over all men, and our wives over us."

Ancient Rome lost its soul in a saturnalis of "wine, women and song"—and circuses. The Romans were ruined by prosperity and enjoyed holidays without end. The citizens were bored. Marcus, the great Roman emperor and philosopher, remarked, "I wouldn't mind the games being brutal and degrading if they weren't so [expletive deleted] monotonous." Another Roman statesman, Savinus, bemoaned, "The Roman Empire is filled with misery, but it is luxurious. It is dying, but it laughs." A contemporary added, "We reached those last days when we could endure neither our vices nor their remedies." "...Death, torture, blood were the only spectacles that could really gratify the people's basic longings. They became drunk on suffering....Gradually the games began to degenerate into spectacles of pointless massacre."[49]

D. L. Moody made the significant statement, "A Christian can see more on his knees than a philosopher on tiptoe." This is particularly true when one tries to evaluate the reasons for the fall of one of the greatest empires of all history.

The answer is spiritual. Rome lost her soul. Victor Hugo wrote concerning Napoleon and Waterloo: "Napoleon had been impeached before the Infinite,

---

## The ancient Romans had everything to live with but nothing to live for.

---

and his fall was decreed....He vexed God." Schaeffer concludes: "Rome did not fall because of external forces such as the invasion by the barbarians. Rome had no sufficient inward base; the barbarians only completed the breakdown—and Rome gradually became a ruin."[50] History has shown that religious faith is necessary if a nation is to survive.

Rome lacked spiritual stability because she lacked spiritual guidance. Schaeffer commented, "But a human god is a poor foundation and Rome fell."[51] The ancient Romans had everything to live with but nothing to live for. Rome had many pagan gods but did not know the true God. Like the men of Athens, their religion was not sufficient. Sir Henry Rider Haggard put it this way:

> Nowhere, not even in old Mexico, was high culture so completely wedded to the lowest barbarism. Intellect, Rome had in plenty; the noblest efforts of her genius are scarcely surpassed; her law is the foundation of the best of our codes of jurisprudence; art she borrowed but appreciated; her military system is still the wonder of the world; her great men remain great among a multitude of competitors. And yet how pitiless she was!
>
> What a tigress! Amid all the ruins of her cities we find none of a hospital, none I believe of an orphan school in an age that made many orphans. The pious aspirations and efforts of individuals never seem to have touched the conscience of the people. Rome incarnate had no conscience; she was a lustful, devouring beast, made more bestial by her intelligence and splendor.[52]

Will Durant lists reasons for the fall of Rome, and some of them have a strange parallel to our day.[53]

"The world of the Roman Empire in the first two centuries is almost frighteningly similar to modern North America in its excesses and in its wealth and, above all, in its devotion to materialistic success at the expense of the spiritual and the intellectual" (W. G. Hardy, *The Greek and Roman World*).

Muller comments: ". . . in ancient Rome he [the Roman] demanded only bread and circuses; he hardly noticed the fall of Rome because the games went on. In America today he glances at the headlines and then turns to the sports page and the comics."[54]

Rome committed suicide. Arnold Toynbee writes of the fall of Rome: "I think [Rome] began to decline in the fifth century before Christ. It died not by murder, but by suicide; and that act of suicide was committed before the fifth century B.C. was out."[55]

George Sweeting has written, "Dying civilizations are the sum total of dying individuals." Rome through the ages has been designated "The Eternal City." However, one must remember that individuals only come in contact with the eternal through Jesus Christ who is "the way, the truth, and the life" (John 14:6). The way to the Eternal City is not found in any city but via the way of the cross and the empty tomb. The ruins of ancient Rome attest to their failure. Christ has triumphed over Caesar!

## Paul at Rome

The coming of Paul to Rome was significant. It had a tremendous impact on the future of Christianity and history itself. Wilbur M. Smith writes of Sir William Ramsay's evaluation of the Apostle Paul:

> Sir William Ramsay, himself a brilliant scholar, a master of classical learning, intimately acquainted with the work of most of the great men of genius of the ancient Greek and Roman civilization, after thirty years spent in studying the life and writings of the Apostle Paul, accompanied by many extended examinations of the country of Asia Minor in which Paul extensively labored, concluded:
>
> "Of all the men of the first century, incomparably the most influential was the Apostle Paul. No one man exercised anything like so much power as he did in molding the future of the Empire.
>
> "Among the imperial ministers of the period, there appeared none that had any claim to the name of statesman except Seneca, and Seneca fell as far short of Paul in practical influence and intellectual insight as he did in moral character.
>
> "Had it not been for Paul—if one may guess at what might have been— no man would now remember Greek and Roman civilization."[56]

It has been said that the epistle to the Romans has changed the history of the world.

Augustine was a wayward youth who lived in northern Africa. He fled to Italy to get away from the prayers of his saintly mother, Monica. There he lived a life of dissipation, but he could not get away from the influence and prayers of his mother.

One day he read in the book of Romans, "Let us walk honestly, as in the day; not in rioting and drunkenness, not in chambering and wantonness..." (Rom. 13:13). He was converted and became one of the great church fathers and an influential theologian. His work, *The City of God,* was "a magnificent plea for Christianity to take the place of the dissolving empire."

Martin Luther's study of Romans prepared the way for the Reformation.

The French Revolution engulfed France but never came to the shores of England. Historians say that one man had much to do with it—Charles Wesley. This influential figure was converted by reading *Luther's Preface to Romans.*

The book of Romans is absolutely necessary for the understanding of the Bible. Throughout history, to depart from Paul has been heresy. No other writing so powerfully influenced the church. The first chapter of Romans is a description of the corruption of ancient Rome. The book has been designated as "an epistle against the Romans."

The book of Acts relates the narrative concerning Paul in Rome. Paul was in Rome because of a burning desire. According to the sovereign plan of God, he was to have his ardent wish fulfilled. He came to Rome a prisoner of Caesar; he departed Rome a liberated captive of Christ.

Not only was it Paul's design to appeal unto Caesar (Acts 25:10-12) but also to share the message of the Gospel in this noted city. Note Paul's fervency: "...I must also see Rome" (Acts 19:21); "So, as much as in me is, I am ready to preach the gospel to you that are at Rome also" (Rom. 1:15); "...and having a great desire these many years to come unto you" (Rom. 15:23).

Little did the apostle realize that, when he appeared in Rome, he would be "an ambassador in chains." Paul was to go to prison, but out of that Mamertine incarceration were to come the glorious prison epistles. Like John Bunyan's writing of *The Pilgrim's Progress* in jail, the dungeon in Rome became a pulpit whereby he reached a world! William R. Newell writes:

> ...here is Paul, utterly weak in himself, and with his physical thorn; yet ready, eager, to go to Rome!
>
> And to preach—what? A Christ that the Jewish nation had themselves officially rejected, a Christ who had been despised and crucified at their cries—by a Roman governor! To preach a Way that the Jews in Rome would tell Paul was "every where...spoken against" (Acts 28:22).
>
> Talk of your brave men, your great men, O world! Where in all history can you find one like Paul? Alexander, Caesar, Napoleon marched with the protection of their armies to enforce their will upon men. Paul was eager to march with Christ alone to the center of this world's greatness entrenched under Satan, with "the Word of the cross," which he himself says is "to Jews, an offence; and to Gentiles, foolishness."
>
> Yes, and when he does go to Rome, it is as a shipwrecked (though divinely delivered) prisoner.
>
> Oh, what a story! There, "for two whole years" in his own "hired dwelling" he receives "all that go in unto him" (for he cannot go to them); and the message goes on and on, throughout the Roman Empire, and even into Caesar's household![57]

Before the great missionary of the cross was to reach Rome, he experienced the wrath of a dreadful storm. It seemed as if the Devil and all his cohorts were determined that he should not reach the capital of the Roman Empire. Luke describes the storm in Acts 27:20-25:

> *"And when neither sun nor stars in many days appeared, and no small tempest lay on us, all hope that we should be saved was then taken away.*
>
> *"But after long abstinence Paul stood forth in the midst of them, and said, Sirs, ye should have hearkened unto me, and not have loosed from Crete,*

*and to have gained this harm and loss.*

*"And now I exhort you to be of good cheer: for there shall be no loss of any man's life among you, but of the ship.*

*"For there stood by me this night the angel of God, whose I am, and whom I serve,*

*"Saying, Fear not, Paul; thou must be brought before Caesar: and, lo, God hath given thee all them that sail with thee.*

*"Wherefore, sirs, be of good cheer: for I believe God, that it shall be even as it was told me."*

Humanly speaking, all hope was gone; the Apostle Paul was going down with the ship. But here was a man who was in touch with God. He had "blessed assurance" in the midst of terrible circumstances. What was his secret? He had a vision of a faithful God. Thus he could trust when he couldn't see. And thus through the guiding hand of the Almighty, he safely arrived in Rome.

Paul was now in the greatest city in the world. He had made it to his desired destination, even though the route had been devious. This was the heart of the Caesars, the city of the Roman language, Roman coins, Roman legions. Perhaps the words of Jesus Christ were appropriate: "Render therefore unto Caesar the things which be Caesar's, and unto God the things which be God's" (Luke 20:25).

Rome, the nerve center of the mighty empire, was to play an important role in the closing epoch of Paul's life.

The irony of it all was that the Apostle Paul was "an ambassador in chains." He did not rebel against his fate but accepted it as a part of the sovereign plan of his Father. Humanly speaking, what could he do? His was almost a hopeless case. One insignificant representative of the cross against the vaunted power of Rome!

God used him in spite of his dire circumstances. Paul never lived to see the triumph of his labors, but we are cognizant of them today. He was "the corn of wheat" which fell into the ground of Rome and died (John 12:24), and today in Christianity we enjoy the fruit.

> Despite all obstacles, the message which he carried found a welcome in most unexpected quarters. The Word of God could not be bound, and but for his captivity and chain, the apostle would not, humanly speaking, have carried out so far-reaching a ministry.

> The influence of this prison-ministry made itself felt in many directions. It moved upwards and touched the lives of men and women in the highest circles of society in Rome. It penetrated to the lowest deeps of humanity and regenerated the outcast. It spread—and is still spreading in ever-widening circles—to far distant lands. By the letters which he dictated

in his Roman prison, the apostle has left an enduring memorial, a pattern of Christian faith to shape the life of the church in all ages. . . .

What a life Paul would have lived had he been free to do whatever he pleased, to go wherever he liked.

It is notorious that, when a man is made a bishop, his days become so crowded that it is a rare thing for him to produce his greatest books! And who knows but that if this great apostle had had more temporary freedom we might have had less permanent fruit. Sometimes the Lord permits our seclusion in order that we may do a larger work. His merciful sight has long range, and that is why our immediate circumstances are often so contradictory to our aspiration and prayer. The Lord looks beyond the temporary bondage to the ultimate freedom.[58]

Paul and Nero represent a study in contrasts. Paul languished in prison, the Emperor Nero was worshiped as a god; Paul suffering in a dank, dark, dismal cell; Nero enjoying all the luxuries of royalty. The one the most godly of his day; the other, the most wicked.

Note some further contrasts. Their positions: Nero was an absolute dictator; his will was law. Paul was a common criminal (no lowly slave in Rome would exchange places with him). What a difference in character! Nero was a sensualist; Paul was spiritual. Nero was a glutton and drunkard, and there was not a sin so vile in which he was not indulgent; Paul's life revealed a holy discipline. He was "temperate in all things," and he "kept his body under."

Their contrast in wealth was most glaring. Nero spent money like a crazy man, as if there were no tomorrow. "He played dice for $16,400.00 per point. . . . He never wore the same garment twice. He fished with a golden net drawn by cords woven of purple and scarlet threads. It is said that he never made a journey with less than one thousand carriages, his mules shod with silver."[59]

What a contrast with the lowly maker of tents whose only possessions consisted of a cloak, a few books and parchment!

Not only in their lives was there a distinct contrast but also in their deaths. The ungodly do not know how to die. Poor Nero didn't even know how to commit suicide. Before his aid drove the dagger into his throat, he lamented: "To live despoiled, disgraced—this does not become Nero!" It is also reported that he exclaimed, "What a great artist dies with me!"

How different the triumphant death of the Apostle Paul! In anticipation of his release from mortal life, he wrote: "I have fought a good fight, I have finished my course, I have kept the faith" (II Tim. 4:7).

After Paul's arrival in Rome, he began that which was the driving thrust of his ministry—witnessing. The writer of Acts supplies us with the details:

*"And it came to pass, that after three days Paul called the chief of the Jews together: and when they were come together, he said unto them, Men and brethren, though I have committed nothing against the people, or customs of our fathers, yet was I delivered prisoner from Jerusalem into the hands of the Romans.*

*"Who, when they had examined me, would have let me go, because there was no cause of death in me.*

*"But when the Jews spake against it, I was constrained to appeal unto Caesar; not that I had ought to accuse my nation of.*

*"For this cause therefore have I called for you, to see you, and to speak with you: because that for the hope of Israel I am bound with this chain."*—Acts 28:17-20.

This cause was the motivating force in his life. A psychological assessment is made of the Apostle Paul by Ernest White:

> We see in St. Paul's life and writings that his love was something very much more than a tender sentiment or a kindly feeling. It was a mighty driving force which urged him on through hundreds of miles of journeyings by land and by sea, through hunger and thirst, through poverty and hardships, through shipwrecks, through beatings, stonings and prison, and finally to the martyr's death. For love of Christ, and for love of his fellows, he allowed nothing to daunt him. His love, like his Master's, was sacrificial.[60]

It was for this cause that Paul died.

How did this great preacher of righteousness fare in this idolatrous metropolis? In Thessalonica he "turned the world upside down"; in Athens he was laughed out of town, but in Rome there was neither extreme:

*"And when they had appointed him a day, there came many to him into his lodging; to whom he expounded and testified the kingdom of God, persuading them concerning Jesus, both out of the law of Moses, and out of the prophets, from morning till evening. And some believed the things which were spoken, and some believed not."*—Acts 28:23,24.

He did not preach, of course, from a cathedral pulpit. He was chained to a Roman soldier—a prisoner of Rome. His congregation came to him. His preaching was very personal.

Note his method: "He expounded"—that is, "to expose or declare"; Paul declared definite facts concerning the kingdom of God. His method was expository. Like Nehemiah of old, "So they read in the book in the law of God distinctly, and gave the sense, and caused them to understand the reading" (Neh. 8:8).

He "testified." He did not preach beyond his experience. Exposition and testimony of life go hand-in-hand. The early Christians declared, "For we cannot but speak the things which we have seen and heard" (Acts 4:20).

He persuaded ("persuading them concerning Jesus"). The word *persuade* means "to convince." He preached for results.

Paul was a fundamentalist in his theology. His text was "both out of the law of Moses, and out of the prophets." He was biblical in his presentation. The declaration was "thus saith the Lord."

Paul could not be accused of laziness. His ministry extended "from morning till evening."

What were the results of Paul's preaching? "And some believed the things which were spoken, and some believed not." Lenski writes this interesting paragraph:

> We feel safe in saying that in all of Paul's career he scored no greater success in a single day's work than on the day Luke describes in verse 23 and following. He converted half of the rabbis and leaders of the eleven synagogues in the capital of the world![61]

Whether this is true or not, the fact remains his ministry was effective for time and eternity.

However, it should be noted that there was also rejection of his message. Consider Acts 28:25-28:

*"And when they agreed not among themselves, they departed, after that Paul had spoken one word, Well spake the Holy Ghost by Esaias the prophet unto our fathers,*

*"Saying, Go unto this people, and say, Hearing ye shall hear, and shall not understand; and seeing ye shall see, and not perceive:*

*"For the heart of this people is waxed gross, and their ears are dull of hearing, and their eyes have they closed; lest they should see with their eyes, and hear with their ears, and understand with their heart, and should be converted, and I should heal them.*

*"Be it known therefore unto you, that the salvation of God is sent unto the Gentiles, and that they will hear it."*

Paul elucidates the reasons why his message was rejected at Rome. Using the quotation from the book of Isaiah, he declares that they heard, but they did not hear; they heard, but they did not understand; they saw, but they did not see; they received, but they did not comprehend. Their spiritual lack of sight, dullness and lack of comprehension was their own choice. He then turned to the Gentiles. In essence he was saying, "If you as Jews do not want to hear the message, I'll go to those who will—the Gentiles."

This great veteran of the cross spent "two whole years in his own hired house" (Acts 28:30). How blessed those brief years must have been! Although still a prisoner, he was able to unfold the wonderful counsels of God.

It is believed by most Bible scholars that he was released for a period, then returned back to prison. He made the most of his circumstances. Writing to the church at Philippi, he explained:

*"But I would ye should understand, brethren, that the things which happened unto me have fallen out rather unto the furtherance of the gospel;*

*"So that my bonds in Christ are manifest in all the palace, and in all other places;*

*"And many of the brethren in the Lord, waxing confident by my bonds, are much more bold to speak the word without fear."*—Phil. 1:12-14.

The last view we have of Paul in Acts 28:31 informs us that he was "preaching" and "teaching." Like Jeremiah of old, "his word was in mine heart as a burning fire shut up in my bones. . . and I could not stay" (20:9). He was absolutely devoted to the realm of the spiritual—"preaching" and "discipling." The writer of Acts informs us that his ministry was "unhindered"—"no man forbidding him."

A prisoner—yet free.

And now it's curtain time for the aged apostle. The drama of life is just about over. This is his last appearance on the stage of life. The inevitable final curtain of death is about to come down on his last performance.

Phillips comments concerning his ministry: "When he preached. . . at Athens, the intellectual center of the world, he was mocked. When he preached. . . at Rome, the legislative center of the world, he was martyred. He was ready for that."[62]

God's ambassador was ready for martyrdom. He had been treated like a common criminal by the august city of Rome. He accepted his fate without a whimper. He knew how to live and how to die.

W. M. Taylor penned these words:

> . . .Paul proved the Lord at Damascus, and that gave him courage at Jerusalem; then he passed up and up through the Lystra assault, and the Ephesian riot, and the Caesarea imprisonment, and the Maltese shipwreck, and his first experiences at Rome, until he reached that lofty landing place whereon he contemplated martyrdom without a quiver.
>
> Not all at once, by one spasmodic and emotional bound, did he attain the serene altitude of this sublime assurance: he reached it after the climbing of a lifetime; and he reasoned that He who had been with him through thirty years of life with their hardships and dangers, would not desert him in death. "I know whom I have believed!"[63]

The Bible does not record any of the events of Paul's martyrdom. His biographers have attempted to do that. J. Patterson Smyth gives this account:

We have no details. There is a persistent tradition that, like his Master, he "suffered without the gate" at the Pyramid of Cestius on the Harbour Road.

We can easily picture the scene: the hot, white road, with the yelling mob, the small, quiet old man walking silently amid the guards with the light of another world in his eyes.

One hopes that they were men of the old Praetorian Guard who knew him and would shield him from the insults of that howling mob.

Then the halt—the headsman's block—a broad sword flashing in the sunlight—and an old white head lying dishonoured on the ground. Not even the band of Christians, as in Stephen's day, "to make much lamentation over him."

The further scene is not for us to paint, when those eyes that closed thus in the darkness of death opened on "a light that never was on sea or land," and the poor humble soul who felt himself "the chief of sinners" was again with the Jesus of the Damascus road to give up the commission which he had received that day.

Doubtless, there were more glorious commissions for him now.

> **"We doubt not that for one so true**
> **God will have other nobler work to do."**[64]

Frederic W. Farrar gives us this description:

They who will may follow him in imagination to the possible scene of his martyrdom, but every detail must be borrowed from imagination alone.

It may be that the legendary is also the real scene of his death. If so, accompanied by the centurion and the soldiers who were to see him executed, he left Rome by the gate now called by his name. Near that gate, close beside the English cemetery, stands the pyramid of C. Cestius, and under its shadow lie buried the mortal remains of Keats and Shelley and of many who have left behind them beloved or famous names.

Yet even amid those touching memorials, the traveller will turn with deeper interest to the old pyramid, because it was one of the last objects on which rested the eyes of Paul.

For nearly three miles the sad procession walked; and doubtless the dregs of the populace, who always delight in a scene of horror, gathered round them. About three miles from Rome, not far from the Ostian road, is a green and level spot, with low hills around it, known anciently as Aquae Salviae, and now as Tre Fontane. There the word of command to halt was given; the prisoner knelt down; the sword flashed, and the life of the greatest of the Apostles was shorn away.[65]

The veteran of the faith must have been magnanimous in his death. Note this further description of his martyrdom by Basil Matthews:

> ...the time came when, as an ancient tradition that bears upon it the stamp of truth declares, he walked out with firm step along the path of death to the place of the Three Fountains; and there laid his head upon the block, while the sword of the Roman executioner ended that dauntless life.
>
> Silence and dense darkness are over it all. Yet out of the prison, out of the silence and darkness, comes a Voice.
>
> It is the voice of the hero who, trembling and astonished, had long years before laid down the flail of the persecutor at the feet of his risen Lord on the road to Damascus and had in that hour begun to run the course of his great adventure; a course that had carried him up the steep ascent over mountain pass and by robber den, under blazing sun and through blinding blizzard, travelling on in peril from city to city across the Empire, often without food and in rags, labouring with his own hands, tossed on the sea and, shipwrecked, stoned by the Jews, beaten with Roman rods and torn with scourges, chained, imprisoned and at last led out to his death, yet unafraid to the end.
>
> And that valiant Voice out of the darkness rings triumphantly across the centuries:
>
> "I HAVE FOUGHT THE GOOD FIGHT;
> I HAVE RUN MY COURSE;
> I HAVE KEPT THE FAITH."[66]

## In Retrospect

"Sic transit gloria." Like Athens of old, the glory of mighty Rome had faded. "All roads lead to Rome" to view the ruins of another faded glory. The historian, Hendrik William van Loon, writes:

> Then at last the imperial city sank into a state of utter neglect and despair. The ancient palaces had been plundered time and again. The schools had been burned down....The rich people had been thrown out of their villas....The roads had fallen into decay....Civilization—the product of thousands of years of patient labor on the part of Egyptians and Babylonians and Greeks and Romans, which had lifted man high above the most daring of his earliest ancestors—threatened to perish from the western continent.[67]

To think that a nation which gave us Roman letters, much of our spoken vocabulary and the fundamentals of our science and learning, could ever sink into oblivion! The Almighty plays no favorites. Ancient Rome had her day, but God had the last word.

There is always a day of reckoning. Jesus Christ Himself declared, "Thou fool, this night thy soul shall be required of thee" (Luke 12:20).

Rome had religion, but it failed. The gods of the Greeks and Romans were not sufficient to meet the needs of those who are totally depraved. For the most part, the Romans possessed only "kindly protection during mortal life, but...nothing to look forward to after death but cheerless underworld of departed shade." Francis A. Schaeffer explains:

> The Greeks and later the Romans also tried to build society upon their gods. But these gods were not big enough because they were finite, limited. Even all their gods put together were not infinite. Actually, the gods in Greek and Roman thinking were like men and women larger than life, but not basically different from human men and women.
>
> As one example among thousands, we can think of the statue of Hercules, standing inebriated and urinating. Hercules was the patron god of Herculaneum which was destroyed at the same time as Pompeii.
>
> The gods were amplified humanity, not divinity. Like the Greeks, the Romans had no infinite god. This being so, they had no sufficient reference point intellectually; that is, they did not have anything big enough or permanent enough to which to relate either their thinking or their living. Consequently, their value system was not strong enough to bear the strains of life, either individual or political.
>
> All their gods put together could not give them a sufficient base for life, morals, values, and final decisions. These gods depended on the society which had made them, and when this society collapsed, the gods tumbled with it.
>
> Thus, the Greek and Roman experiments in social harmony (which rested on an elitist republic) ultimately failed.[68]

If the Caesars were to return to earth today, they would be shocked to see the striking parallels between their day and ours. It would be well for our generation to heed the warning of Arnold Toynbee: "Of the thirty-two civilizations the earth has seen, over half have collapsed, and the rest are in a terminal condition....Death the Leveler will lay his icy hand on our civilization also."[69]

In his book, *Childe Harold,* Lord Byron wrote:

> **While stands the Colosseum, Rome shall stand;**
> **When falls the Colosseum, Rome shall fall;**
> **And when Rome falls—the world.**[70]

The Colosseum has fallen, yet it remains in rugged ruins; but the Rome of the Colosseum is buried in antiquity, and the fall of the world is not in the hands of men but the sovereign God. Vance Havner has made this observation: "Today we have moved from the catacombs to the Colosseum and revised our standards to meet a generation of pleasure-lovers who do not love God."

Paul's epistle to the Romans has been described as a "little Bible." It contains the basic doctrines of the Christian faith. The failure of the Romans to take heed to its teachings helped to bring about the eventual fall of a nation. And to think that the United States of America has an entire Bible! Our generation needs to heed the words of Christ: "For unto whomsoever much is given, of him shall be much required: and to whom men have committed much, of him they will ask the more" (Luke 12:48).

In comparison with some of the nations of antiquity, America is young. Rome was not young when she died (she was a power for almost a thousand years). Both Rome and America have the same malady. Their problem was spiritual. It seems certain that the God in Heaven will not wait eight hundred or a thousand years for America to terminate her illness. The death rattle may already be in her throat.

## Rome Today

The ruins of ancient Rome are still visible in the city of Rome today. Three words are characteristic of that historic metropolis: ruins, relics and religion. Her ruins attract scholars, her relics attract pilgrims, and her religion encircles the globe.

Rome's religion is personified in magnificent buildings. They reflect somewhat the grandeur of another glorious (but departed) day. Peter would stand in awe at the church erected in his name. He would be amazed at the opulence and grandiosity of religion. When he was on earth, he confessed: "Silver and gold have I none. . . . Stand up; I myself also am a man" (Acts 3:6; 10:26).

The story is told that one of the Popes, seeing the Sistine Chapel completed, inquired, "Why have you omitted the gold trimmings on the saints and the apostles?" To which Michelangelo replied, "Holy Father, in those days the men and women were poor and honest. They had faith, but they had no gold."

The paganism of ancient Rome still triumphs today. Her pagan teachings are still found not only in doctrine but in her buildings. In St. Peter's Basilica, "the high altar once formed a part of the temple of Minerva." Consider these words: "It is an old thought that the Caesars brought to Rome the marble which the Popes have made into churches; but wheresoever you look, your eyes light upon some column, some architrave, some stairway of pagan Rome now serving a different purpose in Christian Rome."[71]

The tragedy is, the religion of Rome today is a combination of Paganism, Judaism and Christianity.

Wilbur M. Smith gives us the following quotations:

> . . . Uhlhorn closes his epochal *Conflict of Christianity and Heathenism*

with this sentence, "Stronger almost than ever, the heathen spirit in modern guise is wrestling against Christian thought and life, and it almost seems as if the questions of the time should be gathered up into the question: Shall we remain Christian, or become pagan again?" (p. 479).

Gilbert K. Chesterton, in his *Heretics* (1905), argues that, inasmuch as the paganism of the ancient world was followed by Christianity, so it will again follow this neo-paganism.... "Nobody in the nineteenth century, indeed nobody in the last five hundred years, thought that paganism had any future before it.... Today, however, in the most scientific age of the world's history, when the earth is yielding up all her secrets and the cold clear light of science pierces into every human heart, there is not only a revival of a heathenish view of life, but also a cult of pagan rites in at any rate one great European country."[72]

Matthew Henry remarked: "The church at Rome was then a flourishing church; but since that time, how is the gold become dim! The Epistle to the Romans is now an epistle against the Romans."[73]

It is ironic that in the Eternal City, the Communist Party should play such a strategic role. While the power of ecclesiastical Rome is great, there are signs that her pillars are beginning to crumble, thus preparing the way for the Antichrist.

## Rome Tomorrow

It is the belief of most Bible scholars that the ancient Roman Empire will be revived. In other words, Rome in resurrected glory will again appear on the scene. This great revived Empire will play a strategic role in Bible prophecy. It is to be remembered that this ancient Empire was extensive and influential. The Antichrist will emerge from this great confederation. *The Coming Antichrist* is the title of a book by Walter K. Price. In the book he predicts:

The fact that ancient Rome lived on in spirit and even manifested itself in a revived form during the Renaissance, leads us to believe that it is not impossible for the ancient Roman empire to actually live again during the last days....

Though historians assure us that the spirit of ancient Rome is very much alive today in the realm of ideas, it is the prophetic Word of God that assures us that the very structure of the ancient imperial empire will live again during the tribulation period; and that a new Caesar, more powerful than any of his ancient predecessors, will lead that revived Roman empire to universal dominion.[74]

Bible scholars believe that Daniel 2:7-45 gives an historical outline of the empires of history until Christ establishes His own kingdom. The fourth world empire is that of Rome. Note Daniel 2:40-43:

*"And the fourth kingdom shall be strong as iron: forasmuch as iron breaketh in pieces and subdueth all things: and as iron that breaketh all these, shall it break in pieces and bruise.*

*"And whereas thou sawest the feet and toes, part of potters' clay, and part of iron, the kingdom shall be divided; but there shall be in it of the strength of the iron, forasmuch as thou sawest the iron mixed with miry clay.*

*"And as the toes of the feet were part of iron, and part of clay, so the kingdom shall be partly strong, and partly broken.*

*"And whereas thou sawest iron mixed with miry clay, they shall mingle themselves with the seed of men: but they shall not cleave one to another, even as iron is not mixed with clay."*

Ancient Rome is described as being "strong as iron." It ruled with an iron hand. The Roman Empire was noted for its military might.

The great image degenerates in quality and strength until in the toes there is utter deterioration: from an absolute monarchy in Babylon unto a form of government in which the people largely have the say. Someone has analyzed it thus: "The move from a republican form of government to a mob rule democracy is apparent. In other words, 'the voice of the people is the voice of God!'" As in the final days of the Roman Empire, the voice of the mob prevailed.

Much speculation abounds concerning the Common European Market and Bible prophecy. It is believed that there will be an amalgamation of distinct nations for economic and political reasons. In the end time there will be a United States of Europe. The federation will be composed of ten kingdoms. Daniel 7:24,25 gives the details:

*"And the ten horns out of this kingdom are ten kings that shall arise: and another shall rise after them; and he shall be diverse from the first, and he shall subdue three kings.*

*"And he shall speak great words against the most High, and shall wear out the saints of the most High, and think to change times and laws: and they shall be given into his hand until a time and times and the dividing of time."*—Dan. 7:24,25.

The coming Antichrist will have universal control of the world system. John on the Island of Patmos prophesied:

*"And the ten horns which thou sawest are ten kings, which have received no kingdom as yet; but receive power as kings one hour with the beast.*

*"These have one mind, and shall give their power and strength unto the beast.*

*"These shall make war with the Lamb, and the Lamb shall overcome them: for he is Lord of lords, and King of kings: and they that are with him are called, and chosen, and faithful."*—Rev. 17:12-14.

Out of the Common European Market will emerge a new world leader, a superman who comes out of a corrupt system. The revived Roman Empire presents that opportunity. Revelation 13:3 informs us: "And I saw one of his heads as it were wounded to death; and his deadly wound was healed: and all the world wondered after the beast." Lehman Strauss writes:

> Three times in this one chapter the wound of the beast is mentioned, and in all three verses it is made clear that the wound brought death but that the beast was restored to life again (vss. 3,12,14).
>
> Some teachers see here the political death in the fall of the Roman Empire, which will be restored again. Others see in the Antichrist a man who has been here on the earth before and has died, but whom Satan will raise from the dead. Both views are tenable.
>
> I believe that we will see a revival of the Roman Empire. Actually, Rome has never been destroyed completely. This political-religious combination has continued to smolder from underneath the ruins of the old Roman Empire.
>
> The Roman Catholic Church will play an important role in both the political and religious activity in the end times. We must bear in mind that the beast, though a man, is likewise representing a kingdom (Rev. 17:3,9,10), and I understand this kingdom to be the revived Roman Empire. This forthcoming Roman Empire, being revived before our very eyes, will be resurrected through the genius and personality of a human being.[75]

Nothing but doom is in store for Rome. Revelation 18 makes this plain. J. Dwight Pentecost summarizes the situation:

> . . . [the] destruction of Rome, the Roman system, and the Vatican state, is described for us in chapter 18. . . . There you will find that multitudes from all over the world will watch this great holocaust and will lament and mourn because the splendor of this system is no more. That which this passage we have been examining reveals is that God is going to let this system continue till it has gotten a stranglehold on the world. Then God is going to move all these puppets who are subservient to it, to rise up to destroy it. The destruction, first of all, of world communism and second of Romanism clears the way so that the Beast and the False Prophet can come to world-wide power and world-wide authority, ruling by Satan's power over every kindred and tongue and tribe and nation.[76]

All roads will eventually lead back to Rome. As we have seen, Bible prophecy indicates that the revived Roman Empire will yet play a dominant role in the affairs of the world. But the fate of Rome is unequivocally sealed in the hands of the sovereign God. The empire, which once ruled its world with a rod of iron, will discover that it had only feet of clay. The mighty empire that had no time for the lowly Nazarene will one day bow to His majestic rule.

The empire that refused the message of the Apostle Paul will realize to its everlasting shame its tragic mistake.

Who would ever think that the glorious grandeur of Rome would one day become ignominious rubble! And the decaying rubble of the once all-conquering Rome cries out, "Thou hast conquered, O Galilean!"

Rome, too, committed suicide.

## ENDNOTES:

[1]Will Durant, *Caesar and Christ*, vii.

[2]Dero A. Saunders, ed., *The Portable Gibbon: The Decline and Fall of the Roman Empire*, x.

[3]Peter Quennell, *The Colosseum*, 56.

[4]Mortimer Chambers, *The Fall of the Roman Empire, Can It Be Explained?*, 111.

[5]Cyril Bailey, ed., *The Legacy of Rome*, 9.

[6]Saunders, 9, 10.

[7]*Ibid.*, 604.

[8]Fulton Sheen, *This Is Rome*, 32, 33.

[9]*Ibid.*, 34.

[10]Quennell, 166.

[11]Suetonius, *The Lives of the Twelve Caesars*, 260, 261.

[12]Quennell, Introduction.

[13]Daniel P. Mannix, *Those About to Die*, 47.

[14]Quennell, 52.

[15]Sheen, 78.

[16]Suetonius, 23.

[17]William Stearns Davis, *A Day in Old Rome*, 1.

[18]W. A. Criswell, *Expository Sermons on Galatians*, 209.

[19]Davis, 126, 127.

[20]National Geographic Society, *Greece and Rome (Builders of Our World)*, 362.

[21]Mannix, 6.

[22]Davis, 102.

[23]*Ibid.*, 102 [footnote].

[24]*Ibid.*, 106.

[25]Suetonius, 258, 259.

[26]Davis, 377.

[27]*Ibid.*, 374, 375.

[28]Mannix, Flyleaf.

[29]*Ibid.*, 8, 13.

[30]Harold Mattingly, *The Man in the Roman Street*, 60, 83.

[31]Sholem Asch, *The Apostle*, 686.

[32]Mrs. Charles Rundle, *Martyrs and Saints of the First Twelve Centuries*, 19, 20.

[33]Quennell, 60.

[34]Michael Grant, *The Fall of the Roman Empire*, 301.

[35]Herbert J. Muller, *The Uses of the Past*, 210.

[36]R. A. Lafferty, *The Fall of Rome*, 291, 292.

[37]Saunders, ix.

[38]Durant, 665.

[39]*Ibid.*, 665-668.

[40]Muller, 213.

[41]Saunders, 621.

[42]*Ibid.*, 17.

[43]Francis A. Schaeffer, *How Should We Then Live?* 227.

[44]Leonard Ravenhill, *America Is Too Young to Die*, 51.

[45]Schaeffer, 26.

[46]Saunders, 589, 624.

[47]Durant, 363.

[48]Mannix, 96.

[49]*Ibid.*, 88, 129.

[50]Schaeffer, 29.

[51]*Ibid.*, 22.

[52]Sir Henry Rider Haggard, *Pearl Maiden*, 15.

[53]Durant, 665.

[54]Muller, 225.

[55]Arnold J. Toynbee, *Civilization on Trial*, 227.

[56]Wilbur M. Smith, *Therefore Stand*, 246, 247.

[57]William R. Newell, *Romans Verse by Verse*, 17.

[58]James Hastings, *The Speaker's Bible, the Acts of the Apostles*, Vol. 2, 229, 231.

[59]Suetonius, 260.

[60]Ernest White, *Saint Paul, the Man and His Mind*, 77.

[61]R. C. Lenski, *Interpretation of Acts*, 1124.

[62]John Phillips, *Exploring Romans*, 19.

[63]William M. Taylor, *Paul the Missionary*, 539.

[64]J. Patterson Smyth, *The Story of St. Paul's Life and Letters*, 245.

[65]Frederic W. Farrar, *The Life and Works of Paul*, 245.

[66]Basil Matthews, *Paul the Dauntless*, 360.

[67]Hendrik William van Loon, *The Story of Mankind*, 119.

[68]Schaeffer, 21.

[69]Geoffrey F. Albert, *After the Crash*, 32.

[70]Quennell, 89.

[71]Sheen, 36.

[72]Smith, 563.

[73]Newell, 11.

[74]Walter K. Price, *The Coming Antichrist*, 172, 173.

[75]Lehman Strauss, *The Book of the Revelation*, 248, 249.
[76]J. Dwight Pentecost, *Prophecy for Today*, 138.

## 6 Is America a Christian Nation?

*"Righteousness exalteth a nation: but sin is a reproach to any people."*—Prov. 14:34.

History dogmatically attests that nations, like men, are mortal. Some nations live to a senile old age, while others bloom for a comparatively short time. In comparison with other countries, America is still a young nation. What a pity if she should die at such an early age!

Nations, like men, commit suicide. Suicide has been defined as "self-murder, the act of willfully and designedly destroying one's own life"—literally, "killing one's self." Suicide, therefore, is an act of the will. It does not have to be. The act of self-destruction can be brief or executed over a long period of time. "To be or not to be: that is the question." America may not have as much time as did Rome.

### God Has Blessed America

Psalm 85:1 declares, "Lord, thou hast been favourable unto thy land." Few nations have been the recipients of such divine favor as America. W. W. Reid penned these words:

> Everywhere in America—from every hamlet and home, from every field and factory, from every city and shop—men and women and little children raise their voices in praise and thanksgiving to God and pray: "God bless America, land that we love."
>
> The farmer astride his tractor presses the plow through row upon row of the good earth, sure of tomorrow, heart and machine attuned to the song of his God.
>
> The truckman and his motor hum merrily along the highway carrying harvest fruit to the thankful city.

The rhythmic beat of the oil driller's hammers is his confident song that in earth's deep recesses God has stored up wealth and power for mankind.

The cook is thankful for the succulent plenty from God's acres that fills her pots and pans, and for song in the laughter and smiles of those she serves.

The minister of the Sacred Gospel is on his knees, grateful for the privilege of relating man to God, for the right to help lift a fallen brother, for the freedom to criticize wrong even in high places.

The mother sings a glad lullaby as she foresees a good life for her child among a people dedicated to righteousness and justice.

The student makes a joyful noise unto the Lord, happy that he can search deeply into the mysteries of the universe and apply new truths to the blessing of all mankind.

These men and women, endowed with diverse gifts and skills by their Maker and Master, sing in chorus and pray in unison: "America gives thanks to God. . .God bless America. . .stand beside her and guide her."

Divine munificence has been our portion. "Thou crownest the year with thy goodness; and thy paths drop fatness" (Ps. 65:11). It has been said of the United States that "everybody in the world looks in our direction." Our free enterprise system must work. United States Senator Jesse Helms reminds us that we define poverty at a level higher than median income in Russia.[1] Alistair Cooke's book on *America* is a survey of our nation from its early beginnings. He writes concerning our wealth:

The enviable richness of America's natural resources is a theme that Europeans like to dwell on whenever they are feeling peevish about some new American achievement like a moon shot. . . .

While the Europeans attribute America's bounty to the luck of her resources, Americans, on the other hand, like to ascribe it to nothing but character. It usually required a combination of both, as the dramatic history of this country, including the actual invention of a nation, will show.[2]

We are the most affluent nation on the earth. "Yesterday's luxuries have become today's necessities."[3] Someone has gathered this information: "In one year Americans smoked 550 billion cigarettes, chewed 6 billion pieces of gum, ate 2 billion pounds of candy, drank 2 billion gallons of beer, took 16 billion aspirin tablets and ate 3 billion quarts of ice cream. We spend more on dog food than we do for baby food."

Statistics speak for themselves.

. . .[the] United States represents but one-sixteenth of the world's population, yet we have created more new wealth than all the other millions of people in the world; and the benefits of this great wealth have been more widely distributed here than in any other country—at any time. In addition to, or rather as a result of, such accomplishments, we have more churches, more schools, more libraries, more recreational facilities, more hospitals.

Americans have gone farther than any other people in the elimination of abusive child-labor practices, the reduction of back-breaking drudgery, the spread of literacy, enlightenment, health, longevity, general well-being, and good will toward others.[4]

Thomas Jefferson wrote of the United States: "Its soul, its climate, its equality, liberty, laws, people, and manners—my God! How little do my countrymen know what precious blessings they are in possession of, and which no other people on earth enjoy!"

Every American citizen should have a deep respect for the Declaration of Independence and the Constitution of the United States. William Gladstone, famous British statesman, described the American Constitution as "the most wonderful work ever struck off at a given time by the brain and purpose of man."

Have you ever wondered what happened to those men who signed the Declaration of Independence?

Five signers were captured by the British as traitors and were tortured before they died. Twelve had their homes ransacked and burned. Two lost their sons in the Revolutionary Army. Another had two sons captured. Nine of the 56 fought and died from wounds or hardships.

What kind of men were they? [24] were lawyers and jurists, [11] were merchants, [9] were farmers and large plantation owners, men of means, well educated. But they signed the Declaration of Independence knowing full well that the penalty would be death if they were captured.

They signed, and they pledged their lives, their fortunes and their sacred honor. Carter Braxton of Virginia, a wealthy planter and trader, saw his ships swept from the seas by the British navy. He sold his home and properties to pay his debts, and died in rags.

At the Battle of Yorktown, Thomas Nelson, Jr., noted that the British General Cornwallis had taken over the Nelson home for his headquarters. The owner quietly urged General George Washington to open fire, which was done. The home was destroyed, and Nelson died bankrupt.

Francis Lewis had his home and properties destroyed. The enemy jailed his wife, and she died within a few months.

John Hart was driven from his wife's bedside as she was dying. Their 13 children fled for their lives. His fields and grist mill were laid waste. For more than a year he lived in forests and caves, returning home after the war to find his wife dead, his children vanished. A few weeks later he died from exhaustion and a broken heart.

Such were the sacrifices of the American Revolution. These were not wild-eyed, rabble-rousing ruffians. They were soft-spoken men of means and education. They had security, but they valued liberty more. Standing tall, straight, and unwavering, they pledged: "For the support of this declaration, with a firm reliance on the protection of the Divine Providence, we mutually pledge to each other, our lives, our fortunes, and our sacred honor."

—J. Eugene White

## How Christian Is America?

It has been repeated often that America had a spiritual beginning. There may be differences of opinion as to the spiritual nature of its beginning. One historian characterized our origin thus: "The pilgrims came for God, not gold." The seeds of liberty and justice were brought from the Old Country and were permitted to bloom on new soil. It cannot be denied that some of our founders sought divine guidance as they formulated the creed which became the guiding light for future generations. However, not all.

Perry C. Cotham points out that all of the early statesmen in the United States would not be considered evangelicals.

That political leaders such as Franklin, Jefferson and Washington should be so highly esteemed by ministers in conservative and evangelical churches today is somewhat ironic, for if they were living today and advocating the same religious convictions and lifestyle, many of these same ministers would feel bound to disfellowship them.

Some, Franklin and Jefferson not excluded, were less than morally impeccable in their sexual behavior. Many were deistic, believing that God effects His providence only through natural, immutable laws, that the Bible is the best but not a perfect or even consistent revelation of His nature, and that Jesus Christ was an ideal man whose system was as complete as any man could devise.

Franklin's motion for prayer at the Constitutional Convention is often cited as an index to his spiritual life, and there is no reason to doubt his sincerity; the fact that the motion was defeated, however, is not widely circulated.... [5]

Harold O. J. Brown gives this evaluation:

The United States was not, in fact, founded as a Christian nation. A certain religious orientation was more or less taken for granted by the Founding Fathers, it is true. It would not have occurred to them to contest the existence of God or the necessity of dependence on Him. It was not their purpose to form a secular, anti-Christian state. Still, they had no intention of establishing any particular form of Christianity. Many of them were merely vaguely deistic in their convictions. The "Christian America" for which they laid the foundation resulted from their tolerance, but not from their deliberate design.[6]

While it may be true that some of the influential Founding Fathers were deists, the foundling nation adhered to Christian principles.

John Warwick Montgomery states that our nation was "Christian in spite of itself." Note his explanation:

> The single most paradoxical aspect of American history is that, though the country's Founding Fathers were deists and not Christians, the nation got off to a Christian start nonetheless. Both the American Revolution and the founding documents arising from it turned out to be—often in spite of the motives of their creators—fully compatible with historic Christian faith. In this sense, our national origins might be said to exemplify the fundamental principle of divine economy that men are saved by God's free grace and not by their own works—"lest any man should boast"![7]

Our Founding Fathers sought divine wisdom in establishing America:

> Reverently and humbly, the founders of our nation sought divine guidance in writing the creeds that became the guiding light of this new and independent country.
>
> The first sentence of the Declaration of Independence speaks of "the Laws of Nature and of Nature's God"; and its final sentence expresses a "firm reliance on the protection of Divine Providence."
>
> The Articles of Confederation, which preceded the Constitution, declare, "It has pleased the Great Governor of the world to incline the hearts of the legislatures we respectfully represent in Congress to approve of, and to authorize us to ratify, the said Articles of Confederation and perpetual union."
>
> Engraved on the hearts of these Americans who had just won freedom from big government in England was the belief that a force greater than man had created the universe and in so doing had imposed certain natural laws which would always prevail over man-made laws.
>
> Here, for the first time in human history, man called upon God to aid him in forming a government dedicated to the principle that each individual citizen, answerable ultimately only to God, should be free to work out his own spiritual and material destiny.[8]

William Penn declared, "If you are not governed by God, you will be ruled by tyrants." To be governed by God meant to accept "The Bible Charter of Freedom." Thus it has been stated, "The reverence for God of our Founding Fathers, coupled with the principles of liberty established in the Holy Bible, have provided the basis upon which the United States of America has been founded."

Norman Cousins in his book, *In God We Trust* (The Religious Beliefs and Ideas of the American Founding Fathers), gives us the following information:

> All these groups had their own religious experiences and outlooks, divisions and subdivisions, branches and sub-branches. Far from representing any weakness of the whole, they provided strength. As Jefferson and various others have pointed out, what was true of America politically was true in the reverse spiritually. In politics it was: United we stand, divided we fall. In religion: Divided we stand, united we fall....
>
> It is significant that most of the Founding Fathers grew up in a strong religious atmosphere. Many had Calvinist family backgrounds. In reacting against it, they did not react against basic religious ideas or what they considered to be the spiritual nature of man. Most certainly they did not turn against God or lose their respect for religious belief. Indeed, it was their very concern for the conditions under which free religious belief was possible that caused them to invest so much of their thought and energy into the cause of human rights....
>
> To repeat: Not all the founders acknowledged a formal faith, but it was significant that their view of man had a deeply religious foundation. Rights were "God-given"; man was "endowed by his Creator"; there were "natural laws" and "natural rights"; freedom was related to the "sacredness" of man. The development of a free man was not divorced from the idea of moral man any more than religious man could be separated from moral man.
>
> There was also strong spiritual content in the confidence of the American founders in the capacity of man to govern his own affairs, to hold the ultimate power in the operation of his society, and to be able to decide correctly when given access to vital information.[9]

It cannot be denied that America has a Christian heritage. One has written:

> It is worth remembering that 48 of the 50 states refer to a deity in their Constitutions; that the Pilgrims, on landing, wrote a compact which began: "In the name of God, Amen." Our coins have historically borne the legend, "In God We Trust." Our Congress and legislatures open daily with prayer.

All of this is not accidental.

## The Greatness of America

The oft-quoted words of the French statesman and philosopher Alexis Comte de Tocqueville (1805-1869) are worth considering. In his treatise, *Democracy in America* [a systematic analysis of democratic institutions in the United States], he asserted:

> I sought for the greatness and genius of America in her commodious harbors and her ample rivers. . .and it was not there; in her fertile lands and boundless prairies. . .and it was not there. Not until I went to the churches of America and heard her pulpits aflame with righteousness did I understand the secret of her genius and power. America is great because she is good. . .and if America ceases to be good, America will cease to be great.

The psalmist declared, "Except the Lord build the house, they labour in vain that build it. . ." (Ps. 127:1). No one can doubt the greatness of America. We have "greatness to spare."

But the remark has been made that "the flag is losing color." David A. Norris urges a return to the principles which made our nation great:

> This discouragement among Americans, especially biblical Christians, over trends in society and the confusing inability to get corrections, can be cleared up by a re-examination of this unique heritage. The philosophy spelled out in the Declaration of Independence and implemented by our national Constitution has been sufficient; it is only a matter of returning to and reapplying those principles. . . .
>
> America's hope for future greatness lies in the grass-roots self-education in the unique civilizing and liberating principles that were stressed educationally until the early 1900's. Our system of government still retains the procedures whereby the principles "under God" can be reinstituted by the people.
>
> In understanding, there is power. Willful deception becomes powerless before serious patriots whose actions and opinions are stayed on the fundamentals of freedom's heritage.[10]

The blessings of a nation are dependent upon the favor of a sovereign God. His direction is to be recognized. The Pledge of Allegiance to the American flag dogmatically proclaims, "one nation, under God." Historically our leaders have sought the guidance of the Almighty. A nation sometimes forgets the roots of her greatness. Charles Dickens commented, "The memory of those who lie below passes away so soon."

America was born in greatness. The smile of Deity was upon us. The hand of God is seen in American history. George Boddis expressed it this way: "The providence of God is no more clearly seen in the history of any nation than in that of America. Indeed, if we read our national history in the light of the Scripture, we can see God's hand in American history as clearly as that in Israel."

We owe the Pilgrims an eternal debt of gratitude. Despite their shortcomings, they did much to establish Christian principles in our nation. They believed the Bible. Alistair Cooke informs us that

> they truly believed that the simple faith of Christ had been corrupted by the Church of England, and they accordingly renounced it. They looked in the Second Book of Corinthians and read: "Come out from among them, saith the Lord." So they became "Separatists."[11]

Their journey to America was most impressive. Kate Caffrey has written an interesting book, *The Mayflower*. From that informative book come the following facts:

> It [the *Mayflower*] was a sizeable ship for its time—about 90 feet long (only 12 feet shorter than a tennis court), just over 26 feet at its widest (shorter than the world record long jump), and 180 tons in weight. Four hundred and fifty such vessels would add up to the tonnage of the *Queen Mary*; eleven such, in a line, would not equal the *Queen Mary*'s length....
>
> Most of the sleeping and living space for the passengers was in the low-ceilinged great cabin, 25 by 15 feet at its largest, and on the main deck, 75 by 20 feet at most. Below decks anybody five feet tall could never stand fully upright.
>
> ...In an area that size, depressingly similar to a grave space, each person had to...survive for eight months—the time it took to get ready, make the crossing, and establish the settlement on the shores of the New World.[12]

"They came to America looking for peace, not fame." They were a courageous lot. "The sixty-five day voyage took a grim toll during the following winter on land: over half of all the people who made the journey died of scurvy, or 'general debility.' "[13] And yet when the *Mayflower* returned to England, not a single survivor volunteered to return to the Old Country.

William Bradford wrote of their landing:

> ...Being thus arrived in a good harbor and brought safe to land, they fell upon their knees and blessed the God of Heaven, who had brought them over the vast and furious ocean and delivered them from all the perils and miseries thereof, again to set their feet on the firm and stable earth, their proper element.
>
> ...Being thus passed the vast ocean, and a sea of troubles before in their preparation, they had now no friends to welcome them, no inns to entertain or refresh their weather-beaten bodies, no houses, much less towns, to repair to, to seek for succour.
>
> It is recorded in Scripture as a mercy to the apostle and his shipwrecked company that the barbarians showed them no small kindness in refreshing them, but those savage barbarians, when they met with them...were readier to fill their sides full of arrows than otherwise.[14]

Their future was as bleak as the land, yet their faith was as strong as the symbolic Plymouth Rock. "The Mayflower Compact" is a significant historic document in that it declares the Pilgrims' reliance on the Almighty God and the seeking of His blessing upon the establishment of a Christian colony in the New World.

Though these stouthearted pioneers suffered many privations, they were grateful to their Maker for all His provisions. William Bradford, governor of the colony, wrote these words of gratitude:

PROCLAMATION TO ALL YE PILGRIMS:

Inasmuch as the great Father has given us this year an abundant harvest of Indian corn, wheat, peas, beans, squashes, and garden vegetables, and has made the forests to abound with game and the sea with fish and clams, and inasmuch as He has protected us from the ravages of the savages, has spared us from pestilence and disease, has granted us freedom to worship God according to the dictates of our own conscience; now I, your magistrate, do proclaim that all ye Pilgrims, with your wives and ye little ones, do gather at ye meeting house on ye hill, between the hours of 9 and 12 in the day time, on Thursday, November ye 29th, of the year of our Lord one thousand six hundred and twenty-three and the third year since ye Pilgrims landed on ye Pilgrim Rock, there to listen to ye pastor and render thanksgiving to ye Almighty God for all His blessings.

With the apparent blessing of God upon them, this infant nation grew to be the greatest and most powerful on earth. Her affluence was recognized by the nations of the world.

But it has been noted that "the highest power may be lost by misrule." Francis Bacon wrote: "It is a strange desire to seek such power and to lose liberty; or to seek power over others and to lose power over a man's self." It is possible for a nation to be rich in possessions but poor in spirit. Jesus Christ warned, "Take heed, and beware of covetousness: for a man's life consisteth not in the abundance of the things which he possesseth" (Luke 12:15).

We have forgotten history. We have forgotten God. Jeremiah, the weeping prophet, lamented, "...yet my people have forgotten me days without number" (Jer. 2:32). The Prophet Hosea declared, "...their heart was exalted; therefore have they forgotten me" (Hos. 13:6). Are the words spoken of the pitiful Samson true of our nation, "...And he wist not that the Lord was departed from him" (Judges 16:20)?

## What Happened to America?

*"Are not these evils come upon us, because our God is not among us?"*—Deut. 31:17.

*"Sirs, ye should have hearkened unto me. . . ."*—Acts 27:21.

The mighty nation of America has fallen on hard times. There are those who contend that with the outlawing of prayer from the public schools we have become a secular state. We are still highly favored among the nations of the world, but there is an aching void in our midst. We have lost our sense of direction.

An old Scottish proverb declares, "If you don't know where you are going, any road will take you there." In the past, blind leaders have led us astray. "A nation of sheep" have followed tragically.

Is America on the road to ruin? Is America over the hill? Could it be that we died spiritually because of atheism, apostasy, avarice? Did our demise take place because of prosperity, politicians and false prophets?

---

## There are those who contend that with the outlawing of prayer from the public schools we have become a secular state.

---

Columnist Max Lerner wonders if America may not be

> a dying civilization. Americans have always turned inward, into an awareness of themselves as a people. Lately this self-awareness has taken on overtones of a sense of being at the end of the tether, a mordant feeling of disintegration and decay . . . a Hamlet-like loss of self-confidence, with an apocalyptic sense of doom for the civilization.

America bows before the god of materialism. We are enamored with things. John Steinbeck, the noted author, commented:

> . . . we are also poisoned with things. Having many things seems to create a desire for more things—more clothes, houses, automobiles. Think of the pure horror of our Christmases when our children tear open package after package; when the floor is heaped with wrappings and presents, say, "Is that all?" Two days after the smashed and abandoned things are added to our national trash pile, and perhaps the child, having got in trouble, explains, "I didn't have anything to do." And he means exactly that— nothing to do, nowhere to go, no direction, no purpose, and worst of all, no needs. Wants he has, yes, but for more bright and breakable "things." We are trapped and entangled in things.

*—America and Americans*

Harold Lindsell writes:

> In the United States, perhaps the richest of all nations, more Christians have capitulated to materialistic lives than anywhere else. In the final analysis it is no more than putting *things* before God, of seeking first the kingdom of man rather than the kingdom of God. It is easy to forget the biblical principle that the things that are seen are temporal, while the things that are not seen are eternal.
>
> To suppose that materialism is limited to the possession of money, lands, houses, and furniture would be imprudent. The materialist may also seek for himself the more intangible trappings of power, fame, and applause, although these are rarely attained without money and other material things. But they are an expression of materialism and represent a commitment to priorities other than God.[15]

T. Walter Brashier puts it this way:

> A distinguished Britisher said recently that he visited an American home that seemed to have everything: two cars in the garage, a beautiful living room with expensive furniture, a color TV set, a kitchen filled with the latest gadgets, and a large pool and beautiful patio. However, the lady of the house was reading a book entitled *How to Be Happy*.
>
> The number one book sellers today are books on peace and happiness.

Someone has quipped: "If anyone can be happy in times like these, he ought to have his TV set examined."

Is America laughing at her own funeral? Is America laughing her way into oblivion? America finds sin exceedingly funny. "The sin clowns" on television are disgusting. This is a day of jokes. While our nation stands in jeopardy, we poke fun at that which is sacred. Radio and TV commentators joke about drunkenness, divorce and juvenile delinquency. This generation needs to awaken to the fact that sin is no joke. Can we be engaged in foolish chatter while the very existence of our nation is at stake?

Laurence M. Gould remarks:

> I do not believe the greatest threat to our future is from bombs or guided missiles. I don't think our civilization will die that way. I think it will die when we no longer care—when the spiritual forces that make us wish to be right and noble die in the hearts of men....
>
> If America is to grow great, we must stop gagging at the word "spiritual." Our task is to re-discover and re-assert our faith in the spiritual values on which American life has really rested from its beginning.

Which way is America going economically? It has been said that "the laws of economics are just as unrelenting as the laws of physics." Professor William

H. Peterson points out that we cannot get "something for nothing," and it is impossible to thumb our noses at the future for the sake of the present. Note his simple logical deduction: "He perforce must consume only to the extent he produces—he must live within his means. Or else. So must a family. Or else. So must a corporation. Or else. And so must a nation. Or else." Or else—bankruptcy! According to a leading economist, "America is heading for a full-blown crisis, maybe bankruptcy."

The Welfare State and Socialism have done their deadly work. We are now reaping the bitter harvest. Socialism is dangerous.

Bryce MacKasey, a former Postmaster General of Canada, spoke these poignant words of wisdom:

> Keynes destroyed our belief in the discipline of money. Freud destroyed our belief in sexual discipline. Spock almost destroyed our belief in discipline for children. Einstein destroyed the discipline of absolute values. We gave up the goal of Heaven for heaven on earth.

He further adds:

> Ours is a very depressing moment in the so-called enlightened men. The ghosts of dead civilizations seem to haunt every serious writer. The consensus appears to be that democracy is ungovernable and inflation is administering the last rites to free enterprise. . . . Except for lemmings, who get this off urge to rush to their destruction, no animal species but man commits suicide.
>
> The more I read about what's happening, the more incredible it seems. Here we are with an economic system of free enterprise—it has given the average man luxury and leisure for the first time. Does he support it? Does he work for it? Look at the figures on absenteeism, the figures on labor turn-over. Productivity is falling in every area but crime.
>
> Our system has given us the most enlightened citizens in history, yet we're racing along a road that plunges down the abyss of ignorance. So we are with a stranger-than-fiction paradox. We've the most successful economic system ever devised, the most humane and enlightened system of government that ever evolved. Yet. . .the system is like a machine without brakes. It's running out of control.
>
> Appeals to reason don't work. For more than half a century we've been fighting communism because it opposes all our beliefs. Its government is monolithic. Its economy is controlled. Its values are materialistic, and individual liberty is repressed. And all the time we've been fighting state control, we've been moving toward it, the slaves of our own inventions: our machines and our institutions.[16]

> **Ill fares the land, to hastening ills a prey**
> **Where wealth accumulates and men decay.**

America has lived beyond her means. She is now hopelessly in debt, and there is coming a day of reckoning. Read these pertinent sayings: "There is no Santa Claus; there is no free lunch." We should learn from Rome. A nation cannot survive without fiscal responsibility.

"God gives every bird its food, but He does not throw it into the nest"; or to put it more bluntly, "The world owes you a living only when you have earned it."

"It's all right with the Lord if you pray for a good harvest, but He expects you to keep right on plowing."

"The only lasting favor which the parent may confer upon the child is that of helping the child to help itself."

Genesis 3:19 plainly declares, "In the sweat of thy face shalt thou eat bread, till thou return unto the ground. . . ." Second Thessalonians 3:10 plainly states: "For even when we were with you, this we commanded you, that if any would not work, neither should he eat."

"If you take care of a person from the time he is born until he leaves this earth, you destroy his self-respect."

"You cannot strengthen the weak by weakening the strong."

## The Foundations Are Being Destroyed

*"If the foundations be destroyed, what can the righteous do?"*—Ps. 11:3.

Is America on a "moral toboggan-slide"? Arnold Toynbee, the eminent historian, observes, "Moral decay from within has destroyed most of the world's great civilizations." Few can deny that our great nation is in the last stages of moral deterioration.

The *Wall Street Journal* predicts, "The decade of the '80s promises to be an absolutely ghastly period." On his 75th birthday, October, 1965, President Eisenhower warned of America's "moral decay" and added: "We are going too far away from the old virtues and rules of life . . . there are certain values we should keep, values like decency in our conduct and dealings with others, pride in ourselves, self-reliance, dedication to our country, respect for law and order."

The United States of America is committing moral suicide, and we don't seem to care. A "Flood of Filth" has overwhelmed our nation, but we have been designated "The Unshockable Generation." It has been said: "We used to blush with shame when we were ashamed; now we are ashamed when we blush. There is no fear of God before our eyes."

Listen to Ezra as he confesses to God the sins of Israel: "O my God, I am ashamed and blush to lift up my face to thee, my God: for our iniquities are

increased over our head, and our trespass is grown up unto the heavens"
(Ezra 9:6).

Ancient Corinth could not blush. A city without shame—but ancient Corinth is gone. When a nation loses its sense of shame, it is headed for destruction.

The spiritual nature of a nation can be determined by how she spends her money. Americans (like the Romans of old) are addicted to pleasure. We spend $83 billion a year for leisure activities. Americans spend $13 billion for Christmas. That's over $60.00 for every man, woman and child in the U.S.A. As much is spent for dog and cat food as half of the missionary budget of all the churches in the United States. In one day Americans consume 28 tons of aspirin, tranquilizers and sleeping pills. In order to shed weight, our nation pays out $10 billion a year.

---

## "We used to blush...when we were ashamed; now we are ashamed when we blush."

---

Note this definition of a civilized country: "A nation living on reducing pills while the rest of the world is starving." It looks like America qualifies.

It would be well for our nation to learn from England and pre-war Germany. It has been pointed out that a country can "buy survival at the cost of conscience." A tourist visiting England remarked: "They live like an utter bankrupt, not caring what the morrow may bring...." The same sins that were rampant in Hitler's day are common in America today.

Richard Hanser, in his book, *Putsch,* has a chapter entitled "Fever Chart" which deals with the moral conditions in Germany. The similarity between pre-war Germany and our nation is amazing. George Clemenceau's prediction was fulfilled not only in France but in Germany: "You will live the gamy peace of decadence.... It will be filthy and delicious...as when the ancients opened their veins in a bath of milk."[17]

What happened to America? How did we get this way? A good indication of our present condition today is a bumper sticker with the words: DON'T FOLLOW ME—I'M LOST! Daniel Webster's famous "Reply to Hayne" contains these words of wisdom:

> When the mariner has been tossed for many days in thick weather and on an unknown sea, he naturally avails himself of the first pause in the storm, the earliest glance of the sun, to take his latitude and ascertain how far the elements have driven him from his true course. Let us imitate

this prudence; and before we float farther on the waves of this debate, refer to the point from which we departed, that we may, at least, conjecture where we now are.[18]

It has been said that "America is running on the momentum of a godly ancestry; and when the momentum is spent, God help America!" "The 4-F's of our day are not just those unfit for military service: they're the frightened, fearful, futile and frustrated." When a nation loses its character, her doom is not far off. R. E. Maxwell writes of "Character Pollution":

> Oh, the mental and moral and spiritual "fall-out" that has polluted and perverted millions of young people in our Western world! We are reminded of the plague of Black Death in Europe in the 14th century. That plague, so very contagious and accompanied by fever and prostration, was usually fatal.
>
> Fleas from infected rats were the carriers of that awful scourge. But today we have a polluting plague worse than the Black Death, a plague carried by that brood of infected moral rats—the writers of pornography, the promoters of sex literature, the pushers of drugs, the peddlers of dope. And what might we not say of professors and philosophers who peddle atheistic evolution and God-hating communism and Christ-denying education? Was not China thus taken over by the power of the polluting pen?
>
> —*The Prairie Overcomer*, March 1972

Law and order are necessary for the survival of a nation. The famous Roman political writer Cicero (106-43 B.C.) gave sound advice when he contended that "the very idea of existence was linked to that of law and government, 'without which existence is impossible for a household, a city, a nation, the human race, physical nature, and the universe itself.' "[19]

J. Edgar Hoover made these remarks:

> Communists recognize that they cannot infiltrate and undermine American society unless they first turn the people against established authority. To accomplish this, they try to influence and turn people against law and order and to smear and discredit constituted authority.[20]

The idea of permissiveness has wrought havoc on American society. Dr. Boris Sokoloff points out that the ancient civilizations which practiced permissiveness became decadent nations and ultimately fell.

> Promiscuity and excessive sexuality, unlawful behavior of citizens, growing crime and general use of narcotics, all this was a part of the permissive syndrome in past civilizations.[21]

He further adds that

we are now witnessing a fascinating phenomenon in this country. The "flower" of our society, the intellectuals and the wealthy, promote and defend an extreme permissiveness, without even realizing that they are contaminated by the Freudian ethic, the ethic which declares that all is permitted, that the permissive syndrome is the natural drive of a human being to be free from society, and that it should not be repressed or even controlled.[22]

Permissiveness leads to rebellion, and rebellion to revolution. Revolution is a distinct possibility. The riots of the 60s are an evil memory. Back in 1967 Gary Allen wrote a revealing book, *Communist Revolution in the Streets.* In the last chapter he presents a frightening picture of what could happen to our country:

Imagine how easily a mere handful of trained Revolutionaries could destroy billions of dollars' worth of property in every major city in the United States. The frightening fact is that this would only take a small handful in each urban area to cause fantastic dislocations.

A half dozen people could trigger enormous brush and forest fires surrounding metropolitan areas, poison the water supply of an entire metropolitan area, or a few could blow up the dams which provide water and power to huge urban areas. The 1965 blackout of the northeastern section of the United States has demonstrated that our power distribution system is vulnerable.

The object of all this sabotage would be to cause panic and try to precipitate mob warfare. During this period, supermarkets would become prime targets as a food shortage would give rise to roaming gangs of hungry people, just as occurred in Russia in 1918. This is the logical and planned culmination of civil disobedience. At such a time panic would prevail through the land and the citizenry would gratefully allow the federal government to seize complete control over the lives and property of Americans, thereby establishing total dictatorship.[23]

Moral decay is certain when God is ruled out of our lives. David A. Norris comments:

When men cease to believe in God, their standards fade. Hence, no dependable standards can be translated into law. As we are finding, men who do not believe in God have few moral ideals upon which to erect a moral law. When faith in God disappears, moral standards disappear, individuals and families are torn apart and the civilization crumbles. Selfishness takes its toll in ignorance and distrust of the guidelines of a sovereign God, given to us to make true happiness possible.[24]

The Prophet Jeremiah asked the question, "And what will ye do in the end thereof?" (Jer. 5:31). America must be awakened. The stakes are high. The country we lose could be our own. You have heard this statement, a true one: "God is a sure paymaster. He may not pay at the end of every week or month or year, but remember, He pays in the end." The law of the harvest is inevitable. Is it time for America to reap what she has sown?

A millionaire, turned bootlegger, was serving a long prison term when a friend of his visited him one day. The millionaire was sitting cross-legged with an enormous needle and a ball of twine, sewing burlap bags. "Hello," said the friend. "Sewing, eh?" "No," said the prisoner, "reaping."

God's Word is true: "For they have sown the wind, and they shall reap the whirlwind" (Hos. 8:7).

Jeremiah the prophet exclaimed, "Her sun is gone down while it was yet day..." (Jer. 15:9).

America is too young to die unless she commits suicide!

## ENDNOTES:

[1] Jesse Helms, *When Free Men Shall Stand*, 34.

[2] Alistair Cooke, *America*, 20.

[3] Paul Blumberg, *Inequality in an Age of Decline*, 20.

[4] Phillip Abbot Luce and Douglas Hyde, *The Intelligent Student's Guide to Survival*, 107.

[5] Perry C. Cotham, *Politics, Americanism and Christianity*, 522.

[6] Harold O. J. Brown, *The Protest of a Troubled Protestant*, 73.

[7] John Warwick Montgomery, *The Shaping of America*, 57.

[8] A. G. Heinsohn, Jr., *Anthology of Conservative Writing in the United States, 1932-1960*, 1.

[9] Norman A. Cousins, *In God We Trust*, 6, 9, 10.

[10] David A. Norris, *Before You Lose It All*, 10, 11.

[11] Cooke, 76.

[12] Kate Caffrey, *The Mayflower*, 11, 69.

[13] Cooke, 77.

[14] Francis Bretano, *Nation Under God*, 8.

[15] Harold Lindsell, *The World, the Flesh, and the Devil*, 49.

[16] John Wesley White, *W. W. III*, 134, 135.

[17] Richard Hanser, *Putsch*, 222.

[18] James Burnham, *Congress and the American Tradition*, 1.

[19] William Ebenstein, *Great Political Thinkers*, 123, 124.

[20] J. Edgar Hoover, *On Communism*, 102.

[21] Boris Sokoloff, *The Permissive Society*, 14.

[22] *Ibid.*, 22.

[23] Gary Allen, *Communist Revolution in the Streets*, 113, 114.

[24] Norris, 94.

# 7   Is America Terminally Ill?

*"In those days was Hezekiah sick unto death. And the prophet Isaiah the son of Amoz came to him, and said unto him, Thus saith the Lord, Set thine house in order; for thou shalt die, and not live."*—II Kings 20:1.

*"It is of the Lord's mercies that we are not consumed, because his compassions fail not."*—Lam. 3:22.

An ailing individual may suspect that he has cancer. A visit to his physician confirms the fact. The diagnosis is: "terminal cancer"! In other words, he is going to die! Is America terminally ill? Is our nation going to die? Most Americans are abhorrent at such a thought. We reason it just simply can't be! It is imperative that we go to the Bible for our diagnosis. The Word of God gives a detailed account of our terminal illness. It is found in the first chapter of Isaiah.

Isaiah was a prophet. He was called to a particular task. W. E. Vine in his commentary on *Isaiah* informs us: "As with Amos in Israel so with Isaiah in Judah, they were called to declare that the time of God's longsuffering was coming to an end."[1] Henrietta C. Mears in her book, *What the Bible Is All About*, explains the character of the prophets:

> The prophets were fearless men. They denounced the sins of their day. They called men away from idols back to God. It is true that the prophets were concerned about the moral and political corruption of the nation, but the fact that the people were worshipping idols was their greatest concern. The nation had a wrong attitude toward God....
>
> The prophets exposed the cold formalism of their religion. They constantly reminded the people that Jehovah was the only true God. They pointed men to the law. They were statesmen of the highest order. They were prophets in that they came to tell forth what God said. They were not only "forth-tellers" but "foretellers"....

The prophets were the most unpopular men in their day, for they dealt with the moral and religious conditions of the hour! Generally the state was bad. Prophets were sent when the nation was out of step with God—when they were walking in disobedience. The words which the prophets used to rebuke or exhort the people were very pointed. . . .

The kingdoms of Judah and Israel had become so weakened by idolatry and corruption that the enemies swept down upon them from the north "like a wolf on the fold." First, Israel rolled in the dust under the tramp of the terrible Assyrian hosts (722 B.C.), and then Judah fell with the Babylonian thundering at her gate and breaking down her walls (586 B.C.). Both kingdoms ended, and her people were carried into captivity. Isaiah lived and prophesied in Jerusalem at this time.

Isaiah spent his life trying to get Judah to become acquainted with God and His Word. He wanted them to trust wholly in God's guidance.[2]

America while still young in years has grown tragically old—a nation that has grown old too soon. The Prophet Hosea describes her condition: "Strangers have devoured his strength, and he knoweth it not: yea, gray hairs are here and there upon him, yet he knoweth not" (Hos. 7:9). Leonard Ravenhill makes this astute observation:

Compared with hoary dynasties and the empires of the ages, America is but a prattling child in a crib playing with its toes. Compared with the ancient civilizations, America was born only yesterday. But, and here is the rub, she is dying today, and she will be dead tomorrow unless there is a spiritual awakening. . . .

In a day when men ignore the diagnosis of history and pretend that America does not have the disease that destroyed every major civilization there ever was, it is time to tell the truth with all the passion and zeal that pure love for one's country can produce![3]

President Carter in a nationally televised speech spoke of "America in the grip of a national malaise." A former United States Senator has remarked: "America is sick with a sickness that goes very deep. The sickness has spread into our schools, our industries, our unions, even our churches." The late Noel Smith commented: "If America ever crumbles it will be because she, like a good watch, has become unwound. If America dies, she will die of apathy and laziness. If America dies, it will be because she has forgotten the price of living" (*Baptist Bible Tribune*).

## Brainwashing a Nation

*"The ox knoweth his owner, and the ass his master's crib: but Israel doth not know, my people doth not consider."*—Isa. 1:3.

"Look out the window, and you will see the bird after the worm, the cat after the bird, and the dog after the cat. It gives you a little better understanding of the news." Someone has quipped, "The American people are the best misinformed people in the world." Ours is the day of "the manipulated society," "managed news," "distortion by design." Something evil is happening to us (in spite of all the positive thinkers). We are unknowingly being manipulated by nefarious forces. A philosopher put it bluntly, "We are stewing in our own juices."

---

## "If America dies, it will be because she has forgotten the price of living."

—*Noel Smith*

---

Blase Pascal in his *Pensés* has remarked, "Thought makes the whole dignity of man; therefore, endeavor to think well, that is the only morality." But today our thinking to a great measure is controlled by the media. Abraham Lincoln declared: "In this and like communities, public sentiment is everything. With public sentiment, nothing can fail. Without it, nothing can succeed. Consequently, he who moulds public sentiment goes deeper than he who enacts statutes and pronounces decisions." Alexander Solzhenitsyn has put it this way:

> Your judgment is only as good as your information. If they are controlling your information, they are controlling you. . . . "If you want a nation of hopheads, sex maniacs, alcoholics, psychos, and maddened mobs, then just you—and the rest of our American population—keep on laughing at things like. . .dirty movies, filthy books, and crude, cheap, and profane language."
>
> In keeping silent about evil, in burying it deep within us, so that it appears nowhere on the surface, we are implanting it, and it will rise up a thousandfold in the future.

The awesome power of the media is frightening! It has patterned the thinking of our nation. "The news media have in their hands today a power that pales even that exercised by public leaders. They can create heroes or villains almost overnight. Or make or break a business."

Will Durant is reputed to have said, "It may be true. . .that 'you can't fool all the people all the time,' but you can fool enough of them to rule a large country." Isaiah warned, "Woe unto them that call evil good, and good evil; that put darkness for light, and light for darkness; that put bitter for sweet, and sweet for bitter!" (Isa. 5:20).

Fred W. Friendly, former president of CBS News, in commenting on the influence of TV, remarked, "No mighty king, no ambitious emperor, no pope, no prophet dreamt of such an awesome pulpit, so potent a magic wand."

Malcom Muggeridge in his book, *Christ and the Media,* has written: "The media in general, TV in particular, are the greatest single influence in our society today. This influence is, in my opinion, largely irresponsibility arbitrarily, and without reference to any moral or intellectual, still less spiritual guidelines whatever."[4]

The late Eric Severeid, after many years as a radio and TV commentator, boasted, "We have affected our times." The book, *The Culture of Narcissism,* by Christopher Lasch was a nationwide best seller. The author states his views thus:

> The mass media, with their cult of celebrity and their attempt to surround it with glamour and excitement, have made Americans a nation of fans, moviegoers. The media give substance to and thus intensify narcissistic dreams of fame and glory, encourage the common man to identify himself with the stars and to hate the "herd" and make it more and more difficult for him to accept the banality of everyday existence.[5]

There is no doubt that America is being brainwashed daily by the news media. George C. Roche III in the Introduction of his book, *Legacy of Freedom,* makes this statement: "Yet mass communications, public school education, and public entertainment consistently reflect the values of the 'intellectuals' who would destroy the tradition of our civilization."[6]

It has been said that "we live in a day...in which public opinion is moulded like wax." Harry Schultz has commented that "people assume most of the news on TV, radio and newspapers are factual accounts...when in reality, up to 75% is often a gross distortion, outright fiction or false information; furthermore, the big media in the U.S. is largely in the hands of the liberals, who usually report the most controversial part of a speech, while ignoring 95% of what may be constructive talk" (*Harry Schultz Letter,* 9-8-80).

Fred Friendly declared that "broadcasting is going to determine what kind of people we are...." The fate of America seems to hang in the balance between two cities—Moscow or Washington. This is a day of battle for the minds of men.

Newspapers are fast becoming a monopoly. "There are 1,760 daily newspapers in the United States. Nearly 1,100 are now owned by large media chains, and more and more are gobbled up at the alarming rate of 50 per year. Independently owned newspapers are disappearing like family farms."

Joseph Pulitzer voiced a truism when he asserted, "Our Republic and its press will rise and fall together."

Tim LaHaye, in his book, *The Battle for the Mind,* makes this observation:

> Even though a newspaper is privately owned, it is dependent on the two
> wire services (Associated Press and United Press International) for its daily
> source of world and national news. This news is carefully edited before
> being sent out to the daily papers. Who does the editing? Who hired the
> editors, and what are their beliefs? Anyone really familiar with humanism
> can recognize its influence in the way the news is managed. Remember,
> a reporter cannot possibly report everything that is said or done. He must
> edit it down to what he thinks is important. If he is a humanist, what
> he considers important is inevitably colored by his humanistic outlook.
> If one of his favored politicians says something wrong or harmful to his
> image, that statement can be edited. If, however, a politician represent-
> ing traditional moral values or economics makes a misstatement that can
> put him in a bad light, it hits the front page of every paper in the country.[7]

*The Opinion Makers* is the title of a book by William L. Rivers. He states
that "much of the history of American governments pivots on the use of the
press as an instrument of political power."[8]

Henry Luce of *Time* magazine ["in a moment of candor"] confessed: "I don't
pretend that this is an objective magazine. It's an editorial magazine from the
first to the last, and whatever comes out has to reflect my view, and that's
the way it is."[9]

"You Can't Trust the News" is the title of an article by William Simon which
appeared in *The Saturday Evening Post* for December 1980. In that revealing
article he makes these statements:

> They [the press] are not merely "reporting news but actively involved
> in making [or suppressing it], then solemnly passing the results along to
> the American people as 'the way it is'"....By constantly pushing the
> country toward collectivist regimentation, they are creating a controlled
> society which can affect press freedoms as well as others....Freedom is
> indivisible, and those media spokesmen who have been working overtime
> to deny liberty to others may someday discover too late that they have
> forfeited their own.

A reporter for a nationally known newspaper is reported to have said, "It's
almost a perverse pleasure. I like going out and finding something
wrong...and then putting it into the newspaper."[10]

It is a common saying, "You are what you eat." Perhaps the words should
be paraphrased, "A nation becomes what it reads—and what it sees." The
remark is often heard that "the world watches America, and America watches television." Television has been defined as "a box that throws light without
illumination." "What TV gives you is just what you'd expect to get from a
vacuum tube." "Television is all sight and no vision."

Whether you like it or not, "the one-eyed monster" is here to stay. "Ninety-eight percent of all homes in America have at least one television set, while eighty-five percent have one bathtub; which only goes to show that more brains are washed than bodies." You can't feed garbage into your mind without having some of it come out. According to a report from the Associated Press from New York, "Consumers own more television sets than either telephones or automobiles!"

"How much time do we spend watching TV? In some nations adult TV viewing ranks only behind sleep and work for time consumed by a single activity." According to the A. C. Nielsen report: "Adult women average 30 hours and 14 minutes a week before the television set; children from 2 to 11 average 25 hours and 35 minutes; adult men average 24 hours and 25 minutes a week; teenagers 12 through 17 average 22 hours and 36 minutes."

---

## "What TV gives you is just what you'd expect to get from a vacuum tube."

---

Mary Lewis Coakley in her book, *Rated X (The Moral Case Against TV)*, writes:

> Whether we like it or not, TV is an integral part of our lives. It is not just another form of entertainment, comparable to the movies, or a bridge game, or bowling, or golf. It is not something that some of us leave our homes to do once a month, or once a week, or three times a week. It is right there in the house, as much a fixture as the kitchen sink, and it runs every day, and in some families, all day long. . . .

> Moreover, every year the vast army of TV viewers grows, despite a declining birth rate, because families are no longer content with one or two sets. Sets are scattered all through the house because each child now wants a set for his or her bedroom, Mom wants a portable mini-set to take with her into the kitchen while she cooks dinner, or into the laundry while she irons, and Dad wants one for his den or the office he fixed up in the room over the garage. The total number of viewing hours is rising with each passing day. . . .

> Apparently, people don't know that they can live without TV. In about 95 percent of the cases of TV breakdown, a repairman is called within 24 hours.[11]

Barry Goldwater was correct when he wrote, "It has been said that television has provided all Americans with a 'window on the world.' "[12]

"The messages of television, with words reinforced by music and pictures and action, received in a darkened room and reiterated over and over, are the most effective communications ever let loose on the world" (Dr. S. I. Hayakawa). It is significant that 34 million households in America view the Network Evening News. There is no doubt about it, the Network Evening News influences a nation—for good or evil.

Television is big business—and it is profitable. The radio and television industries employ over 160,000 people, and in one year the revenue from TV amounted to almost $8 billion. Eliot Daley writing in *TV Guide* comments:

> Television is one of modern man's greatest inventions—especially when it is used for the purpose of mass education. Unfortunately, most of the time it is used simply to attract people to some commercial product. Manufacturers want to sell their products. That's why all of their parents give them their wishes. That's why manufacturers sponsor programs. That's why advertisers worry about program ratings.

Mel White has compiled the following statistics:

> According to a CBS news special on commercials, advertisers spent $23 billion a year to brainwash us! Last year Procter and Gamble was the top advertiser spending almost $200 million to sell us soap and toothpaste while General Foods spent almost $100 million peddling cereals and other foods. Roughly, $400 million advertising dollars are directed against our children. The average child will absorb 220 minutes of commercials every week, more than 25,000 commercials in a year.

Don R. Pember in his book, *Mass Media in America*, makes this observation: Television is "the least grateful, most abrasive, exhausting, money grabbing, coldblooded showplace the world of entertainment has ever known."[13]

> **Sin is a monster of such frightful mien**
> **That to be hated needs but to be seen;**
> **But seen too oft, familiar with its face,**
> **We first endure, then pity, then embrace!**
> —Alexander Pope

The enormous influence of television is tremendous. It has been designated as "the most powerful social force in American culture today." "No modern medium of communication exerts more power than television. The average American spends about eighteen hours each week before the set. By the time he reaches sixty-five, he will have spent over six years of his life watching television." It is acknowledged that television reaches more than 95 percent of the homes in America and the average television set is on almost seven hours a day.

*U.S. News and World Report* asked some 500 business, government and professional leaders to rate, in terms of their influence, 18 of the nation's principal organizations and institutions. Television came in first. It was ranked ahead of the White House and the Supreme Court and the Congress; ahead of education and religion and political parties and all competing media.

Bill Paley, head of CBS in TV's early days, asserted that television was "more dominant in most American lives than newspapers, churches, and often the family itself."

The monster in your living room is ruining our nation and possibly your home. George Gerbner and Larry Cross wrote an article entitled "The Scary World of TV's Heavy Viewer," which appeared in the April, 1976, issue of *Psychology Today.* Note their observations:

> TV has replaced the Church as the toughest means of social control. . . . Television is different from all other media. From cradle to grave it penetrates nearly every home in the land. Unlike newspapers and magazines, television does not require literacy. . . . With virtually unlimited access, television both precedes literacy and, increasingly, preempts it. . . .
>
> Instead of threatening the social order, television may have become our chief instrument of social control.

"Some admit to being 'TV-intoxicated,' needing a 'daily fix' of it, as a drug addict would need drugs."

Bruce Herchensohn in his book, *The Gods of Antenna,* makes these revealing statements:

> The Founding Fathers could not foresee the day when a multichrome moving image would become more powerful than our elected leaders. That day has come. . . .
>
> The sordid reality was that a piece of furniture had become a member of the family. . . .
>
> Television images can mean life and death to someone. In a larger sense, those images can mean life and death to nations. Those images can be more powerful than a thousand armies—because armies can scorch only the skin, but television can scorch the mind.[14]

This tremendous influence is held in sway by a comparative few. Theodore H. White is quoted as saying: "What worries me most about the cultural pattern in the U.S.A. is its increasing concentration. . . especially in the media. You can take a compass with a one-mile radius and put it down at the corner of Fifth Avenue and 51st Street, and you have control of 95 percent of the entire opinion and influence making in the U.S.A."[15]

"Televisionitis" has become the scourge of the American home. It has been estimated that "the average child has seen 9,000 hours of television before he enters school." It is through this medium that a child may receive his outlook on life. An average child is said to spend more time watching television than is spent in anything else except sleeping. Dexter H. Faulkner relates these searing facts:

> By any measure, whether magnetic appeal, amount of exposure, or power to change behavior, commercial television now wields the major educational impact in the land.
>
> Does that sound like a sensational exaggeration? Then ponder these statistics:
>
> By the time the average American child reaches adolescence he will have spent twice as many hours watching television as he has sitting behind his school desk. Believe it or not, he'll have had 22,000 hours of television 'instruction,' as opposed to 11,000 hours' worth of school instruction.
>
> Even before he reaches age five he will already have spent more time in front of a television than the average student in a liberal arts program spends in the classroom throughout his entire four years of college attendance.

According to a survey of the three major television networks in Washington, D.C., between the hours of 3:00 p.m. and 11:00 p.m., the following facts were disclosed: 113 shootings, 92 stabbings, 168 beatings, 9 stranglings and 10 violent acts. In other words, "There was an act of violence every 17.9 minutes, a killing every 43.8 minutes."

Steve Allen has classified TV as "Junk Food for the Mind." Note his words:

> Most people watch far too much television. A high school graduate may have spent 15,000 hours viewing TV and 12,000 hours in class.
>
> Much of television is what I call junk food for the mind. Like junk food for the stomach, it's not terribly harmful in itself. It's just that it's empty, escapist—just something to pass the time.
>
> I don't see any hope in lifting the quality of commercial television. The people who run the networks are perfectly intelligent gentlemen—responsible citizens. They may personally prefer opera or a Leonard Bernstein concert; but if they put that sort of thing on against some detective thriller, they know what will happen to the ratings: They will go down.
>
> —U.S. News and World Report, March 13, 1978

Erik Barnouw, an authority on television, was asked in an interview: "Is it fair to blame television for increasing violence and crime?" His answer was: "Yes, I think it is. Television changes people's hair styles, clothing, the words they use—almost everything. I can't imagine that this constant display of violence would not affect them in the same way, especially when it's shown as a way of solving problems. We are actually merchandising violence" (U.S. News and World Report, March 1, 1976).

A few years ago the average American parent would not tolerate what is now plainly revealed on the television screen. We have come a long way—the wrong way! Alistair Cooke contends that the influence of a child in development is influenced more by television—"next to Mother and Father and far ahead of school and church." Homosexuality, abortion, prostitution, wife-swapping on television no longer offend an average American audience. Boris Sokoloff in his book, *The Permissive Society*, writes: "The media play so endlessly on themes of violence and aggression that they become, to the young at least, an accepted part of life."[16]

"For a considerable proportion of American children and youth, violence has become a major health problem. For an alarming number it is a way of life. One major contributing factor is television's massive diet of symbolic crime and violence in 'entertainment' programs" (*New England Journal of Medicine*, April 8, 1976, p. 711). It has been noted that "murder is our fastest cause of death. An American boy born in 1974 is more likely to die by murder than an American soldier in World War II was to die in combat" (Dr. Ronald Ellis).

Does not a nation exhibit a malaise when TV personalities are paid more in a week than Edward Gibbon earned during a lifetime writing *The Decline and Fall of the Roman Empire* (Aaron Stern). Television has made sin respectable. "Should TV Go on the Wagon?" is the title of an article by John Dillon. Note his words:

> A new *Monitor* study of TV drinking finds all three networks continuing to put emphasis on liquor to portray humor, sophistication and tension—despite a quiet campaign by federal officials to get liquor off the tube.
>
> Alcoholic beverages, the *Monitor* has found, are being seen or mentioned during this television season on an average of once every 17 minutes in the primetime period (7 to 10 p.m.).
>
> NBC this season is averaging a scene with alcohol every 15 minutes. CBS averages such a scene every 16 minutes, and ABC every 21 minutes....
>
> Federal watchdogs are concerned, first, with the frequency of TV drinking. Television writers, says one leading official with the federal program, seem to use drinking as a device to give actors something to do with their hands during dull moments on the screen.
>
> Officials also are worried by the way TV shows liquor being used—as a readily available 'problem-solver,' or a joke, or a sophisticated drink.
>
> —*TV Guide*

We live in a day in which television is rapidly becoming more influential than the school or the church in creating public opinion. Ernest L. Boyer states it thus:

One of the unhappy characteristics of our culture is the trend toward increased passivity. We are soaking up the messages of others and becoming less effective in formulating messages of our own.

All across America tonight, millions of families will be transfixed by their glowing television screens. Millions of people will spend from three to five hours in those darkened rooms—watching, listening, absorbing.

They will be sponges—soaking up the messages.

They will be passive, not active, communicators.

—Instead of speaking, they will be listening.

—Instead of formulating their own ideas, they will be the targets of thoughts hurtled at them.

We have, in short, become a nation of receivers, not of senders. Small wonder that signs point to a decline in our ability to express ourselves clearly and precisely.

Television may be robbing your home of a priceless privilege—that of communication. "According to Kay Birdwhistell, communications expert, a study of married couples and communication revealed that couples spend an average of only 27.5 minutes per week talking to each other. One reason: the average household television is on 46 hours a week." Do you realize what TV is doing to your home?

> **In the house**
> **of Mr. and Mrs. Spouse,**
> **he and she**
> **would watch teevee**
> **and never a word**
> **between them spoken**
> **until the day**
> **the set was broken.**
>
> **Then, "How do you do?"**
> **said he to she.**
> **"I don't believe that**
> **we've met yet.**
> **Spouse is my name.**
> **What's yours?" he asked.**
>
> **"Why, mine's the same!"**
> **said she to he.**
> **"Do you suppose that we could be—?"**
>
> **But the set came suddenly right about,**
> **and so they never did find out.**
>
> **—Author Unknown**

However, all is not bad with TV. There are things to be said for it. T. S. Eliot has remarked: "Every social, emotional and political evil is blamed on what is broadcast, and every ignorance and prejudice attributed to what is not."

Television can be an asset in certain fields. Author James Michener predicts a day when "I think we'll develop a society in which about 70 percent of the people will get most of their education and all the news from television."

---

## "Television does not require literacy . . . . With virtually unlimited access, television both precedes literacy and, increasingly, preempts it."

*—George Gerbner and Larry Cross*

---

This medium is being used to propagate the Good News of salvation to the nations of the world. It is said concerning a leading Christian telecast that "more people are hearing the Gospel in that audience than were living when Christ was on earth." What a glorious opportunity to present God's Word to the world in these last days of time.

Can we tame the monster in our living room? Jef Calkins has warned that "the danger of television is that we can literally waste our lives by spending too much time in front of it." Gregg Lewis has asserted: "Most Christian families are as blindly addicted to their [TV] sets as the rest of society." Are we being fair to our children?

Dr. Thomas Harris gives us these facts:

> A three-year-old who sits before a television set many hours a day is recording what he sees. The programs he watches are a 'taught' concept of life. If he watches programs of violence, I believe he records violence. . . . This conclusion is certain if his parents do not express opposition by switching the channel. If they enjoy violent programs the youngster gets a double sanction—the set and the folks—and he assumes permission to be violent provided he collects the required amount of injustices.

How should a Christian react to that which filters into his living room? A TV repair service ad read: "We can fix anything wrong with your TV except the lousy programs." It is time for righteous indignation. Are we going to control television, or is television going to control us? Dr. Hugh F. Pyle protests:

> Why should the language of the gutter be piped into my living room?

Do not the airwaves belong to all of us? Does it ever occur to the meatheads who produce these vulgar and profane shows that millions of Americans do not want their children subjected to the cheap cursing of the locker room and the barroom?...

Television has become a menace and a monster to millions of families. How ridiculous that we in this country mourn over the moral problems and the crimes being committed by children, yet let them continue to receive their training for such crimes from 'the god with the glass face' in the living room of our homes!... If certain people are so low and so vile that they must feed on moral garbage, let them go off to some smoke-filled den and wallow in the slime—but in the name of decency and sanity, don't pipe the junk into our living rooms!

—THE SWORD OF THE LORD

Surely "Christ will not live in the parlor of our hearts if we entertain the Devil in the cellar of our thoughts."

This is a day of image building. Students of God's Word know there is coming a day when the entire world will worship a man—the Antichrist. This will be possible through the medium of television. Aaron Stern in his book, *Me: The Narcissistic American*, writes these prophetic words concerning the media:

In an open society the ultimate control over the abuse of power lies in the collective majority. If we continue to let only narcissistic leaders dominate the media, we forfeit our responsibility....

All of this at a time when the media is on the verge of an almost inconceivable proliferation. It will make everything that has come before minuscule by comparison. Controlling the networks will be like child's play compared with the outcome of the contest over who will control the satellites....

Any stone dropped into the huge ocean of the media generates waves that will pound into infinity. Throughout the ages people have appeared who sought to dominate the entire world—from Genghis Khan to Adolf Hitler. They failed. But they tried to do it the hard way, one territory at a time. The first tyrant to master the media may succeed where others have failed.[17]

Revelation 13:8 declares, "And all that dwell upon the earth shall worship him...." The miracles of the False Prophet which follow in this chapter will doubtless be seen by the nations of the world through television. In Revelation 11 the two witnesses slain during the Tribulation will become a spectacle to the world.

*"And their dead bodies shall lie in the street of the great city, which spiritually is called Sodom and Egypt, where also our Lord was crucified.*

*"And they of the people and kindreds and tongues and nations shall see their*

*dead bodies three days and an half, and shall not suffer their dead bodies to be put in graves.*

*"And they that dwell upon the earth shall rejoice over them, and make merry, and shall send gifts one to another; because these two prophets tormented them that dwelt on the earth.*

*"And after three days and an half the spirit of life from God entered into them, and they stood upon their feet; and great fear fell upon them which saw them.*

*"And they heard a great voice from heaven saying unto them, Come up hither. And they ascended up to heaven in a cloud; and their enemies beheld them."—* Rev. 11:8-12.

The world will be deceived by the Antichrist. Television is preparing the way for his advent.

E. B. White, one of the pioneers of the TV industry, writing in *Harper's* magazine back in 1938 was a prophet when he made these significant statements: "I believe television is going to be the test of the modern world, and that in this new opportunity to see beyond the range of our vision we shall discover a new and unbearable disturbance of the modern peace or a saving radiance in the why. We shall stand or fall by television—of that I am sure."

The closing paragraphs of the book, *The Gods of Antenna*, by Bruce Herchensohn are worth quoting:

> No true historian can feel that our country is immune from the fate of other nations in other times. Although Americans have never elected a dictator, dictators have never been freely elected in any country. They came to power through their own molding of public opinion and psychology and force.
>
> If our civilization should ever end, future historians will not find the weapons of its destruction among the fallen pillars of the White House or the Capitol or the Supreme Court. They will need to search for the suppliers of prejudice that armed the millions of fallen antennas resting on the rubble of rooftops.[18]

Are we committing suicide by default? Are we terminally ill by choice? Is America being lulled into a fatal sleep?

We are told that a frog dropped suddenly into boiling water can always escape because of his fast reflexes. He will leap rapidly, thereby saving his life. However, if a frog is placed in cold water and the water is very slowly heated to the point of boil, he will not move and consequently will die by slow, subtle change.

"This reminds us of the slow, subtle brainwashing that is being done in America. Had it happened suddenly, citizens would have rebelled instantly, and quality standards would have been maintained without fail; but the slow process, carefully planned, allows America to depreciate to the point of death without any particular efforts to withstand the certain degradation."

In a speech before Harvard graduates, Solzhenitsyn gave this evaluation of today's society: "After the suffering of decades of violence and oppression, the human soul longs for things higher, warmer and purer than those offered by today's mass living habits, introduced by the revolting invasion of publicity, by TV stupor and by intolerable music."

How will the world one day worship the Man of Sin (Antichrist)? They will be conditioned by worldwide propaganda. The diabolic system of brainwashing is bearing its evil fruit in our nation. Malcom Muggeridge, British critic, gave these words of wisdom: "Future historians will surely see us as having created in the media a Frankenstein monster which no one knows how to control or direct, and marvel that we should have so meekly subjected ourselves to its destructive and often malign influence."

John Heywood asked:

> **Who is so deaf or blind as he**
> **That willfully will neither hear nor see?**

The prophet was correct: ". . . but Israel doth not know, my people doth not consider" (Isa. 1:3). America is "as blind as a bat at noon." Jesus Christ warned: "Let them alone: they be blind leaders of the blind. And if the blind lead the blind, both shall fall into the ditch" (Matt. 15:14).

The ditch of oblivion may not be too far away.

## Is Big Brother Too Big?

*"When the righteous are in authority, the people rejoice: but when the wicked beareth rule, the people mourn."*—Prov. 29:2.

We are all familiar with the story of a German peasant and his ill wife. The ailing wife continued to visit the local doctor who assured her after each visit (and collecting his fee) that she was much improved. After she died, the bereaved widower was asked the cause of her death. His sorrowful reply was: "She died of improvements!"

For years Americans have been fooled by the quack doctors. We are dying of "improvements"! In our critical condition, we have been taking the wrong medicine. America's problems are mainly spiritual. We have been consulting the wrong physicians.

While admitting our nation may be sick (even terminally ill), we must recognize that our trouble could be with ourselves. There are some things which we must do for ourselves.

Dr. Paul E. Adolph gives us an insight into our medical prognosis:

> That disease symptoms on an emotional basis are frequently encountered in present-day medical practice is abundantly evident. It is conservatively estimated that over fifty percent of the patients who come to the general practitioner's office in our large cities have no demonstratable organic disease. They are, nevertheless, suffering real disease symptoms on an emotional tension basis. . . .
>
> If overloading of the nervous system can be recognized early and corrected, there is hope that the burned-out fuses, as it were, and the accumulation of emotional tensions can be prevented before deep ruts are worn in the road to permanent damage. . . .
>
> Since emotional state is largely a matter of the condition of the soul and spirit, it is our conviction that further discussion of these matters is useless apart from dealing directly with the origin and growth of spiritual life.[19]

Big Brother is getting bigger and bigger. Someone has designated Americans in this way: "Property of the U.S. Government. Do not fold, bend or mutilate."

It has been said that "most bad government has grown out of too much government."

Thoreau's ideal was "a government that governs not at all" [that ideal government will come during the millennium].

Thomas Jefferson asserted: "Were we directed from Washington when to sow and when to reap, we should soon want bread."

Thomas B. Macaulay in a similar vein remarked: "Nothing is so galling to a people, not broken in from birth, as a paternal or, in other words, a meddling government, a government which tells them what to read and say and eat and drink and wear."

In our day, of more recent vintage, economist Milton Friedman has remarked: "If you put government in charge of the Sahara Desert, within five years you would have a shortage of sand."

Note the scope of our government's activities. "A study . . . conducted by the *Chicago Tribune* showed that the federal government . . . is the 'biggest land owner, property manager, renter, mover and hauler, medical clinician, lender, insurer, mortgage broker, employer, debtor, taxer and spender in all history.' "[20]

From David Harrop's interesting book we get the following information:

> The Federal government employs approximately 2.8 million civilians with an aggregate monthly payroll of nearly $3.8 billion. The states employ approximately 3.46 million people with a monthly payroll of $3.2 billion.

City and local governments, taken together, are by far the largest segment of government in the United States, employing approximately 9 million people with an aggregate monthly payroll of $8.08 billion.[21]

"Over the past fifty years," writes U.P.I. Washington correspondent, Donald Lambro, "our federal government has become a bloated, extravagant, paternalistic, remote, cluttered, disorganized, inefficient, frivolous, duplicative, archaic wasteland."

A startling book by Geoffry F. Albert contends that "Your Uncle Is Bankrupt." Note his words:

> Americans believe that "big is better." By this measure, we have a magnificent government. The federal government alone spends an amount equal to almost twenty-five percent of the nation's total production of goods and services. The government owns 760 billion acres—1/3 of the nation's total land. Uncle Sam also holds title to 405 buildings that cost $91 billion to construct. Additionally, the annual bill for rent on another 54,000 office buildings runs to $663 million. In other words, the U.S. government occupies the equivalent space of 96 Sears Towers. . .with 110 floors.
>
> To handle the paperwork generated by federal regulations and procedures, 211,000 clerks, typists, and secretaries are employed. A major portion of their work involves processing 4,504 different federal forms. The material generated by these forms each year would fill eleven Washington Monuments.[22]

It is alarming to know that "the American taxpayers are paying for their own destruction." Statistics reveal that the United States Treasury "spends more than $1 billion dollars a day for the business of federal government." Such reckless spending is full of dire consequences. The ancient Roman Empire could not get away with it, nor will we.

Joan Beck reports that "most of us pay more for government than we do for food or housing or anything else—most of us aren't getting our money's worth." The title of the article which appeared in the *Chicago Tribune* is appropriate—"Americans Suckered Too Long." Note her caustic words:

> But we don't dare lose our sense of outrage about federal spending. We are being stung, taken, bamboozled, boondoggled, flimflammed, hoodwinked, misled, exploited, suckered and robbed by an army of bureaucrats that has swollen out of control. We are being forced to buy more government than most of us can afford. . .and more than most of us want. . . .
>
> We now work, on the average, four months and 11 days every year just to earn enough to pay our taxes.

One of the reasons for the fall of the Roman Empire was its weak leadership. It is a truism, "A nation like a tree dies from the top down. When our leaders begin to decay, our nation is soon on its way to oblivion."

We usually get the government that we deserve. Plato put it this way: "The punishment which the wise suffer who refuse to take part in government, is, to live under the government of worse men." Thomas Jefferson once spoke of the fact "that we need an aristocracy of character in place of leadership in our government."

America should be thankful for any Moses to help lead us to the Promised Land.

Big government had its origin in the administration of Franklin D. Roosevelt. Since his day, the federal autocracy has snowballed. David Halberstam gives this explanation:

> He was the greatest newsmaker that Washington had ever seen. He came at a time when the society was ready for vast political and economic change, all of it enhancing the power of the President and the federal government, and he accelerated that change.
>
> The old order had collapsed, old institutions and old myths had failed; he would create the new order. In the new order, government would enter the everyday existence of almost all its citizens, regulating and adjusting their lives.
>
> Under him, Washington became the focal point: it determined how people worked, how much they made, what they ate, where they lived.
>
> Before his arrival, the federal government was small and timid; by the time he died, it reached everywhere, and as the government was everywhere, so Washington became the great dateline; as it was the source of power, so it was the source of news.[23]

Ayn Rand suggests that "the only proper functions of a government are: the police, to protect you from criminals; the army, to protect you from foreign invaders; the courts, to protect your property and contracts from breach or fraud to others, to settle disputes by rational rules, according to objective law." Thomas Jefferson asserted: "Government, even at the best state, is but a necessary evil; at the worst state, an intolerable one."

It is reported that the United States is "going deeper and deeper in the hole." The government is caught in a vicious circle of printing more money to cover deficits. More than ever, the American economy is riding on a mountain of debt.

Let's face it: "There is no free lunch!" The famous declaration, "Give me liberty or give me death," has now been reduced to mere "gimme." Lewis Albert Aleson writes of "the flight from responsibility":

> When the historian of the future applies the tools of the archaeologist in an attempt to understand and to explain your America and mine of today, he will have no hesitancy in pronouncing the chief and outstand-

ing characteristic of our time to be the flight from personal responsibility. He will record the fact, incredible as it will then seem, that . . . the chief
concern of the young American high school or college graduate seeking
employment in his chosen field was not an interest in the opportunities
offered for advancement, the ultimate of which would be a chance to
become the firm's head, but, rather, a concern with the number of vaca-
tions with pay, the sick leaves, the unemployment compensation and, of
course, the opportunity to retire on a pension at an early age.

The significant and arresting attribute of the present American citizen
is the complete change in his character that has been wrought over a short
period of years in which he has been transformed from a lover of individual
freedom and one who scorned external interference with his personal and
private affairs, to one who has come to rely upon government largesse
and to accept government dictation in each and every phase of his activity, however personal that may be. This is the trend in our country today.[24]

The goal of Big Government is to provide security from the cradle to the
grave. "Welfare—dole as a way of life—is increasingly becoming a part of the
American scene." In other words, "There is something for everyone" "from
the womb to the tomb."

---

## If you put government in charge of the Sahara Desert, within five years you would have a shortage of sand."

—*Milton Friedman*

---

It must be remembered that "government was instituted to provide protection for its citizens, not merely possessions." Abraham Lincoln wisely declared,
"You cannot help men permanently by doing for them what they can and
should do for themselves." The statement has been made: "Give a child a present, and he is ecstatic beyond description; give a child two presents, and he
is interested in only a third" (Alan Saperstein).

What most people are looking for these days is less to do, more time to do
it and more pay for getting it done.

O. A. Battista writes: "There is a lesson for us all in this: God gives us
wheat, but we must bake the bread. He gives us cotton, but we must convert
it into clothing. He gives us trees, but we must build our homes. He provides the raw materials and expects us to make the finished product with
them."

A. G. Pigou, noted economist, put it plainly: "As time goes on, the realization grows that the welfare state is not a way of getting something for nothing, and that every piece of welfare has to be paid for."[25]

A European newspaper correspondent, interviewing residents of a Chicago slum, asked one teenage girl what she wanted to do when she grew up. "To draw," she replied. The newsman, pleasantly surprised to find artistic interests in such unlikely surroundings, pursued his inquiry: "What kind of pictures do you like to draw?" "Not pictures," replied the girl. "Draw welfare like Mother does."

One poet says, "God loves the rainbow, but His clouds first worked to set the stage." And, "If you take care of a person from the time he is born until the time he leaves this earth, you destroy his self-respect."

Discerning students of economics are aware that creeping socialism has become galloping socialism. Modern socialism is the assumption by the state of responsibility and authority for control of the economic system (Fred DeArmond).

It has been said that "socialism is the fiction that everyone can feed off everyone else." The daughter of Stalin remarked that "people who want to change democracy for socialism are blind." A wit has exclaimed: "Socialism will steal you blind so it can give you contact lenses." It has also been designated "a mailed fist in a velvet glove." Note the remark of Professor Mortimer Adler: "The average citizen is unaware just how socialistic this country has become."

Is it possible that we are moving toward socialism while talking about free enterprise and competition? Norman Thomas, the Socialist Party candidate for President from 1928-1948, admitted: "The American people will never knowingly adopt socialism, but under the name of liberalism they will adopt every fragment of the socialist program until one day America will be a socialist nation without knowing what happened."

Our nation has been deceived. Henry Knickerbocker, Jr., explains: "The many crimes that add up to socialism are sold to you and me in small pieces, wrapped in yards and yards of good deeds ribbon."

Could it be that the threat of socialism is greater than that of communism? The statement has been made that "socialism is just soft communism; communism is hard socialism." Lenin declared, "Striving for socialism, we are convinced that it will develop into communism." Kruschev explained that "society cannot leap into communism from capitalism without going through a socialist stage of development. Socialism is the first stage to communism, and thus you are now in this first stage if you advocate socialism."

Gus Hall, leader of the Communist Party in the United States, predicted that "the United States will move gradually from socialism to the higher state

of communism." Herbert Hoover, whose wisdom was spurned by this generation, remarked that "the real threat to American freedom is not presented
by the few hundred thousand communists in America, but by their fellow
travellers and sympathizers, who 'are engineering a compromise between
free men and these European infections.' "[26]

Socialism was given a great thrust forward under President Franklin D.
Roosevelt. Ebenstein in his *Great Political Thinkers* remarks:

> Important as the knowledge of the principles of Marxist communism
> is to Americans, the proper understanding of the main ideas of democratic
> socialism, particularly as it has developed in Britain, is even more vital.
>
> In the last half century the trend all over the world has been toward
> more public responsibility and collective action. In the United States this
> tendency found expression in. . . Franklin D. Roosevelt's New Deal. What
> was a generation ago considered in the United States intolerable in-
> terference in fields like labor, social security and education, has gradual-
> ly been accepted by the public as just and inevitable.[27]

Our political leaders have been wrongly influenced by what is known as
Fabian Socialism. Loyd Wright in the opening paragraph in the Foreword of
Rose L. Martin's book, *Fabian Freeway,* writes:

> The American people have been and are completely unfamiliar with com-
> munism's helpmate, Fabian Socialism. For over fifty years, but especial-
> ly since the middle 1930's, there have been insinuated into high places
> in our government at Washington men whose collaboration in this
> socialistic movement has been greatly responsible for breaking down our
> constitutional form of government and substituting therefore the socialist
> idea of centralized government.[28]

Fabian Socialism began in ancient Rome and was copied by the British
socialists.

> Shortly after Marx died, the Fabian Society was founded in 1884; it was
> named after a Roman General, Quintus Fabius Maximus Cunctator, the
> "Delayer." The early motto of the Fabian Society was: "for the right mo-
> ment you must wait, as Fabius did; but when the right moment comes
> you must strike hard, or your waiting will be fruitless."[29]

This was often accomplished by underhanded methods. Great Britain has
been the leading exponent of Fabian Socialism. Today this once "great" nation is a Welfare State and bankrupt. It is no longer "great." The decay of
the ancient Roman Empire was long and gradual; the British have decided
to commit suicide much quicker.

The economic policies of John Maynard Keynes are helping America to commit suicide. What is Keynesian economics? According to Ebenstein, "In the field of investment, Keynes holds that the traditional methods of relying solely on private initiative have failed, and that 'socialization of investment will prove the only means of securing an approximation to full employment.' "[30]

John A. Stormer remarks:

> As collectivists have grabbed for control of the federal government they have skillfully used the "economic" theories of John Maynard Keynes, a British Fabian economist, as the vehicle for buying the votes and support of the masses with their own money.
>
> Today's advocates of Keynes and his theories present him respectably as the "last hope for saving free enterprise," in typical Fabian fashion of "never calling socialism by its true label."[31]

Geoffry F. Albert makes this observation:

> In 1933 Franklin Roosevelt took office. He adopted the economic policies of John Maynard Keynes. . . an English economist. Keynes' basic idea was that there was no reason for countries to have to back their money with gold. In fact, Keynes suggested that the responsibility of government was to get the ball rolling by spending money—even if the government was broke. His plan was to create money by deficit spending. . . .
>
> Roosevelt became one of the most popular presidents ever. People were happy. They were working. They weren't too happy about the way government and taxes were growing. And they didn't like the fact that they were paying more all the time for the same goods and services. The inflation roller coaster had been boarded. The inflationary ascent would be gradual at first, but ever increasing. Nobody stopped to recognize that the idea of spending money without having it had been tried repeatedly in the economic history of the world—and had never worked.[32]

And that is how we got this way. Again note the words of Rose L. Martin:

> Although Lord Keynes died peacefully in 1946 and was interred with all the pomp an admiring Labour Party Government in Britain could provide, the mischief he compounded lives on. If his influence was vast during his lifetime, it has been enormously magnified since his death. In the pantheon of Fabian Socialism, even a demigod is not irreplaceable: there are always trained heads and hands prepared to push his theories, with appropriate variations, to their unnatural conclusion.
>
> The cult of national suicide, initiated by Keynes and known as the New Economics, is not only preserved but expanded by his sophisticated followers, operating through the twin channels of politics and higher education with the blessing of the Socialist International.
>
> An entire generation of political economists has been reared in Keynes' image; and Keynesian cliches have become the debased tender

of intellectual exchange from Washington and London to Calcutta and Damascus. As *The New York Times* proclaimed in a banner headline on September 9, 1963: "Once revolutionary, the economics of Keynes now is orthodox."[33]

Should we abolish the capitalistic system for socialism? Dan Smoot has this answer:

> Historically, Socialism has an unbroken record of failure. Whenever it becomes total, it brings grinding poverty and crushing tyranny.
>
> The American business system, on the other hand, has produced more prosperity, more widely distributed, than any other economic system has ever produced. It has created more schools, universities, art galleries, theaters, orchestras, publishing houses, churches, hospitals, clinics, beautiful parks, magnificent recreational facilities, comfortable dwellings, means of travel, and means of communication than have ever been enjoyed anywhere else.[34]

It has been contended by some liberal theologians that Jesus Christ was a socialist. Dr. I. M. Haldeman was pastor of the First Baptist Church of New York City from 1884 to 1933. Back in 1913 his book, *The Signs of the Times,* was published. One of the chapters of the book was on the subject of "Socialism." [He wrote the Preface to the book in 1910.] Note his words:

> Socialism may be described under various titles. There is a scientific and radical socialism. There is yet another which is the latest thoroughly startling—it is known as Christian socialism. This new cult of socialism might be called "ministerial socialism," for it is among Christian ministers that it finds its expression and power. . . .
>
> Was Jesus Christ a socialist? Was He a reformer? I answer in the negative. He was neither a socialist nor a reformer. . . .
>
> Not once did He intimate that His teachings followed out through the coming centuries would cause the elimination of poverty, the decrease of the poor. Instead, He said that so long as the church should continue in the world, poverty would remain, the poor should continue. It was the plain denial that He expected the church to work, testify, or legislate against poverty. It was the plain denial that He was a socialist—a plain denial that the church would be the advocate of socialism. . . .
>
> The church is not to go out and raise the false, delusive hope that man can be repaired like a broken piece of furniture and made as good as new, or that he is like a colored telescope, only needing to be opened out that he may get the true and delivering view of God. . . . The church is to point the world to the only hope—the coming of the second and perfect Man, the true King and Saviour of the earth.[35]

Big brother is not always a big brother. Sometimes he's a bully! Thomas

Jefferson was very dogmatic when he declared, "I have sworn upon the altar of God eternal hostility against every form of tyranny over the mind of man." Woodrow Wilson warned:

> The history of liberty is a history of the limitation of governmental power, not the increase of it. When we resist, therefore, the concentration of power, we are resisting the processes of death, because a concentration of power is what always precedes the destruction of liberty.

Note the words of Herbert Hoover:

> My word to you, my fellow-citizens, on this 75th birthday is this: The Founding Fathers dedicated the structure of our government "to secure the blessings of liberty to ourselves and our posterity." A century and a half later, we of this generation still inherited this precious blessing. Yet as spendthrifts, we are on our way to rob posterity of its inheritance.[36]

What does the future hold for us? Leroy Pope makes this prediction:

> The survival of free-enterprise economics in the world for the next 50 years is doubtful, says Prof. Richard Eells of Columbia University Business School.
>
> "Private ownership of business probably will not disappear," he says, "but private control very well may.
>
> "Control will rest increasingly with company directors representing various segments of the public economic and political sectors whose selection is made mandatory by law or custom."
>
> —*American Business*, July, 1980

Spruille Braden warns:

> The Hammurabi Code promulgated earlier than 2,000 B.C. by imposing controls over wages, prices, production, consumption and all the rest of the economy, wrecked Babylonia. Governmental extravagance and a bloated bureaucracy killed individual initiative and led to the fall of ancient Greece. A planned economy of state maintenance for the slothful and excessive taxation brought the collapse of the later Roman Empire and regression of a civilized society into the Dark Ages. The Welfare State of the Incas became so debilitated as to become easy prey for Pizzaro and his "Conquistadores". . . .
>
> For the same reasons, the British Empire is now dissolving before our eyes. God forbid that the U.S.A. follow any further down these disastrous trails than it already has! . . .
>
> Moreover, no major civilization ever perished primarily because it was murdered by an external enemy. In each case, the victim first was weakened fatally by its own internal measures; in effect, it really committed suicide.[37]

All is going according to God's prophetic plan. Students of Bible prophecy know that there is a day coming when a one-world government headed up by the Antichrist will take charge of the nations during the Tribulation Period. He will be an absolute dictator. The power of Big Brother will be enormous. In Revelation 13:16, 17 we read of that commercial power:

*"And he causeth all, both small and great, rich and poor, free and bond, to receive a mark in their right hand, or in their foreheads: And that no man might buy or sell, save he that had the mark, or the name of the beast, or the number of his name."*

Again, consider the words of I. M. Haldeman:

Socialism, as expressing the latest effort of the natural man to go out like Cain from the presence of God and build a city, a society and a civilization in defiance of divine order, divine law, divine revelation and divine warning, is a witness that the world, like the ship now on the breakers, requires only one more wave to dash it to pieces. It is the sign that the world needs the hand and touch of its true and coming King.
It is a warning that the coming of the Lord draweth nigh.[38]

The biggest and best of all governments will be when Jesus Christ returns to establish His millennial reign on earth.

## Suicidal Inflation

*"Now therefore thus saith the Lord of hosts; Consider your ways.*

*"Ye have sown much, and bring in little; ye eat, but ye have not enough; ye drink, but ye are not filled with drink; ye clothe you, but there is none warm; and he that earneth wages earneth wages to put it into a bag with holes."*— Hag. 1:5, 6.

One of the sure signs of our national illness is our economy. Today we are experiencing "the high cost of staying alive."

There is a humorous side of inflation. Someone has defined inflation as "that period during which a fellow goes broke by just staying even." "These days most Americans are in the middle age bracket—they make too much money to buy food stamps and not enough to buy postage stamps." A frustrated husband, struggling with the family budget, was heard to remark: "Now I wish we had saved money during the Depression so we could live through prosperity."

But inflation is no joking matter. It is terribly cruel. Inflation, like big government, is a Frankenstein that can destroy its creators. Speaking before a Joint Session of Congress, April 8, 1974, President Ford said: "Inflation, our public enemy number 1, will, unless whipped, destroy our country, our homes, our liberty, our property...as surely as any well armed enemy." Inflation is personal, but some feel its pangs more than others.

The poor, those on pensions and Social Security, those with their life's savings in the bank are all victims of this evil. According to Hans F. Sennholz, noted economist, "The American dollar lost 80 percent of its purchasing power and is losing more every day. Inflation is winning all the battles." As a result, there are those who "pay more in taxes than for our combined costs for food, clothing and shelter." As stated before, inflation is cruel. Back in 1970 Barry Goldwater made this prophetic statement:

> Inflation will run rampant, the purchasing power of the American dollar will melt away like snowdrifts in the spring sun and our hard-working and thrifty people will watch in stupefied dismay as the value of their savings, their insurance, their pension funds diminish each day, ultimately perhaps to vanish almost entirely.[39]

Ed Wynn, popular comedian of another decade, made sense [cents] when he commented, "What this country needs is a good 5-cent nickel." Said Ludwig Von Mises: "Government is the only institution that can take a valuable commodity like paper and make it worthless by applying ink."[40]

The statement has been made that "runaway inflation is playing havoc with the lives of Americans, creating an atmosphere of fear and distrust unlike anything this nation has seen in decades." Again note the words of Hans Sennholz: "Few policies are more calculated to destroy the existing basis of a free society than the debauchery of its currency. And few tasks, if any, are more important to the champion of freedom than to secure a sound monetary system."

Inflation is dangerous to a nation. The demon of inflation can bring disaster to our country.

In an article, "Let's Face the Facts of Inflation," Fred C. Clark gives this simple reason for inflation:

> If you are average citizens, you are, according to the polls, ignorant about the basic causes of inflation and high prices. And you have every reason to be, because the average citizen does not go to college and the basic laws of economics are not taught in our high schools....
>
> If we stick to simple fundamentals, we do not have to be political scientists to understand what has been going on; we merely need to discard the ten-dollar words and the technical phrases that are now hiding the truth from us.... The basic cause of high prices is the whopping amount of new unearned money that has been pumped into the American economic system.[41]

To put it simply, "What causes inflation is government spending more than it takes in and simply printing money to back up the difference." A nation, like a household, cannot spend more money than it takes in without dire consequences.

> Gradually our currency and our nation's world financial position are turned into fool's gold by the economic practices of our government. These practices are the direct result of the economic preachings of Keynesian economists. . . . What Keynes told his disciples was that inflation is not only good for the economy, it is necessary for a strong economy.[42]

It has been remarked that, "without inflation, neither Lenin nor Mussolini nor Hitler could have come to power." Lenin knew "that the best way to destroy the capitalist system was to debauch the currency." Germany provides a tragic example of the economic devastation that inflation can bring upon a country. Richard Hanser gives us these details:

> . . . No currency in history had ever depreciated like the German mark, and the toboggan slide of its descent was a disaster that turned into the wildest absurdity without becoming any less disastrous. Strings of ciphers that had hitherto applied only to astronomical distances now applied to pocket money; the number of marks needed to buy a newspaper reached figures that only the mind of a trained mathematician could hope to comprehend. . . .
>
> An egg that cost twenty-five pfennings in 1918 came to 80,000,000,000 (billion) marks in 1923, and what was once a seventeen-pfenning glass of beer was priced at 150 billion marks. Based on the value of the prewar mark, a 1923 postage stamp would have cost $11,900,000,000 in American money.
>
> The German inflation was an economic convulsion that unhinged itself from economics and drifted into sheer delirium, taking the German people with it.[43]

"Hyper-inflation is considered the worst thing that can happen to any nation." Hitler took over Germany and bathed Europe in blood because of the economic conditions in Germany following World War I. An eyewitness of the tragedy was Otto Strasser, who described the scene:

> These were days of dark uncertainty. Events moved so rapidly that it was impossible to predict what was going to happen next. With Depression hanging like a black pall over the country, there was uncertainty and confusion and the ever-present menace of strikes and revolution. Men struggled for power against a background of human misery. Starvation was common—indeed, it was rare to see a person who was not suffering from obvious malnutrition. . . .
>
> Money was worthless. Earlier, the German government had decided to meet its obligations and running expenses by the simple process of printing numbers on worthless paper and calling the banknote, so obtained,

"money." Due to this ridiculous process, the mark that already had stood 160,000 to the dollar early in July, 1923, fell to more than 1,000,000 to the dollar at the end of the month.

With the demand for notes that followed, the printers found it difficult to keep pace. For instance, it required 30 paper factories, 133 printing offices, and 1,783 printing presses working at top speed to meet the demand.

Late in 1923 the government owed the Reichsbank about 190 quintillion (190,000,000,000,000,000,000) marks. The mark was now quoted at 2.5 trillion to the dollar in Berlin, and at 4 trillion in Cologne, and one should always bear in mind that before the war a single mark was worth 23.82 cents. One quart of milk at this time cost 250 billion marks, and an ordinary postage stamp cost 12,000,000,000 marks.

The government ceased printing notes on both sides because the cost of printing alone was more than even the astronomical numbers indicated on the face of the bill—and citizens used these notes for scratch paper and memoranda slips because it was cheaper than buying such paper in the stores! Baskets were used now instead of wallets.

The people cried for a change in government. They did not know what they wanted, but anything was better than what they had now.[44]

There are some economists who feel very strongly that America is headed for financial ruin. Senior citizens remember Tuesday, October 29, 1929, the day the stock market crashed, bringing with it financial chaos and a rash of suicides. Will Rogers in the same year quipped: "The situation has been reached in New York hotels where the clerk asks incoming guests, 'You wanna room for sleeping or to jump out of.'"

*The Day the Bubble Burst* by Gordon Thomas and Max Morgan-Witts is an interesting book describing in detail that historic day. I quote from the Author's Note:

> The Wall Street Crash of 1929 was the most climactic disaster in his [our] history. It still affects our lives today. . . .
>
> . . . The Crash affected everyone; it was the precursor to the Depression; as such, it was not only a financial collapse but a human tragedy. In a way it was worse than war. . . .
>
> Few man-made events, short of World Wars, created so much pain and bitterness and the fear it could occur again.
>
> Perhaps the only protection against that happening is to have an understanding not only of why it happened but of what it was like to be there when it happened.[45]

Today anxious investors are concerned if another stock market crash could take place. In the closing chapter, "Aftermath," of the same book, the author made this observation:

Could it—will it—occur again?

It cannot happen again for the same reasons: Too many of Wall Street's barn doors were closed by the mass of legislation introduced as a direct result of the Crash. But only a fool would say that other circumstances could not contrive to make another crash occur. . . .

Most Wall Streeters dismiss talk of another great crash as mischievous speculation. They have faith in America, and in an old Street dictum about the market: It is like a dog's tail; its wagging is controlled by the economic-cum-political body of the nation it is joined to, but it does not cause the body to wag.

There are others to be found in the Street, respected elder statesmen, who say quite definitely that another crash is coming. . . .

And, of course, there are those, equally eminent, who believe the market is on the eve of the "biggest and strongest economic boom in history."

There is only one thing to worry about in those words. They have been used before. On the eve of the day when the bubble burst.[46]

Where do we stand today? Is the hour too late for help? In an article, "Toward a Point of No Return," Robert C. Tyson writes: "Yes, I personally am certain that we have not passed a point of no return. The American Golden Goose is a tougher bird than most people realize. But I am entitled to a shiver as I attempt to point out how close we may be to a point of no return."[47]

Dan Smoot points out that "the goose that laid the golden egg is in trouble. She may not be in the oven yet; but the poor creature, already severely plucked by government, is cornered, menaced by many foes with sharp and gleaming axes. Rescuing her will take courage, as well as effort."[48]

It has been said that "ignorant men raise questions that wise men answered a thousand years ago." A nation (as well as an individual) cannot spend more than it receives.

Jack Kahn asks the question:

Do we have to wait until all is taken from us by inflation and taxation to pay for increasing federal spending. . .? Or can we recall that free private enterprise can do what government cannot, and make government give back the freedoms so that private enterprise can again function fully? Later it will be too late, and we won't have a choice.

There are those who paint a dark picture of the future. Their viewpoint is to be objectively considered. Robert L. Preston warns:

If the inflation is not held back, then the economy goes berserk. The paper dollars drop in value faster; wages and prices rise and rise faster and faster, finally just skyrocketing; the government printing presses are going twenty-four hours a day trying to keep up; the prices are changing hourly. And finally it is hopeless, and the money is completely worthless; no one will take it.

Then all the factories and stores shut down. Rioting, robbing, looting and all types of crime begin to stalk the streets. The cities turn into concrete canyons, with savages hunting down their prey of other human beings who might have food and drink. Blood flows like rain water in the gutters.

It has happened before, in France and in Germany. Only this time, it will be worse than ever before. It will be worse because there are large segments of the population which have been brought up without morals. They will have no compunction in imitating the worst scenes from the most vile and savage books they have read and movies they have seen. They will torture without mercy and kill without reservation to get the things they are after.

This will be the terror that is coming if we have runaway inflation.[49]

Such conditions perhaps will take place during the Tribulation Period. Worldwide inflation may be one of the means to bring in the reign of the Antichrist. Severe economic conditions will require the abilities of a Superman. The Antichrist will be that financial genius. Conditions that existed in prewar Germany will find parallel conditions (to a great extent) in the Tribulation.

Revelation 6:5,6 gives this description:

*"And when he had opened the third seal, I heard the third beast say, Come and see. And I beheld, and lo a black horse; and he that sat on him had a pair of balances in his hand.*

*"And I heard a voice in the midst of the four beasts say, A measure of wheat for a penny, and three measures of barley for a penny; and see thou hurt not the oil and the wine."*

Thus we see that "uncontrollable inflation is followed by famine." There will be worldwide famine on the earth, and those who do not receive the mark of the Beast (Rev. 13:16,17) will be forced to starvation. Theodore H. Epp gives this commentary:

A "penny" was a normal day's wages in New Testament times. A measure of wheat is about one quart, or that which is sufficient for one meal. During the Tribulation enough wheat for one meal will cost about a day's wages. Barley was used mostly for livestock, but in times of famine it is used for human consumption. During the Tribulation three measures of barley (enough for three meals) will also cost a day's wages.

In New Testament times a penny (a day's wages) bought eight quarts of wheat or 24 quarts of barley. Therefore, a penny bought eight times as much during the Apostle John's time on earth as it will during the Tribulation. No doubt the reason for this inflation is that almost all money will have been appropriated for military use, and famine will result.

The voice which the Apostle John heard also said, "See thou hurt not the oil and the wine." Oil speaks of the toiletries and beauty aids; wine refers to liquor. Although most people will be poverty-stricken during the Tribulation, the rich will have plenty. We see this even today in dictatorial countries. The masses of people are poor, but those in control are extremely rich.[50]

Basically, inflation may be but a sign of a decaying nation. In that sense, that problem is one of morality. "Inflation springs from the desire of the people to accumulate material things excessively." Jesus Christ warned: "Take heed, and beware of covetousness: for a man's life consisteth not in the abundance of the things which he possesseth" (Luke 12:15). He also said, "But seek ye first the kingdom of God, and his righteousness; and all these things shall be added unto you" (Matt. 6:33).

Is it not high time that we set our financial house in order before it's too late?

## Let Freedom Ring

*"...Proclaim liberty throughout all the land unto all the inhabitants thereof...."*—Lev. 25:10.

*"And the chief captain answered, With a great sum obtained I this freedom. And Paul said, But I was free born."*—Acts 22:28.

Freedom is priceless. In anticipation of a possible British victory, Samuel Adams warned: "Our towns are built of brick and wood; if they are burned, we can rebuild them; but liberty, once gone, is gone forever." Archibald McLeish wrote these significant words: "There are those, I know, who will say that the liberation of humanity, the freedom of man and mind, is nothing but a dream. They are right. It is. It is the American dream."

But all today do not believe in that "American dream." The late J. Edgar Hoover remarked: "Today patriotism seems to be out of style. Those who express their love of country are often looked upon as paranoiac patriots or right-wing extremists." Charles M. Crowe comments:

> In certain quarters in the United States patriotism seems to be considered strictly out of date, old hat, if not actually un-Christian....
>
> To hold that it does not matter under what political arrangement Christianity lives is a difficult position to defend....
>
> We are at a critical juncture of history, and the fate of mankind is inevitably linked with the fate of freedom in America....
>
> Instead of being so critical and apologetic, American Christian leaders need to be profoundly grateful for this land of ours—and not ashamed to say so![51]

William K. McComas makes this observation:

> I sometimes wonder why that lady we know as the Statue of Liberty doesn't turn about face, descend her pedestal, extinguish her torch in the briny waters of the Atlantic, bow her face in the sand and cry out in despair from the acts of high treason going on behind her. The word *freedom* is being batted around like a ball on a tennis court by those who would destroy it and have no idea of its price.
>
> —SWORD OF THE LORD

It is a privilege to be an American. Louis Hirsch has expressed it this way: "America is a place where the people have a right to complain about the lack of freedom." On a wall in another country was a sign with the usual "Yankee Go Home." Underneath someone had written, "And take me with you."

According to a survey by Freedom House, "Only one in five in the world lives in freedom."

> Only 19.8 percent of the world's population live in virtually complete freedom. . . . By far the biggest group—1,823 million in 65 nations and 3 dependencies, or 44.9 percent of that total population—live under dictatorships or other forms of government that deny people most all political and civil rights.
>
> —*U.S. News and World Report*

One has expressed, "*Freedom* must be one of the most misused words in the English language. *Patriot* is derived from the Greek *patrio* referring to 'fatherland.' It denotes 'one who loves and serves his country.'"

Funk and Wagnall's *Dictionary of the English Language* defines *patriotism* as "love of and devotion to one's country, the spirit that, originating in love of country, prompts to obedience to its laws, to support and defense of its existence, rights, and institutions, and to the promotion of its welfare."

"Freedom is a precious thing today. Those who have it cherish it; those who fear it want to destroy it; and those who don't have it will still fight for it," wrote Harvey C. Jacobs. Bertel Sparks has declared: "I am convinced that the freedom-of-choice principle is so woven into human existence that any effort to curtail it is an attempt to curtail life itself. To lose our freedom to choose is to lose our humanity."

Every true American should thrill at the famous words of Patrick Henry: ". . . Is life so dear, or peace so sweet as to be purchased at the price of chains and slavery! Forbid it, Heaven! I know not what course others may take, but as for me, give me liberty, or give me death!"

Ancient Rome was the victim of a bad bargain when she offered security for her freedom. "There is no freedom on earth or in any star for those who deny freedom to others," Elbert Hubbard declared. Herbert Hoover warned that "they that give up essential liberty to obtain a little temporary safety deserve neither liberty nor safety." Edmund Burke, 18th-century British statesman, showed shrewd political insight when he declared: "People never give up their liberty except under some delusion."

Hear these lines: "There are strange times for our country when patriots are vilified and traitors glorified." "The primary threat to freedom and independence is communist totalitarianism. The over one billion people who live under communism can attest how serious that threat is."

Those who are unfortunate to reside in communist countries are prisoners in one vast prison. As one inhabitant has testified: "You are in prison even though you are free." Fred Schwartz has commented appropriately that "communism in power creates one vast prison in which every prisoner is confined by potential starvation." It has been remarked that "the communists are staking their future on the idea that slaves dragging their chains can overtake free people dragging their feet."

Liberty is a gift of God. It is acknowledged that some of the Founding Fathers were deists and some even atheists; yet Thomas Jefferson in his *Notes on the State of Virginia* [1782] asserted: "And can the liberties of a nation be thought secure when we have removed their only firm basis, a conviction in the minds of the people that these liberties are the gift of God?"

Norman Cousins writes that

> it has often been asked how it was that within a short span of time on the east coast of the North American continent there should have sprung up such a rare array of genius-men who seemed in virtual command of historical experience and combined moral imagination with a flair for leadership. Part of the answer, at least, is that these men knew how to invest their combined strength in a great idea.[52]

This "great idea" of freedom was God-given.

The nations of the earth have learned that there is a mighty Sovereign ruling on this earth according to His divine will. Nations that have ruled God out have suffered the fate of history.

> Beginning with the absolute monarchy of Babylonia, one form of government succeeded another, through Medo-Persia, Greece, Pagan Rome, and on down to our day through nations that have occupied the territory of Old Rome, until every possible form of government, from absolute monarchy to complete democracy, has been tried.
>
> Because the dominant control under each form of government was held by those who wanted freedom from the will of God, every government has muddled on across the centuries until failure has been written upon the

history of each one of them—not because there has been anything inherently defective in any of them, but simply because those in control have been intolerant of the will of God in governmental affairs.

(*The Growing Menace of the Social Gospel,* J. E. Conant, p. 33).

The Apostle Paul wrote these historic words to the church at Galatia: "Stand fast therefore in the liberty wherewith Christ hath made us free, and be not entangled again with the yoke of bondage" (Gal. 5:1).

Dante called freedom "the greatest gift bestowed by God to mankind." America has been called "the last bastion of liberty." Thomas Jefferson exclaimed: "How little do my countrymen know what precious blessings they are in possession of, and which no other people on earth enjoy." The words are often quoted: "Eternal vigilance is the price of liberty." Thomas Paine (although not classified as a Christian) wrote: "What we obtain too cheap, we esteem too lightly; 'tis dearness only that gives everything its value. Heaven knows how to put a proper price upon its goods; and it would be strange indeed if so celestial an article as 'freedom' should not be highly rated."

Our generation needs to prove that we are worthy of such a priceless heritage. It has been said, "Freedom is not free but must be earned anew by each succeeding generation." Freedom involves discipline and responsibility. Of ancient Athens it can be said, "When the freedom they wished for most was freedom from responsibility, then Athens ceased to be free." George Washington at Valley Forge remarked, "This liberty will look easy by and by when nobody dies to get it."

Katherine Lee Bates said, "We sing 'America, the Beautiful.' We must match the greatness of America with the goodness of personal living." Dr. J. Gordon Melton wrote this challenge:

I call upon all committed to preserve the integrity of our religious institutions and the freedom to propagate our beliefs, set our priorities, and participate in the American religious scene, to join forces at this hour. Raise the hue and cry. Let all know that we will not stand by and allow our freedoms to be subverted.

Freedom involves sacrifice—the cost of liberty runs high.

. . . Tso Yiu-kam, a journalist of the *Free China Review,* related this experience as he stood on the shore at Hong Kong opposite the Mainland, night after night, listening as escaping swimmers were machine-gunned in the waters by Red Chinese patrol boats.

The currents are treacherous, the water is full of sharks, and it is an eight- to fourteen-hour swim. After fourteen hours, if you have lost your way in the dark, the tides will wash you to sea and certain death. Yet at the time some seventy people a day— seventy human beings every day—

successfully made that swim to freedom. And every day, three times that many drowned trying . . . or were eaten alive by sharks as they swam. Tso waited helplessly on the shore, listening to the screams of his countrymen in the night.

Each swimmer had a story, but our friend wanted us to know about a young woman named Pan Yuan-chuan. On the Mainland, he explained, permission is required from the communist bosses to marry, and Pan and her fiance were, for political reasons, refused such permission. Well aware of the danger, but very much in love, they determined to try the swim.

They were six hours out into the blackness when Pan's fiance drowned. Exhausted by the currents, he had refused to cry out for help lest she be endangered. Alerted too late to what had happened, but unwilling to leave his lifeless body to be eaten by sharks even if it meant her death also, little Pan Yuan-chuan finished her swim to freedom with one arm around the corpse of the man she loved.

The words of Lord Byron are worth repeating: "Civilization goes like this: first freedom, and then glory, and then corruption, and then barbarism, and then collapse." Precious freedom can be lost by default. It has been said, "If free men lost their freedom, it was because they were too apathetic to take note while the precious waters of God-given freedom slipped, drop by drop, down the drain."

When the French historian Guijot asked James Russell Lowell how long the American Republic would last, Lowell is reported to have said, "It will last as long as the ideals of the founders remain dominant." The words of Winston Churchill are appropriate for Americans today:

> If you will not fight for right when you can easily win without bloodshed; if you will not fight when your victory will be sure and not too costly; you may come to the moment when you have to fight with all the odds against you and only a precarious chance of survival.[53]

"Freedom is only a word until you are close to losing it."

A nation must have a personal relationship to its Maker. It is an acknowledged fact that "God can get along without America, but America can't get along without God." Liberty comes from above. The French patriot Frederic Bastiat put it this way: "For liberty is an acknowledgment of faith in God and His works." Frances Bretano writes this significant paragraph:

> Whenever freedom's holy light shines forth it impels liberty of soul and mind and body, lifting men to all their God-given rights. . . . Justice, human dignity, freedom, brotherhood, the right to truth—these are the shafts of Eternal Light, lit by God Himself for mankind.[54]

Someone has asked: "Can the liberties of a nation be thought secure when we have removed their only firm basis, a conviction in the minds of the people that these liberties are the gift of God?" Note the words of Judge Learned Hand: "Liberty lies in the hearts of men and women: when it dies there, no constitution, no law, no court can save it." Nicholai Berdyaev, a former Marxist who was deported and suffered for freedom's sake, has written: "God has laid upon man the duty of being free, of safeguarding freedom of spirit, no matter how difficult that may be, or how much sacrifice and suffering it may require."

When the Declaration of Independence was being signed, a spectator remarked that "there was nobody on the colonists' side but God." Dr. John J. Zubly, the Swiss clergyman who represented Georgia, replied in his heavily accented English, "Dat is enough." Abraham Lincoln said, "I am nothing, but truth is everything. . . . I know that liberty is right; for Christ teaches it, and Christ is God." Therefore, William Harvard was right when he asserted that "the greatest glory of a free-born people is to transmit that freedom to their children."

What does the future hold? George Orwell's penetrating book, *1984*, warns of a coming day when "eternal warfare is the price of bleak prosperity, in which the Party keeps itself in power by complete control over man's actions and thoughts." Erich Fromm, writing in the "Afterword," makes these statements:

> George Orwell's *1984* is the expression of a mood, and it is a warning. The mood it expresses is that of near despair about the future of man, and the warning is that unless the course of history changes, men all over the world will lose their most human qualities, will become soulless automatons, and will not even be aware of it.

In God's Word we discover that there is coming a day of world government, with the Antichrist as the supreme dictator. Freedom as we know it today will be banished from the earth. Nations and individuals will submit to this world dictator or be destroyed. Again note God's warning:

*"And he causeth all, both small and great, rich and poor, free and bond, to receive a mark in their right hand, or in their foreheads:*
*"And that no man might buy or sell, save he that had the mark, or the name of the beast, or the number of his name."*—Rev. 13:16, 17.

The days of freedom for our nation and the world are numbered. Take advantage of them. We need to heed the words of William Cullen Bryant: "Not yet, O Freedom! Close thy lids in slumber, for thine enemy never sleeps."

America may be terminally ill. The dangerous symptoms are obvious. Isn't it time we consulted the Great Physician?

## ENDNOTES:

[1]W. E. Vine, *Isaiah*, 9.

[2]Henrietta C. Mears, *What the Bible Is All About*, 208, 209, 219.

[3]Leonard Ravenhill, *America Is Too Young to Die*, 29, 31, 32.

[4]Malcom Muggeridge, *Christ and the Media*, 23.

[5]Christopher Lasch, *The Culture of Narcissism*, 55, 56.

[6]George Charles Roche III, *Legacy of Freedom*, xiv.

[7]Tim LaHaye, *The Battle for the Mind*, 148.

[8]William L. Rivers, *The Opinionmakers*, 3.

[9]David Halberstam, *The Powers That Be*, 62.

[10]Leonard Downie, Jr., *The New Muckrakers*, 14.

[11]Mary Lewis Coakley, *Rated X: The Moral Case Against TV*, 14-16.

[12]Barry Goldwater, *The Conscience of a Conservative*, 137.

[13]Don Pember, *Mass Media in America*, 187.

[14]Bruce Herchensohn, *The Gods of Antenna*, flyleaf, 20, 27.

[15]Joseph Keeley, *The Left-Leaning Antenna*, 47.

[16]Boris Sokoloff, *The Permissive Society*, 216.

[17]Aaron Stern, *Me: The Narcissistic American*, 144, 145.

[18]Herchensohn, 145.

[19]Paul E. Adolph, *Health Shall Spring Forth*, 14, 15, 16.

[20]Goldwater, 20.

[21]David Harrop, *America's Paychecks: Who Pays Them?* 97.

[22]Geoffrey F. Albert, *After the Crash*, 4, 5.

[23]Halberstam, 8, 9.

[24]Lewis Albert Alesen, *Mental Robots*, 56.

[25]William Ebenstein, *Great Political Thinkers*, 818.

[26]*Ibid.,* 816.

[27]*Ibid.,* 753.

[28]Rose L. Martin, *Fabian Freeway*, vii.

[29]Ebenstein, 752.

[30]*Ibid.,* 634.

[31]John A. Stormer, *None Dare Call It Treason*, 183.

[32]Albert, 66.

[33]Martin, 339.

[34]Dan Smoot, *The Business End of Government*, 212.

[35]I. M. Haldeman, *The Signs of the Times*, 281, 282, 284, 288, 302, 303.

[36]Ebenstein, 830.

[37]Spruille Braden, *Diplomats and Demagogues*, 459, 460.

[38]Haldeman, 309.

[39]Goldwater, 12.

[40]Howard Ruff, *How to Prosper During the Coming Bad Years*, 40.

[41]A. G. Heinsohn, Jr., *Anthology of Conservative Writing in the United States, 1932-1960*, 64, 65, 69.

[42]H. L. Hunt, *Fabians Fight Freedom*, 131.

[43]Richard Hanser, *Putsch*, 288.

[44]Otto Strasser, *Flight from Terror*, 35, 36.

[45]Gordon Thomas and Max Morgan-Witts, *The Day the Bubble Burst*, xi, xiii.

[46]*Ibid.*, 425, 426.

[47]Heinsohn, Jr., 407, 408.

[48]Smoot, 224.

[49]Robert L. Preston, *How to Prepare for the Coming Crash*, 32, 33.

[50]Theodore H. Epp, *Practical Studies in Revelation*, 61.

[51]Charles M. Crowe, *In This Free Land*, 100, 101.

[52]Norman Cousins, *In God We Trust*, 2, 3.

[53]Stormer, 236.

[54]Francis Bretano, *Nation Under God*, 1.

# 8    Isaiah's Prognosis of America

*". . . the whole head is sick, and the whole heart faint."*—Isa. 1:5.

Isaiah was a prophet, not just a foreteller, but a spokesman for God. His ministry was during a period of outward prosperity but spiritual apostasy and moral degeneracy. He has been designated "the contemporary prophet." His name signifies "Jehovah's salvation." F. C. Jennings writes these words:

> In this, how strikingly this "salvation of Jehovah" corresponds with the "Gospel of God" in the New Testament, for that, too, begins at Jerusalem, but also does not end there. . . .
>
> There is, too, a more spiritual correspondence between Isaiah and Romans, the "salvation of Jehovah" and "the Gospel of God," for as in this chapter we have a solemn exposure of sin, so does the New Testament epistle begin with a similar indictment, by which "every mouth may be stopped, and all the world become guilty before God." To convict thus of guilt seems a strange part of "good news," but it is an essential part, for as only the sick send for a physician, so do those only who are convicted of sin care for salvation from its penalty and power.[1]

Isaiah's prophecies are directed against Judah and Israel in view of the coming captivity. This first chapter of Isaiah has a vivid parallel to the United States in the hour in which we live.

Most Americans are not concerned about the evaluation of Isaiah and our nation today. Henry L. Mencken remarked that "it was impossible to overestimate the low taste of the American public." John Warwick Montgomery quotes a key passage from Ethelbert Stauffer's *Christ and the Caesars*:

> Theatres and games and festivals were organized in unprecedented number, grain and wine and money were distributed. . . . But meanwhile the Germanic tribes were breaking through the frontiers, and the old order was tottering to its end. One contemporary account compares the sick

gaiety with the effect of the "Sardonian root," a poisonous plant which forces a convulsive smile across the face of the dying.[2]

Russell Shannon writes: "That our cities are sick is surely no news to anyone who has seen their graffiti-smeared stores and garbage-strewn streets. The disease is chronic, the decay corrosive. The problems exceed the aesthetic: the demoralizing effects on the urban inhabitants defy denial" ("Latrogenic Government," *The Freeman*, December, 1980). Our sick cities are made up of sick individuals.

Winston Churchill declared, "Man has improved himself every way except morally." Sartre the philosopher described our condition as follows: "A morally neutral world where good and evil have been absorbed and made irrelevant." James Reston of the *New York Times* makes this observation: "There is something in the air of the modern world: a defiance of authority, a contagious irresponsibility, a kind of moral delinquency, no longer retained by religious or ethical faith."[3] Isaiah declared that "the whole head is sick, and the whole heart faint." Alas, how true!

## Breakdown of the Family

*"Ah sinful nation, a people laden with iniquity, a seed of evildoers, children that are corrupters: they have forsaken the Lord, they have provoked the Holy One of Israel unto anger, they are gone away backward."*—Isa. 1:4.

America has suffered a severe spiritual relapse with the disintegration of the family. Isaiah cried out in desperation, "Ah sinful nation"—sinful because they had chosen their own way rather than that of Jehovah. The sins of the parents as well as the children brought about their downfall. As goes the home, so goes the nation. The breakdown of the family is a symptom of a dying nation.

The home is the foundation of a nation. It has been described as the oldest institution in the world. "The home is the one divine institution which antedates the Fall. It was constituted in the Garden of Eden when the sun each day looked down upon a sinless world. It is the most important of all institutions."

Today the American family faces obsolescence. The cornerstone of American society is being threatened. The marriage scene in our generation has been described as being "chaotic." Ancient Homer declared that the Grecian ladies counted their age from their marriage, not from birth. Oscar Wilde commented, "The world has grown suspicious of anything that looks like a happy married life."

Modern attitudes toward marriage and family range all the way from the profoundly spiritual to the disgustingly carnal. The steady shift toward the carnal extreme began soon after World War II and has accelerated at an alarming pace. Never before in our history have we had more emphasis on the home through seminars, conferences, films, tapes, etc.; but the American home continues to disintegrate.

The home has a unique place in the lives of its members. It has been said, "Home is a little corner of the earth that a man can call his own." And, "He is happiest, be he king or peasant, who finds peace in his home." It has been designated "the seminary of all other institutions" and "the nursery of the infinite."

T. Cecil Myers declared, "Happiness is homemade. Whether you live in a hut in the hollow or a mansion on the hill, a one-room efficiency or a ten-room penthouse, your home is earth's most important place. Nothing can take its place or substitute for its importance." A Christian home has been described as "an earlier heaven."

It has been noted that "the family is the nearest thing to torture when it is torn by rebel forces, and the nearest thing to God when it cares enough to live, love, struggle and conquer as one great unit."

> The home stands at the center of our civilization. The great need of our time, as in the past, is for Christian homes. But what is a Christian home? That question deserves some serious thought and consideration.
>
> A home is not automatically a Christian home because the father or the mother have their names on the roll of a church. It is not necessarily a Christian home because there are some religious pictures hanging on the wall and a family Bible on the end table. It is not a Christian home just because the whole family may be in worship services fairly regularly on Sunday.
>
> A truly Christian home is one where prayer is heard daily and the Bible is read aloud. It is a home where the principles of Christ are honored. It is a place where people try to show the spirit of Christ in their day-by-day relationships.
>
> Is yours a Christian home?
>
> —*Arkansas Baptist*

We have more houses in America than homes. A sign was seen on a furniture truck, HELP US MAKE YOUR HOUSE A HOME. But it takes more than possessions to make houses into homes. Someone noted that "the American family in one week consumes more energy, such as electricity, natural gas, etc., than all other families of the earth consume in one year." We live in an affluent nation. Years ago John Henry Jowett wrote these words:

> ANYBODY can build a house; we need something more for the creation of a home. A house is an accumulation of brick and stone, with an assorted collection of manufactured goods; a home is the abiding place of

ardent affection, of fervent hope, of genial trust.

There is many a homeless man who lives in a richly furnished house. There is many a modest house in the crowded street which is a beautiful home.

The Bible does not say very much about homes; it says a great deal about the things that make them. It speaks about life and love and joy and peace and rest! If we get a house and put these into it, we shall have secured a home.

The family played an important role in the early history of our nation. It was characterized by a spiritual stamina. The pioneer families endured indescribable obstacles and manifested real courage in the establishment of their homes. It has been declared, "It would seem appropriate to laud 'rugged familyism' rather than 'rugged individualism' as the clue to the greatness and stability of our national heritage."

What is a home without children? Psalm 127:3 declares, "Lo, children are an heritage of the Lord. . . . "

> **In praise of little children I will say**
> **God first made man, then found a better way**
> **For woman; but His third way was the best.**
> **Of all created things, the loveliest**
> **And most divine are children.**
>
> —*Laus Infantium*, William Canton

According to a national poll, it was discovered that a great number of American couples do not want children. The reasons: "more trouble than they're worth"; "too expensive"; "too much responsibility"; "too much trouble."

Some claim that "children are so expensive that only the poor can afford them." Also, "a real family man is one who looks at his new child as an addition—not a deduction." "A house empty of children. . . is as useless and lonely as a railroad station on an abandoned line," said one. Gordon Jaeck has written, "These difficult, mixed-up kids of ours are also the greatest, most lovable and exciting packages of potential that God could give to two parents."

Abraham Lincoln wrote of that potential:

> A child is a person who is going to carry on what you have started. He is going to sit where you are sitting and, when you are gone, attend to those things which you think are important. You may adopt all the policies you please, but how they will be carried out depends on him. He will assume control of your cities, states and nations. He is going to move in and take over your churches, schools, universities and corporations. All your books are going to be judged by him. The fate of humanity is in his hands.

Another has declared, "The wars of the world have already begun in the world's nurseries." Socrates, the Greek philosopher, warned, "If I could get to the highest place in Athens, I would lift up my voice and say, 'What mean ye, fellow citizens, that ye turn every stone to scrape wealth together, and take so little care of your children, to whom ye must one day relinquish all?' "

In these hectic days it takes the grace of God to rear children. "The accent may be on youth, but the stress is still on the parents." William Penn lamented: "Men are generally more careful of their horses and dogs than their children." "The training of children is the one most important thing the Almighty lets us live for. When we fail at this, all of our spectacular successes in other lives crumble up like paper in our hands."

Alice V. Keliher said:

> Everyone who touches the life of a child contributes in some way to the person he becomes. The quality of our society does not emerge accidentally. We create it. In large measure it lies in the children who will become the adult generation.

The breakdown of the home is a national tragedy. Jim Bishop spoke of a time gone by "when Daddy was the font of knowledge at the dinner table; when peace and security were the norm; when an academic argument was a pleasure; when respect was accorded unasked. But," he said, "it's gone, and I extend an empty hand to an empty world." He noted that now the world was filled with international tension, suspicion and hate.

John B. Watson of the behaviorist School of Psychology predicted "that marriage and the family as Americans knew it would be dead in fifty years."

Is the American home doomed? Dr. W. B. Jackson explained that "it is quite possible that by 2014 the family may disappear as a unit of society, and other units based upon age groups and interests may take its place." He said that the home may develop into merely a "breeding, feeding and sleeping station, only with most features automated."

"The family as a unit seems to be falling apart. The old adhesives that held it together seem to be brittle and cracking." Staid Calvin Coolidge remarked: "Look well to the hearthstone; there all hope for America lies." Note the following words:

> As is the home, so will be the church, the state and the nation. By weakening the pillars of the home in the "interest" of the state, ancient Greece sealed its own doom. Because of corruption in the families, the boasted civilization of Rome could not endure. And today the threads of destiny of our own nation are being silently woven within the narrow confines of our family circles.
>
> Upon the walls of every institution which fails to include in its reckoning the home, no matter how glowing its prospects may seem, no matter

how sumptuous and hilarious its feasting may be, there is traced by secret hand the writing: "Thou hast been weighed in the balance and found wanting."

Parents are the key to a happy home. A noted police official has stated that "there is one way to eliminate juvenile delinquency—provide each child in America with competent parents." Parents without convictions are like "the sextant but no fixed star, the material but no blueprints, the means but no ends."

A noted clergyman has commented:

> No wonder many young boys and girls are delinquent. They have no home lives. They eat out of the refrigerator. The members of the family keep different hours. They leave notes for one another. As one suburban mother put it, "My home has been turned into a filling station. My two sons and daughter just come in at meal times to get filled up. Then out they go."

Note the words of Howard Whitman:

> Dr. Freida Kehm of the Association for Family Living in Chicago has put it this way: "A child doesn't need another playmate. He needs a parent, an adult parent. Too many of us have made the mistake of taking parents down to the child's level instead of offering the child a blueprint for adulthood."
>
> Someone has said, "Children nowadays have too many gadgets to fool with and not enough chores."
>
> Parents have been cowed a great deal in recent years. They've been afraid to stand up for what they believe. Children have missed this. As they need their spinach and vitamins, so they need their parents whom they can look up to and, as the Bible says, honor. They're crying out for leadership, for parental values to hold onto, for reliable guides who know the pathways of life and can—and will—direct them.

You've heard the expressions, "a chip off the old block," and "The apple does not fall far from the tree." In other words, your children are going to be like you. I quote another: "If there's one fault all parents have, it may be trying to rear children to be just like them." A high percentage of young people smoke because their parents have set the example. The same is true of drinking.

Edmond and Jovita Addeo in their book, *Why Our Children Drink*, reveal that "a recent study of New York City high school students showed what 80 percent drank to some extent, and that 12 percent could be classified as problem drinkers." How did these students get started drinking? The authors comment: "National statistics state that 7 out of 10 young people under the age of 14 have tasted alcohol, and most of it has been in the home, with parental permission."

A. W. Pink writes these discerning words (written a generation ago but particularly appropriate to our day):

> When there was an ungrieved Spirit in the churches, the restraining hand of God was held upon the baser passions of mankind. That restraint operated largely through parental control—moral training in the home, wholesome instruction and discipline in the school, and adequate punishment of young offenders by the state. But when the Spirit of God is "grieved" and "quenched" by the churches, the restraining hand of the Lord is removed, and there is a fearful moral aftermath in all sections of the community.
>
> When the divine law is thrown out by the pulpit, there inevitably follows a breakdown of law and order in the social realm, which is what we are now witnessing all over the so-called civilized world. That was the case to a considerable extent twenty-five years ago; and as the further an object rolls down hill, the swifter becomes its momentum, so the moral deterioration of our generation has proceeded apace. As the majority of parents were godless and lawless, it is not to be wondered at that we now behold such reprehensible conduct in their offspring.
>
> . . .Child delinquency is one of the plain marks of a time of apostasy.[4]

"Today only 13 percent of American families include a working father, a stay-at-home homemaking and child-rearing mother, and one or more children!"

Aaron Stern makes this observation:

> An infant who is raised without a stable, single mother figure is irreversibly crippled in terms of his potential for loving. This syndrome, called "institutionalism," was observed in a study of the effect of excessive maternal deprivation among foundlings.
>
> In hospital nursing centers and foundling homes, nursing care is provided in eight-hour shifts. A given infant is exposed to at least three—probably more—different mothering figures during the course of each day. This situation is further complicated by the rotation of working schedules to cover holidays and weekends.
>
> Studies of children raised in such institutions from birth reveal that the multitude of maternal figures serves to undermine the effective transition of a child from a narcissistic animal to a caring human being. Research indicates that in the absence of a more constant nurturing source for about the first two years of life, the child's ability to love another is severely hindered.[5]

Napoleon Bonaparte declared, "The future destiny of a child is always the work of the mother." But Mother is too busy these days. The reason: "The father works the night shift, the mother works the day shift—and the kids shift for themselves." Someone wisely remarked, "When most of us were kids, a baby sitter was an individual called 'Mother.'"

In her book, Catherine Marshall quotes from one of the sermons of her late husband:

> Modern girls argue that they have to earn an income in order to establish a home, which would be impossible on their husband's income. That is sometimes the case, but it must always be viewed as a regrettable necessity, never as the normal or natural thing for a wife to have to do.
>
> The average woman, if she gives her full time to her home, her husband, her children. . . . If she tries to understand her husband's work . . . to curb his egotism while, at the same time, building up his self-esteem, to kill his masculine conceit while encouraging all his hopes, to establish around the family a circle of true friends. . . . If she provides in the home a proper atmosphere of culture, of love of music, of beautiful furniture and of a garden. . . . If she can do all this, she will be engaged in a life work that will demand every ounce of her strength, every bit of her patience, every talent God has given her, the utmost sacrifice of her love. It will demand everything she has and more. And she will find that for which she was created. She will know that she is carrying out the plan of God. She will be a partner with the Sovereign Ruler of the universe.[6]

> **The men of the earth build houses;**
> **Build turrets, roofs and domes;**
> **But the women of the earth—God knows—**
> **The women build the homes.**

Parents should diligently study the book of Proverbs. "We suspect that some of those who raised their children by Dr. Spock's book might have done better to spank the kids with it now and then." O. A. Battista states that "one of the best things a parent can do after reading a child-guidance book is to lose it." Note the words of Solomon, the wisest of men:

*"He that spareth his rod hateth his son: but he that loveth him chasteneth him betimes."*—Prov. 13:24.

*"Chasten thy son while there is hope, and let not thy soul spare for his crying."*—Prov. 19:18.

*"Train up a child in the way he should go: and when he is old, he will not depart from it."*—Prov. 22:6.

*"The rod and reproof give wisdom: but a child left to himself bringeth his mother to shame."*—Prov. 29:15.

Others have expressed the same thoughts thus:

"Train up your child in the way you know you should have gone yourself" (Spurgeon).

"Just as the twig is bent, the tree's inclined" (Pope).

"Let thy child's first lesson be obedience, and the second will be what thou wilt" (Franklin).

"I was brought up at the knee of a godly mother and over the knee of a Christian father" (Penn).

James Dobson has remarked, "Permissiveness has not just been a failure; it has been a disaster." Did you notice that "everything in the modern home is controlled by switches except the children"? When the Duke of Windsor visited the United States, he observed: "The thing that impresses me most about America is the way parents obey their children."

> ## "I was brought up at the knee of a godly mother and over the knee of a Christian father."
>
> —*William Penn*

What happened to the old-fashioned woodshed? What ever happened to spanking? Have children lost respect for authority? A Brooklyn high school teacher offered her resignation with these words:

> Dear Gentlemen:
>
> In this school system the teachers are afraid of the superintendents, the superintendents are afraid of the members of the school board, the members of the school board are afraid of the parents, the parents are afraid of the children, and the children are afraid of *nobody*....
>
> No longer will I put up with pieces of chalk being thrown at me, or listening to the sullied remarks about me in the corridors of this high school. These children are coming from undisciplined homes, and I cannot teach in a classroom where there is no discipline. Consequently, I tender my resignation.

The root of the problem was the lack of discipline in the home.
James Dobson pens these words:

> It is most important that a child respect his parents, not for the purpose

of satisfying their egos, but because the child's relationship with his parents provides the basis for his attitude toward all other people. His view of parental authority becomes the cornerstone of his later outlook on school authority, police and law, the people with whom he will eventually live and work, and for society in general.

The parent-child relationship is the first and most important social interaction an infant will have, and the flaws and knots in that interaction can often be seen in later relationships.[7]

There is a potential delinquent in every home where the principles of God's Word are not taught. Luther Burbank, the noted horticulturist, warned: "If we paid no more attention to our plants than we have our children, we would be living in a jungle of weeds." An unknown author has written the following:

I must not interfere with any child, I have been told; to bend his will to mine, or try to shape him through some mold of thought. Naturally as a flower, he must unfold.

Yet flowers have the discipline of wind and rain, and though I know it gives the gardener much pain, I've seen him use his pruning shears to gain more strength and beauty for some blossoms bright. And he would do whatever he thought right.

I do not know—yet it seems to me that only weeds unfold naturally.

There is a misconception that our children are basically good: all they need is a little encouragement and direction. This is a fallacy. The Bible teaches the total depravity of man which also includes our children. A. W. Pink gives this explanation:

"Foolishness is bound in the heart of a child; but the rod of correction shall drive it far from him" (Prov. 22:15). This foolishness is not merely intellectual ignorance but a positive principle of evil, for in the book of Proverbs the "fool" is not the idiot but the sinner.

This corruption is deep-rooted. It does not lie on the surface, like some of the child's habits, which may easily be corrected. That moral madness, as Matthew Henry pointed out, "is not only found there, but bound there; it is annexed to the heart." It is rooted and riveted in him from the first breath he draws. This is the birthright of all Adam's progeny. "The little innocent" is a misnomer of fondness and fancy.

John Bunyan said: "I do confess it is my opinion that children come polluted with sin into the world, and that oft-times the sins of youth, especially while they are very young, are rather by virtue of indwelling sin than by examples that are set before them by others; not but they may learn to sin by example, too, but example is not the root, but rather the temptation to sin."

The rod of correction (not of caprice or passion) is the means prescribed by God, and under His blessing it will prevent many an outburst of the flesh. . . . C. Bridges agreed: "Discipline is the order of God's government. Parents are His dispensers of it to their children." The child must be broken in, to "bear the yoke in his youth" (Lam. 3:27). Let reproof be tried first; and if it succeed, let the rod be spared (Prov. 17:10). If not, let it do its work."

If parents fail to do their duty, there will be sad consequences. . . .

As E. Hopkins said, "Take this for certain—that as many deserved stripes as you spare from your children, you do but lay up for your own backs."

A child does not have to be taught to sin. Remove all inhibitions and prohibitions and he will bring his parents to the grave in sorrow. . . .

Every parent is the channel of moral contagion to his offspring, who are by nature "children of disobedience" (Eph. 2:2). Original sin is transmitted as leprosy is conveyed to the children of lepers.[8]

There are insidious forces marshalled against the home. Sociologists inform us that "the American family is falling apart." There are damaging attacks from almost every quarter. According to the Family Service Association of America, the "family breakdown is fast reaching epidemic proportions and now ranks as America's Number 1 social problem."[9] It has been noted that the family "is near the point of complete extinction."[10]

Paul Popenoe has declared that "no society has survived after its family life deteriorated." It has been noted that "whenever a nation has permitted its family structure to break down, that nation has always ended in overthrow and destruction." A noted psychologist has remarked, "The family is no longer necessarily the basic unit of our society."

The home is the absolute bulwark of the nation. J. Edgar Hoover manifested a concern: "The home is the citadel of American life. If the home is lost, all is lost." Louis H. Evans has made this observation:

> Marriage is a nation's business. When a pier juts out into the ocean, it is utterly at the mercy of the individual pilings on which it stands. Strike out a piling from beneath it and the whole structure suffers a shock and the pier is weakened.
>
> Every nation juts out into the social sea, resting upon the pilings of its individual homes. Every time a home is destroyed, the whole nation suffers a severe thundershock. No nation can stand for long with one-quarter of its pilings gone or damaged.[11]

According to a Gallup poll, "close to half of all Americans believe family life has deteriorated in the last fifteen years, and almost four in 10 (37 percent) are worried about the future facing them and their families." Billy Sunday, the famous evangelist, warned, "God pity the country when the Devil gets the home."

There are various reasons why the American home is falling apart. One has said, "In an era of easy credit and wobbly economics, it's not surprising to learn that 70 percent of the marriages that fail, the root cause is financial pressure."

One major family problem clearly on the upswing, according to Gallup, is excessive drinking. "The proportion of people saying liquor causes trouble in their homes has doubled in the past five years."

It is true that, "if people would take more time courting before marriage, they would not have to spend so much time in 'the courts' after marriage." An unequal yoke in marriage seldom works out. You have heard this saying, "If a child of God marries a child of the Devil, the child of God is sure to have trouble with his father-in-law."

---

## "Every parent is the channel of moral contagion to his offspring, who are by nature 'children of disobedience' (Eph. 2:2)."

*—A. W. Pink*

---

Sometimes the problem is communication. A study of married couples by speech communications expert Ray Birdwhistell reveals "that couples spend an average of only 27.5 minutes per week talking to each other. One reason: the average household television is on 46 hours a week."

In his book, *Don't Fake It—Say It With Love,* Howard S. Hendricks writes:

> There's another tragedy, not as heralded but just as lamentable as a legal divorce. That is the psychological divorce: a couple who continue to live together but with minimal communication. The relationship is shattered, and for all practical purposes the marriage is dead.
>
> The joke about the silent couple who hadn't been communicating for some time isn't far from reality. They were riding on a Sunday afternoon in the country, and he spotted two mules on the other side of the fence. For the first time in three weeks he spoke to his wife. "Some of your relatives?" he asked. She was equal to the occasion: "Yes, on my husband's side." And back into their stewing silence they went.

"Be it ever so humble, nobody stays home." Home should be more than a filling station.

A real estate salesman tried to sell a house to a newly married couple. Said the wife, "Why buy a home? I was born in a hospital, reared in a boarding school, educated in a college, courted in an automobile, and married in a church. I get my meals in a cafeteria, live in an apartment, spend my mornings playing golf and afternoons playing bridge; in the evenings we dance or go to the movies; when I'm sick, I go to a hospital; and when I die, I shall be buried from a mortuary. All we need is a garage with a bedroom."

There are enemies confronting the children in our homes. Dr. Max Rafferty enumerates:

THE ENEMIES. Who are they? They are the MUCK MERCHANTS, who prey upon puberty. They are the DOPE PUSHERS, who transplant cancers from the old to the young. They are the ENTERTAINERS, some of whom create an atmosphere for youthful audiences which is an odious cross between a brothel and a gang rumble. They are the RELATIVIST PREACHERS, who set up such a sterling example for their juvenile parishioners by mouthing "God-is-dead" slogans, supporting homosexual dance clubs, violating democratically enacted laws, and eroding our entire Judaeo-Christian moral heritage with silent smiles of slow disparagement.

They are the "PROGRESSIVE" EDUCATORS, who for almost a generation now have been promoting the philosophy of John Dewey, singing the praise of permissiveness, assiduously massaging each other's ego while oleaginously assuring one another that teaching organized, disciplined, systematic subject matter to children is far less important than indoctrinating them in togetherness, ingroupness, life adjustment, and democratic socializing with their peer group.

With this bleating band of permissive pedagogues must be included also the LEFTIST COLLEGE PROFESSORS, who throughout the past decade have lip-smackingly encouraged the violent young to become thugs, the unpatriotic to become treasonable, and the obscene to become unspeakable.

I detest these people.... I've had a first-hand view of the chaos they have caused, the young lives they have ruined, the hearts they have broken.

The act of marriage has become a scrap of paper. In fact, marriage in some circles has become a joke. "Marriage is a proposition that ends in a sentence." "These days people still marry for better or for worse, but not for long." "A marriage may be a holy wedlock, or an unholy deadlock." According to a French proverb, "Marriage is either a duet or a duel." "Marriage too often changes an ideal to an ordeal." It has been said "that, according to national figures, we Americans change cars every two-and-a-quarter years, friends every four years, and wives every seven years."

A news commentator remarked, "We live in a society that has learned to accept divorce as a way of life."

"Divorce is no longer an automatic tragedy, at least among the liberal middle class, but a statistically significant trend, even a media-sanctioned 'lifestyle'... nothing to feel eternally guilty about" (*Ms. Magazine*, April 1981).

Margaret Mead, noted anthropologist, remarked, "The most serious thing that is happening in the United States is that people enter marriage with the idea that it is terminable."

In America today we have a divorce rate that "compares with that of ancient Rome in the days of its decadence." The divorce rates vary, but whatever their number the results are tragic.

A professor of sociology in California completed an extensive study of couples who had been married between 20 and 35 years. His conclusion was that only six couples out of every hundred were satisfied and fulfilled by their marriage relationship.

Divorce is making shambles out of our homes. A Chinese proverb attests, "In a broken nest there are few whole eggs." "A broken home is the world's greatest wreck."

Let's face it—the family today is in trouble. According to the F.B.I., "Every 18 seconds a woman is battered by a man. Nationwide, one-fourth of all murders occurred within the family and one-half of these were husband/wife killings."

Divorce is but a symptom of the trouble in the home. More divorces are granted in the United States each year than in the rest of the world combined. Marriage has become a scrap of paper.

> In addition to these breakups, thousands of other homes are suffering from "emotional divorce." In such a situation husband, wife and children walk on the same carpets and eat at the same table, but socially and emotionally they are miles apart. They stay together only because of religious, economic, or other pressures. Such a home provides a cold emotional climate for children.
>
> —B. David Edens

This is not a healthy condition.

Augustine was right—"The union of man and wife is from God, so divorce is from the Devil." Shakespeare once said, "You take my house when you take the prop that sustains my house." The props of our homes are being kicked away. Only the sure foundation of the Word of God can withstand the onslaughts of the enemy.

Not only is divorce threatening the American home, but so is government interference. The government should not interfere with the family. Government experts are not needed to rear our children. "The family is the buffer between the government and the individual." Christopher Lasch writes these words:

> As the family loses not only its productive functions but many of its reproductive functions as well, men and women no longer manage even to raise their children without the help of certified experts. The atrophy of older traditions and self-help has eroded everyday competence in one area after another and has made the individual dependent on the state, the corporation and other bureaucracies.[12]

There is inherent danger in permitting the "certified experts" to guide your family. "Government should get out of the way of the traditional family and should stop searching for 'alternatives' to it." Wisely said: "Happy are the families where the government of the parents is the reign of affection; and the obedience of the children, the submission of love."

The Feminist Movement is threatening the very foundations of our Republic. The advocates of ERA (Equal Rights Amendment) would take the mother out of the house. However, the Bible is clear in its declaration: "She looketh well to the ways of her household..." (Prov. 31:27); "That they may teach the young women to be sober, to love their husbands, to love their children, To be discreet, chaste, keepers at home, good, obedient to their own husbands, that the word of God be not blasphemed" (Titus 2:4, 5).

And what's wrong with being a mother, a homemaker? The late Dr. M. R. DeHaan wrote, "A mother in the home has a more important task than the preacher or the teacher or the highest official in the world. Before there could be any of these, there had to be a mother."

And what a role a mother plays: "wife, homemaker, teacher, maid, chauffeur, referee, philosopher, rescue squad, tutor, psychiatrist, example—all put together spells Mother!" (Mrs. Mel Rutter). Women's vaunted position is described by Rosalie Mills Appleby thus: "Woman is God's poem in whom the rhythm of righteousness and the beauty of holiness are expressed in the highest terms."

Dr. Myrnia F. Farnham gives this testimony:

> There is one type of woman rarely seen in a psychiatrist's office—the woman who is glad she is a woman. Although now a minority in our female population, she honestly enjoys homemaking, and more than anything in the world wants to raise a family of healthy, normal youngsters. During twenty years of listening to distressed patients, I have never met her in my office—because she doesn't need help.
>
> —Quoted by D. M. Panton in *Christian Victory*

Greed for more income is breaking down many homes. *The Rocky Mountain News* published this letter to the newspaper:

Children of today are starved for love. Parents wonder why they are never satisfied to be at home. There is nothing there for them. No one to greet them when they come in from school. No one to care whether they are in or out. Many parents are so busy with other things, they cannot give their families the attention and love they need.

The women of today have raised the standard of the American home so high they cannot live in it. They have to work outside in order to acquire all the household furnishings, gadgets and push-button conveniences they desire—and then they're too worn out to enjoy them. If they wish to sacrifice their children's lives for these material things, then the children deserve our pity.

I always thought it was the father who was supposed to provide for and protect the children, and the mother was supposed to love, teach, guide, and direct them. Let the younger women who are mothers carry on with home responsibilities.

One wisely said: "The Women's Lib Movement has been ventilated, televised, debated, exploited, attacked, defended and, in general, given a thorough public going-over. What seems to be needed now is some insight into the actual effects of this on the normal, mentally alert American woman herself."

In her article, "Women's Lib—Who Needs It!" Mrs. Roman Liechty writes:

> The role of homemaker has too long been downgraded as boring, unfulfilling, intellectually lacking, not stimulating, and very menial.
>
> It is time that the average typical homemaker stand up and be counted. First, if you take seriously your role as homemaker, there is no time or reason to be bored. As to unfulfilling, I am filled to the brim—yes, my cup runneth over. As to intellectually lacking, what other occupation requires such a variety of skills and knowledge? And what is more stimulating than the love, respect and thanks of your husband and children? I must say, for doing such "menial tasks," the pay and fringe benefits are the best in the world.
>
> I resent their attempt to force a reverse role onto society. God created man, then He created woman for the man. I for one am happy with His arrangement.

God's Word is very distinct—"male and female created he them" (Gen. 1:27)—and "never the twain shall meet!" Men are to be masculine, and women are to be feminine.

Years ago before the ERA controversy, Roy L. Smith wrote a tract entitled *Girls Will Be Boys*. Note some paragraphs from that tract:

> I have become firmly convinced of late that I belong to the superior sex. In fact, there seems to be no doubt about it. The women themselves admit it—by imitating us.

But the strange thing to me is that women, instead of beginning on our virtues, have started out by imitating our vices. . . .

The secret of a woman's power has always been in her womanliness, not her masculinity. I know of a girl who is an expert boxer, but I do not know of any man who wants to marry a trained sparring partner.

The Lord made the women beautiful and foolish. Beautiful so that the men would love them and foolish so that they could love the men. . . .

We have complained against the double standard. I am opposed to it. But the only progress we have made in attaining a single standard has been the lowering of women's standards down toward that of the men. . . .

I have the feeling that the modern girl is being swindled. She is trading modesty for recklessness, chastity for sophistication, freedom for danger, womanliness for daring and charm for cosmetics.

It is pathetic when girls will be boys. They fail as girls and make themselves ridiculous as boys.          —Publisher Unknown

The Greek and Roman Empires are illustrative of the importance of the distinctive role of men and women in a nation. When Greece was conquered by the invading Romans, the Greek sculpture and young men were often portrayed as feminine. The Romans maintained their masculinity. However, years later when the Romans were defeated by the barbarians, the Romans had a tendency toward feminization.

Thus the lesson from history is that, when a nation's manhood has deteriorated, that nation is headed for moral disintegration and eventual collapse.[13]

Chesterton's remark, "As are families, so is society," is worth considering. It is well for a nation to ponder that "the security of our nation rests upon the strength of our families." Jane Adams asserted that "America's future will be determined by the home and the school. The child becomes largely what he is taught, hence we must watch what we teach him, and how we live before him." "The home is a barometer which foretells its future and the future of a nation."

According to Dr. James C. Dobson, "If America survives, it will be because fathers begin to put their families at the highest level of priority, and reserve something of their time, effort and energy for leadership within their own homes." Thus parents must lead the way.

Henry Ward Beecher used to say that the first thing for a man to do, if he would succeed in life, is to "choose a good father and mother to be born of." In these days of disrespect for authority, a police chief has admonished: "Training toward acceptable behavior patterns ought to start in the home. The home should be the persuasive force for developing respect for authority generally."

The divine order must be adhered to. In Ephesians 5:22 we read, "Wives, submit yourselves unto your own husbands, as unto the Lord." According to Vine's *An Expository Dictionary of New Testament Words,* the word *submit* is "primarily a military term, to rank under." This is plainly submission to the husband. Verse 23 adds, "For the husband is the head of the wife, even as Christ is the head of the church...." First Corinthians 11:3 gives the order: "But I would have you know, that the head of every man is Christ; and the head of the woman is the man; and the head of Christ is God." This order cannot be broken without causing chaos in the home.

A Christian home, therefore, has one head.

Dr. Kenneth Frederick relates this experience:

> One of the most interesting pictures I have ever seen appeared in the *Des Moines Tribune* several years ago.
> A lad in Florida had found a lizard and it had become the object of fascination because it had two heads. A preacher once told me that "anything that has two heads is a monstrosity...all that God ever made has one head." Well, this lizard certainly was a freak of nature, for there it was— two heads. No tails, just joined at the bodies. Imagine that lizard's consternation when one head wanted to go one way and the other head wanted to drag the entire body in the opposite direction.
> God has ordered the family according to the principle of "headship." There are not two heads but one head to the family unit. Each family member lives under the authority of the "head" whom God has appointed. This principle must be carefully followed, for it is so little understood and much less practiced today. Yet God has made the well-being of the home dependent upon the observance of this divinely appointed order.

"It is not marriage that fails; it is people who fail." "Even when a marriage is made in Heaven, the maintenance work has to be done on earth." "The secret of a successful marriage is to have one partner who makes a living and one who makes living worthwhile." A woman should not get married if she isn't willing to perform the menial tasks of a housewife. A man should not get married if he is not willing to be a provider for the home as well as assume its leadership.

In *The Note Book of Elbert Hubbard,* we find these words:

> It requires two to make a home. The first home was made when a woman, cradling in her loving arms a baby, crooned a lullaby. All the tender sentimentality we throw around a place is the result of the sacred thought that we live there with someone else. It is our home. The home is a tryst— the place where we retire and shut the world out.
> Lovers made a home, just as birds made a nest, and unless a man knows the spell of the divine passion, I can hardly see how he can have a home at all; for of all blessings no gift equals the gentle, trusting,

loving companionship of a good woman.[14]

A study of history will reveal the importance of the home. This was taken from *Christian Victory,* May, 1969:

> The home is America's last line of defense. We are poor readers or interpreters of history. Ancient Assyria was large, victorious, haughty, but she was suddenly destroyed. Why? Happy and healthy domestic life had disappeared. Roman legions conquered the centers of Europe, Asia and Africa, yet the city on the Tiber fell before the barbarians. Why? Because morality gave way to license. Wives could be exchanged, and children sold into slavery. The family collapsed, and when the family collapsed, the Roman Empire collapsed. We in America should heed these lessons, for we are no stronger than our homes.

The Apostle Paul admonished Timothy: ". . . let them learn first to shew piety at home. . . ." (I Tim. 5:4). It has been said, "The family is the nearest thing to torture when it is torn by rebel forces, and the nearest thing to God when it cares enough to live, struggle and conquer as one great unit."

Clergymen down through the ages have asserted that "good family life is, in the last resort, the nation's most precious asset." The hope for the nation's future is dependent on the spiritual condition of the American home today. Therefore, "If you settle Christianity right in the home, it settles all questions everywhere. National life never rises above the home life and never sinks below it."

The greatest mission field is the home. "Keep your home near Heaven; let it face the Father's house." Note what the Bible says:

*"And these words, which I command thee this day, shall be in thine heart: And thou shalt teach them diligently unto thy children, and shalt talk of them when thou sittest in thine house, and when thou walkest by the way, and when thou liest down, and when thou risest up. And thou shalt bind them for a sign upon thine hand, and they shall be as frontlets between thine eyes. And thou shalt write them upon the posts of thy house, and on thy gates."*—Deut. 6:6-9.

Jesus Christ warned of the disintegration of the home. He stated that the enemies of the home would be found in one's own family. In the Olivet Discourse He predicted rebellion in the home:

*"Now the brother shall betray the brother to death, and the father the son; and children shall rise up against their parents, and shall cause them to be put to death."*—Mark 13:12.

*"And ye shall be betrayed both by parents, and brethren, and kinsfolks, and friends; and some of you shall they cause to be put to death."*—Luke 21:16.

These verses have a near and prophetic application.

The cancer of self-destruction has eaten into the vital organs of the American home. The enemies of the family have robbed the home of spiritual vitality. If the family destroys itself, then we will have committed suicide.

## Our Troubled Youth

*". . . a seed of evildoers, children that are corrupters. . . ."*— Isa. 1:4.

It has been said that the young and the old constitute two-thirds of our population. Our greatest treasure is not found in our vast resources nor our prodigious scientific skills but in our youth. Their worth is beyond calculation.

By some, their worth is measured in dollars and cents. Teenagers literally buy billions of dollars' worth of clothing in a year. Their purchase of cosmetics, records, radios and automobiles is phenomenal. In fact, our culture today is geared to glorifying youth. In some respects, the youth have taken over our nation.

The writer of Proverbs declared, "The glory of young men is in their strength" (Prov. 20:29). Goethe remarked, "The destiny of any nation, at any given time, depends on the opinions of its young men under five and twenty."

Do you realize that "twenty-one of the signers of the Declaration of Independence were under forty years of age, and three were in their twenties"?

Note these two significant statements by English statesmen: "The youth of a nation are the trustees of posterity" (Benjamin Disraeli); "Tell me what are the prevailing sentiments that occupy the minds of our young men, and I will tell you what is to be the character of the next generation" (Edmund Burke).

There is much to be said for the youth of the "Now Generation." They demand our attention. George MacDonald expressed it this way: "When we are out of sympathy with the young, then I think that our work in this world is over." A university administrator has made this observation: "I have seen changes in youth. They are now stronger—physically and intellectually. They are more serious; they are better informed; they are more aware of problems and opportunities in their world."

The late Dr. Daniel Poling expressed this optimism:

> They made mistakes. . . as many as we made before them. But I believe that the young people of this generation are intrinsically as fine, as fundamentally forthright and as worthy as young people have ever been. I also believe that youth today faces problems more complex than those faced by youth in any other time. I find them courageous, more intellectually alert than was my general footing. And. . . as quickly responsive to an ideal.

However, we must be realists. All is not well with the youth of our nation. Leslie Thompson has written these words: " 'I wish you and Dad would remember,' quips the kid in the cartoon, 'that I'm not a child anymore. I'm a national problem.' Our analysts, psychologists, historians and magazine writers are all trying to explain the American phenomenon we call teenagers."

Said Herbert Jelley, "We are raising a whole nation of young people whose steady musical diet has been the complaints and the protest and the focus of physical gratification of rock music; never even exposed to the exhilaration of Beethoven, or the tranquility of Mendelssohn or the sheer joy of Mozart. Talk about poverty and underprivilege!"

While not all of the youth of our nation have fallen by the wayside, there is much to be alarmed about at a certain section of the "Now Generation." Jonathan Swift in dismay remarked, "No wise man ever wished to be younger." The ancient Greek philosopher characterized the youth of his day: "The young think they know everything and are confident of their assertions."

The youth of today lack direction. Lord Chesterfield asserted: "The young leading the young is like the blind leading the blind: they will both fall into the ditch." A pastor in Scotland lamented: "The young people of my country used to hike when they went on hikes; now they take taxis to the youth hostels. They are given minds, but they can't think; they are given souls, but they don't know what to do with them. The church has lost youth. . .everyone has lost youth."

The writer of Proverbs gives us these words, which have an apt parallel to our day:

*"There is a generation that curseth their father, and doth not bless their mother.*

*"There is a generation that are pure in their own eyes, and yet is not washed from their filthiness.*

*"There is a generation, O how lofty are their eyes! and their eyelids are lifted up."*—Prov. 30:11-13.

As one witnesses the thousands attending some of the degrading rock festivals, he is tempted to exclaim, "What a waste of youth!" This is an age of rebellion. Today there is a mass movement against all constituted authority, a hatred for established order. A lack of discipline in the school and home results in an undisciplined life. They practice free love but do not know the meaning of real love; they boast of their liberty but are the slaves of habit and passion; they exult in the pleasures of sin but eventually discover that sinful pleasure brings nothing but bitter ashes; they talk about universal love but exhibit hate. In some respects, they act the part of the Darwinian theory— they act like animals!

America stands alone as the leading nation in teenage crime. The statistics today are alarming:

> In the next 30 minutes across the United States, 29 children will attempt suicide; 57 kids will run away from home; 14 teenage girls will give birth to illegitimate babies; 22 girls under 19 years of age will receive abortions to end unwanted pregnancies; 685 teenagers who use drugs regularly will take some form of narcotics; 188 young people will experience a serious drinking problem; 285 children will become victims of broken homes.
>
> —Adon Taft, *The Miami Herald*

According to a recent report, "sexual activity among teens is soaring." Richard Lincoln has stated that sexual activity among teenagers increased two-thirds during the 1970s. According to Lincoln, "It is the exceptional young person who has not had sexual intercourse while still a teenager."

And where are young people looking for help? In a poll of American teenagers, forty percent testified to a faith in astrology. The cults are having a field day with gullible young people. Communism has a strong appeal for misguided youth.

> The communist attack directed at America's youth is designed to (1) split a few disgruntled, hate-driven activists away from the mainstream of American life and train them as revolutionaries, (2) dupe as many non-communist youth as possible into supporting communist causes and programs, and (3) make the remainder of the nation's young people so corrupt and decadent that they will not resist an eventual takeover.[15]

Parents should take their share of blame. Cowper stressed, "Our most important are our earliest years." The home is the basis for the training of Christian character. A free translation of Psalm 11:3 is, "When the foundations were being destroyed, what were the righteous doing?"

Much has been made of "the generation gap." One young man accused his elders, "You are blind to reality, unconscious to love and dead to all the crying." Another exclaimed, "How can they stop us, when they don't even know what's happening?" In other words, the older folks don't understand.

Because of disrespect in the home, we now have demonstrations on the street. Someone has written, "Thank God for the exuberant concert of youth! Without it, boys and girls of seventeen might droop and pine away and perish at the frightful prospect that someday they will be as dumb as their parents." "A child is a person who is going to carry on what you have started."

The question has been asked, "Do we take as much pains to guard our children from moral and spiritual infection as we do from physical infection?" Psalm 78:8 declares, "And might not be as their fathers, a stubborn and rebellious generation; a generation that set not their heart aright, and whose spirit was not stedfast with God."

There is coming a day of reckoning for wayward youth. "Unless a tree has borne blossoms in spring, you will vainly look for fruit in autumn" (Julius Charles Hare). "The majority of men employ the first part of life in making the rest miserable" (La Bruyère). "The excesses of our youth are drafts upon our old age, payable with interest about thirty years after date" (C. C. Colton). In other words, the sins of youth must be paid for in later life.

There is a time of reaping. Parents should be reminded that they too reap what they have sown in their children. And how tragic is that harvest!

Young people (not all, thank God) seldom realize the deceitfulness of sin and its awful consequences. The awkward age has been designated thus: "The awkward age is not so much the age at which a person bumps into things, as it is the age at which a person doesn't know what he is bumping into." Youth has been characterized as "young life plus curiosity minus understanding."

All sin has a payday. "For the wages of sin is death" (Rom. 6:23); ". . . the soul that sinneth, it shall die" (Ezek. 18:4). Most young people have not faced the fact of death. The preacher in Ecclesiastes warns, "Rejoice, O young man, in thy youth; and let thy heart cheer thee in the days of thy youth, and walk in the ways of thine heart, and in the sight of thine eyes: but know thou, that for all these things God will bring thee into judgment" (11:9). Note also these words of wisdom: "Remember now thy Creator in the days of thy youth, while the evil days come not, nor the years draw nigh, when thou shalt say, I have no pleasure in them" (Eccles. 12:1).

Someone asks, "What music is more enchanting than the voices of young people when you can't hear what they say?" What are they trying to tell us? "Blessed is the generation in which the old listen to the young; and doubly blessed is the generation in which the young listen to the old." Josh Billings has put it more crudely: "Young man, sit down and be still; you have plenty of chances to make a fool of yourself before you die."

This is a generation that wants answers, not just the pratings of misguided men. If America is to survive, it must turn to the Book which has the answers— the Bible. The Word of God has stood the test of the ages. "To the law and to the testimony: if they speak not according to this word, it is because there is no light in them" (Isa. 8:20).

Edgar Allan Poe, who died a derelict on the sea of life, despaired over "the fever of living." What an apt description of a Christless life! Young people today are running a high and dangerous fever. Without God and His Son Jesus Christ, that fever culminates in eternal death.

Surely a compassion should be shown the youth of this generation. Jesus

Christ wants to help young people and give them a definite purpose in life. Concerning the rich young ruler it is written, "Then Jesus beholding him loved him" (Mark 10:21).

Young person, "Your life is like a coin: you can spend it anyway you want, but you can only spend it once." Heed the words of the famous evangelist, D. L. Moody: "Give your life to God; He can do more with it than you can."

A nation that has neglected the spiritual training of its youth is committing suicide.

## Abortion Is Wholesale Murder

"... *they have forsaken the Lord, they have provoked the Holy One of Israel unto anger, they are gone away backward.*"—Isa. 1:4.

A nation can lose favor with Deity—the Almighty can be provoked to anger. Murder is a sin that incurs the wrath of God.

In America millions now living will never be born—they will be murdered! Today more lives are lost by abortion than in war. We quote from *Life Messengers*: "Total military losses of the United States in World War II were less than one-half million dead. But today over one million babies are murdered by abortion every year in the United States."

"Every day 4,400 babies are sacrificed to abortion. 1,600,000 babies are killed every single year. In fact, 30 percent of all babies concerned in this country are killed before they see the light of day" (National Right to Life Commmittee).

Wrote Tom Anderson, news commentator, "Murdering babies is now big business. In effect, the mushrooming of abortion clinics' advertisement might read like this: 'Have your baby murdered while you wait!' 'Kill now, pay later.'... 'Ask about our special layaway plan.'"

"It is reported that in certain cities in the United States there are more abortions than live births.... At this rate, we will soon have to apologize to Adolf Hitler."[16]

What is more blessed than a baby? Someone has written these words: "A baby is a small member of the human family who makes love stronger, days shorter, nights longer, the bank roll smaller, the home happier, clothes shabbier, the past forgotten, and the future worth living for." A baby is a priceless commodity, but our generation is guilty of making life cheap. Life in America is now so cheap that any woman may have an unborn child killed and nobody can legally stop her.

United States Senator Jesse Helms has written these words in his book, *When Free Men Shall Stand*:

In the meantime, we must not lose sight of the anomaly, the odd spectacle, that now exists in our country—where there is strong agitation to make tough laws protecting wolves and where it is already a federal offense to destroy an eagle's egg and where all protection has been forfeited on unborn life.[17]

What happened to our sense of values? Has human life become so cheap? How inconsistent we are! "Isn't it strange? With a genuine concern over child abuse, America is moving rapidly to curb the discipline of children. Spankings will probably be illegal. Yet it is legal to kill unborn infants." "Consistency, thou art a jewel!"

Are not babies to be considered people? Yet the Supreme Court has decreed that "certain people, if they are young enough and helpless, may be killed." States Dr. Kenneth M. Mitzner:

> We must protect human life from the moment of conception, not because we are sure that an individual is present, but because we cannot be sure of the contrary.

He also says:

> What is an induced abortion? It is the killing of a distinct, irreplaceable, unique human individual. At best, it is equivalent to killing a person in his sleep. And, as we all know, killing a person in his sleep, even without inflicting any pain, is a more serious offense than causing him painful injuries which are not fatal. This is because the offense lies in depriving the individual of the rest of his life.
>
> —"The Growing Scandal of Abortion," *Applied Christianity,* November, 1974

Is it not a sin of the highest magnitude when "aborted infants lie on tables gasping for breath while doctors pass by ignoring them?" *Moody Monthly* for May 1980 carried an editorial entitled, "What Ever Happened to the Evangelical?" Note the opening paragraphs of that article:

> Could it be that ours is a generation more wicked than any other that has lived upon the earth?
>
> By comparison, the Crusaders, Inquisitors, even the Nazis, were minor leaguers. They destroyed children and adults committed to an ideology. We destroy the unborn....
>
> The United States Supreme Court has given women the right to abortion on demand, making the casual destruction of the unborn the law of the land.

R. F. D. Gardner writes:

> Abortion is more than medical importance, principally because a human life is at stake. The life is only potential, but by the time the woman comes

to see her doctor, the statistical chances are in favour of the fetus going on to safe delivery and becoming a living man.[18]

When does human life begin? The abortionist claims that "the fetus is not human. It is a mass of protoplasm. . . a group of cells. . . a mass of tissue." Bible believers insist that human life begins at conception. Every fetus has the potential of birth. Even the liberal, Dietrich Bonhoeffer, remarked:

> To raise the question whether we are here concerned with a human being or not is to confuse the issue. The simple fact is, God certainly intended to create a human being and that this nascent human being has been deliberately deprived of his life. And that is nothing short of murder.[19]

It has been wisely said, "Is there even the slightest possibility that the fetus is a human being? If so, he must have the right to live." In other words, the prerogative of the fetus' living is in the hands of God, not man.

The Bible confirms the fact that an unborn child is a human being. Note again the words of R. F. D. Gardner:

> . . . The Old Testament reminds us that God is the giver of life, the One by whose power fetal development occurs, and to whom every living soul belongs. This being so, life is not to be taken on one's own initiative, not even for that most inescapable of obligations, the blood feud. Man is not to cause the death of the innocent and guiltless, for the blood of the innocent cries to God from the ground.[20]

It has been noted that Isaac, Samson and Samuel were individuals whose lives were predicted before conception. Their capacity "to serve the purposes of God clearly depended on an uninterrupted gestation period."

Consider these Bible references:

*"For thou hast possessed my reins: thou hast covered me in my mother's womb.*
*"I will praise thee; for I am fearfully and wonderfully made: marvellous are thy works; and that my soul knoweth right well.*
*"My substance was not hid from thee, when I was made in secret, and curiously wrought in the lowest parts of the earth."—* Ps. 139:13-15.

*"Thus saith the Lord, thy redeemer, and he that formed thee from the womb, I am the Lord that maketh all things. . . ."*—Isa. 44:24.

*"Then the word of the Lord came unto me, saying,*
*"Before I formed thee in the belly I knew thee; and before thou camest forth out of the womb I sanctified thee, and I ordained thee a prophet unto the nations."*—Jer. 1:4,5.

*"And Mary arose in those days, and went into the hill country with haste, into a city of Juda;*

*"And entered into the house of Zacharias, and saluted Elisabeth.*

*"And it came to pass, that, when Elisabeth heard the salutation of Mary, the babe leaped in her womb; and Elisabeth was filled with the Holy Ghost:*

*"And she spake out with a loud voice, and said, Blessed art thou among women, and blessed is the fruit of thy womb.*

*"And whence is this to me, that the mother of my Lord should come to me?*

*"For, lo, as soon as the voice of thy salutation sounded in mine ears, the babe leaped in my womb for joy."*—Luke 1:39-44.

*The Bible on Abortion* is the title of a pamphlet written by Dr. Harold O. J. Brown (from his book, *Death Before Death*). The author quotes Tertullian, the church father, on page 12:

> For us, murder is once-for-all forbidden; so even the child in the womb, while yet the mother's blood is being drawn on to form the human being, it is not lawful for us to destroy. To forbid birth is only quicker murder. It makes no difference whether one take away the life once born or destroy it as it comes to birth. He is a man, who is to be a man; the fruit is always present in the seed.

America is acting like a pagan nation. God has judged America for killing unborn babies. Abortion has been called "the number one moral issue of our day."

I quote another:

> Once the United States was known as the world's chief advocate of dignity, the sanctity, and the inherent rights of each human life. Once we were the world's leading defender of every human being's right to life, liberty, and the pursuit of happiness. We are losing ground in all three of those inherent rights, but in none so much as in the defense of the right of human beings to live.

If the unborn do not have a chance in our society, what about the unwanted? Is euthanasia next? There are those who believe that abortion and euthanasia are "ethically inseparable." Have we opened up Pandora's box?

Dr. C. Everett Koop makes this observation: ". . . in a sinful world, liberty leads to license. If the law does not protect the life of an unborn baby, where will this lead? It will lead to infanticide and euthanasia among other things" ("Where Is the Abortion Decision Taking Us?" *Eternity,* October, 1973).

It may be that euthanasia is just around the corner. Here's something else to think about: "If we are going to make it legal to destroy the unborn child because he might be deformed, then will we later adopt laws to permit the legal execution of those deformed at birth—or who were unwanted at birth?"

Rome, like America, aborted babies. A striking similarity is noted between the United States and ancient Rome in her decline: "...abortion and infanticide become acceptable; prostitution is legalized, and homosexuals are recognized as the third sex."

The early church was opposed to abortion, Schaeffer points out:

> ...In the pagan Roman Empire, abortion was freely practiced but Christians took a stand against it. In 314 the Council of Ancyra barred from the taking of the Lord's Supper for ten years all who procured abortions or made drugs to further abortions.[21]

There are those who contend that the killing of the unborn represents "the greatest crime of history." John Warwick Montgomery points out: "If God did not tolerate the Nazi extermination of six million Jews, what makes us think that He will continue to ignore our mounting toll of infanticides?"

Abortion is murder in the sight of God.

Henry M. Morris writes:

> ...the current sudden increase in legalized abortion practice is very disturbing. Regardless of what changes may be taking place in legal and medical practice, abortion is still murder in the sight of God. The parents, the abortionist and all who participate in this denying a helpless infant his right to see the world outside his mother's womb, will someday have to face him again at the throne of God.[22]

The murder of unborn infants may be "the last straw" with our Maker. As some have pointed out, such action may be the turning point of our history—it could be the point of "no return." This should be a day of weeping and humiliation: "In Rama was there a voice heard, lamentation, and weeping, and great mourning, Rachel weeping for her children, and would not be comforted, because they are not" (Matt. 2:18). The judgment of the Almighty is upon us. The Word of God is true: "Whoso sheddeth man's blood, by man shall his blood be shed: for in the image of God made he man" (Gen. 9:6). Again, "Thou shalt not kill" (Exod. 20:13).

This is one of the surest signs that America is committing suicide.

## ENDNOTES:

[1]F. C. Jennings, *Studies in Isaiah*, 19, 20.

[2]John Warwick Montgomery, *The Shaping of America*, 24.

[3]Arnold Lunn and Garth Lean, *Christian Counter-Attack*, 53.

[4]Arthur W. Pink, *Gleanings from Elisha*, 47.

[5]Aaron Stern, *Me: The Narcissistic American*, 33.

[6]Catherine Marshall, *A Man Called Peter*, 54, 55.

[7]James Dobson, *Dare to Discipline*, 11.

[8]Arthur W. Pink, *Gleanings from the Scriptures*, 78, 79.

[9]J. Allan Petersen, *The Marriage Affair*, 2.

[10]Larry and Nordis Christenson, *The Christian Couple*, 15.

[11]Petersen, 9.

[12]Christopher Lasch, *The Culture of Narcissism*, 37.

[13]Petersen, 255, 256.

[14]Elbert Hubbard, *The Note Book of Elbert Hubbard*, 19.

[15]John A. Stormer, *The Death of a Nation*, 69, 70.

[16]Tim LaHaye, *The Battle for the Mind*, 113.

[17]Jesse Helms, *When Free Men Shall Stand*, 68.

[18]R. F. D. Gardner, *Abortion: The Personal Dilemma*, 116.

[19]*Ibid.*, 122, 123.

[20]*Ibid.*, 120.

[21]Francis A. Schaeffer, *How Shall We Then Live?* 222.

[22]Henry M. Morris, *The Bible Has the Answer*, 183, 184.

# 9 fatal Symptoms of Decadence

*"From the sole of the foot even unto the head there is no soundness in it; but wounds, and bruises, and putrifying sores: they have not been closed, neither bound up, neither mollified with ointment."*—Isa. 1:6.

Isaiah is in the role of a physician. In chapter 1 of the book he gives "a prediction of the probable course of a disease and the chances for recovery." It is to be remembered that he is writing by divine revelation. His prognosis of a nation's illness would not be favorably received in our generation.

In his commentary, W. E. Vine writes:

> How fearfully the spirit of rebellion had permeated the nation is vividly portrayed in verses 5 and 6: "the whole [or rather, 'every'] head is sick and the whole heart faint." The head represents the outward controlling power; the heart the inward emotions.
>
> The whole condition was a Divine judgment. They were like a diseased body throughout. If the head and the heart are unsound, the entire body is affected. From the sole of the foot to the head there was nothing sound, but "wounds, bruises, and festering sores."[1]

A gentleman stopped to talk to a small girl who was making mud pies on the sidewalk. "My word!" he exclaimed; "you're pretty dirty, aren't you, little girl?"

"Yes," she replied, "but I'm prettier clean."

America was much prettier when she was clean.

Our nation has let down the bars. We have become a hedonistic society. Our age is characterized by the adage: "If it feels good, do it; if it tastes good, eat it; and if it looks good, buy it." We have become a nation of sensualists. *Lasciviousness* in the New Testament is also translated "wantonness" or "sensuality." Lightfoot renders the word, "so much in the grip of sin, so much under its domination, that he does not care what people say or think so long as he can gratify his evil desire. He is the man who is lost to shame."

Herbert Miller makes this comment: "Like the Hebrew people in the Old Testament, Americans have set up a golden calf to worship. The only difference is that our golden calf is made up of chrome, steel, glass, and new-smelling upholstery."

Americans, like the Romans of old, are addicted to pleasure. That is why in one year our nation spends $244 billion just for leisure.

Nothing can become so foul as that which was once beautiful. "Lilies that fester smell worse than weeds."

---

## Our age is characterized by the adage: "If it feels good, do it; if it tastes good, eat it; and if it looks good, buy it."

---

It was reported that within a few blocks of the nation's Capitol there was a nauseating odor. An investigation revealed that "trash cans containing the bodies of aborted babies behind an abortion clinic had been overturned."

Have you visited Times Square lately? What a "spewed-out flotsam and jetsam of human life!" What a stench it must be in the nostrils of God!

A physician, before he can successfully treat a patient, must make a proper diagnosis. Back in 1937 J. E. Conant in a pamphlet, *The Growing Menace of the Social Gospel,* wrote these words on pages 9 and 10:

> The disease must be diagnosed before the prescription can be written. And we can never arrive at a correct diagnosis by such incorrect reasoning as the social doctors seem to be doing, neither can we even guess at a cure from such a superficial diagnosis as their upside-down logic leads them to.
>
> We must therefore isolate and bring into full view the ultimate general cause of all our ills before we can hope to make even a start in finding our way to the cause of our particular ills, or to arrive at the cure that will work.

Isaiah diagnosed, "the whole head is sick . . . . From the sole of the foot unto the head there is no soundness in it." We are what we think. There are those who "live lives of quiet desperation." "The evidence is strong that human society is in a stage of comprehensive breakdown." America is having a nervous breakdown. According to a government report, "Officially 15 percent of the population in any given year—more than 32 million people—are suffering mental disorders." In other words, 32 million Americans are "unable to cope with the daily hazards of a fast-changing and competitive society, foundering marriages, rebellious children, job or school tensions, or pent-up hostility toward others and themselves." Another report revealed that "$40 billion is spent each year in an attempt to maintain or regain mental health."

## The Signs of the Times

*"O ye hypocrites, ye can discern the face of the sky; but can ye not discern the signs of the times?"*—Matt. 16:3.

America has been playing with sin. We no longer fear the judgment of God. A survey of contemporary life will reveal our low spiritual ebb. How sick we are is manifested in our culture.

Consider art. It has been said, "What garlic is to salad, insanity is to art." "The climate of values and criticism in the art world has been so perverted that a few blobs or smears on a canvas are often judged by art 'critics' for showing alongside or ahead of the great works of the masters" (L. H. Johnson).

Schaeffer points out the absurdity of modern art: "The historical flow is like this: The philosophers from Rousseau, Kant, Hegel and Kierkegaard onward, having lost their hope of a unity of knowledge and a unity of life, presented a fragmented concept of reality; then the artists painted that way."[2]

Richard Hanser explains art in pre-war Germany:

> The alienation of intellectuals like Grosz was finding its wildest expression in the "Dada" movement, which was started by a group of poets, painters and musicians in the Cafe Voltaire in Zurich during the war.
>
> "Dada"—the word was chanced upon in a French dictionary. It meant hobby-horse, and the nursery-nonsensical sound of it was exactly in keeping with the spirit of the movement. The idea was to mock, deride and spit at all the beliefs and standards of a system that had brought mankind to the bloody catastrophe of a world war.
>
> "Dada" staged art exhibits that would have been acceptable to an Andy Warhol a generation later: old rags, rusty nails and cigar butts were posted on canvas and offered . . . as ["garbage pictures"].[3]

Much of today's art represents a culture that is sick.

Music plays a major role in the character of a nation. Someone has observed, "Tell me who writes its songs, and I'll tell you who controls its destiny." A Turkish proverb declares, "As the music is, so are the people of the country."

Thoreau was more specific: "Music will destroy England and America." In other words, "Songs have overthrown kings and empires."

Modern rock 'n' roll has been called an American disease. An observer has remarked, "I have just spent an hour and a half watching high school kids dance. My blunt, frank opinion is that rock 'n' roll is full of lust, sex and downright obscenity. The lyrics of many formulate a meaning that can be categorized only in the bracket of sex."

Rock music has become big business. The sales of records and tapes continue to increase each year. Rock singers (with mediocre talents) have amassed fortunes. Steve Allen, commenting on a particular performer, remarked: "The fact that someone with so little ability became the most popular singer in history says something significant about our cultural standards." What about our spiritual standards!

It has been said, "We tend to live on the level of the music we listen to." The danger of contemporary music (of this type) is that it suggests "premarital and illicit sex, drugs, the occult, even revolution." One rock leader boasted, "Our music is intended to broaden the generation gap, alienate children from their parents, and to prepare for revolution." Phil Kerr, a former band leader, wrote these words:

> In our opinion, the only difference between the leader of a modern "swing" orchestra and a jungle medicine-man is that the former is wearing a dress suit instead of a grass skirt, and has a slim baton in his dainty hand instead of a ring through his nose! The effect of his music is the same as that of the medicine man. Savage impulses stirred in the breast of a tuxedo-garbed American are as vicious and dangerous as the appetites stirred in the breast of the half-naked African by the same Satanic music!
> —*Music in Evangelism*

Ancient Rome lost her soul in a saturnalia of "wine, women and song." America is going down the same pathway. Her degenerate music is hastening her demise.

Music has been defined as "the speech of angels." America should have no time for that which savors of the pit!

## A Sex-Crazy Nation

"666" is the mark of the beast. It has been suggested that the number be changed to "sex-sex-sex." Surely sex is a characteristic of our day. The glorification of sex is a sign of America's decadence. Sex itself is God-given, pure, holy and good. Sex that is perverted is from the pit of Hell. Our nation is now in the throes of a sex obsession unparalleled in our nation's history.

Pitirim A. Sorokin has written: "Our civilization has become so preoccupied with sex that it now oozes from all the pores of American life." The statement has been made, "We are on a sex binge never before equalled in modern times." Jeremiah the prophet exclaimed, "For the land is full of adulterers" (Jer. 23:10).

Our moral values have sadly deteriorated. What was considered gross sin a decade or so ago is today accepted conduct. Our attitude toward extramarital sexual relations is much different from what it was for our parents.

Alvin Toffler of *Future Shock* observed, "Seldom has a single nation evinced greater confusion over its sexual values." Sex was an obsession with Freud, and his philosophy of "pleasure by sexual satisfaction" has pervaded our society. A noted author and psychologist has stated, "Virginity is about as useful as your appendix"—which has prompted another to assert, "If you have to go down in your morals to get up in society, then stay on the level."

Statistics concerning the sexual revolution vary, and they are alarming. Note these figures: "Morals declined last year more than in the last twenty years"; "Gonorrhea and syphilis are now out of control"; "In the United States, one million unmarried teenage girls become pregnant every year"; "43 percent of teenage girls believe there is nothing wrong with premarital sex, and 36 percent intend to live with a man before marriage or are doing so (60 percent of 18- and 19-year-olds)" (*Seventeen* magazine); "Over 80% of young girls who are married have had sex relations before marriage" [another report states 50%]; "Over two-and-a-half million American men and women avoid marriage altogether, yet live together as unwed heterosexuals or as homosexuals."

What is the price we are paying for all this indulgence in illicit sex? One has given this report:

> Venereal disease now constitutes a public health emergency of the first order . . . killing and seriously endangering the mental and physical well-being of millions of people. Gonorrhea is the leading reported communicable disease in this country and syphilis is third. Venereal disease strikes someone in the United States every 12 seconds . . . 5 new victims every minute.

Another lists these figures:

> Just since 1900—in the lifetime of many living today—various forms of syphilis alone have killed 100 million people. During the same period in the United States, it is estimated that syphilis has killed more than three million babies and more than a million adults. . . . One-half to two-thirds of the babies born alive to mothers with syphilis will bear congenital syphilis in some form.

Herpes, a form of a venereal disease, "has infected from five to fourteen million in this country—and the sad fact is that it is considered incurable!"

What a price to pay for momentary indulgence! Sin pays high wages.

What does the Almighty think of unlawful sex? In His Word we see that

He is against sexual perversion. He destroyed Sodom and Gomorrah because of this sin (Gen. 19:24). In Romans 1:24-32 God warns concerning the awful penalty of sexual deviation. First Corinthians 6:9,10 informs us:

*"Know ye not that the unrighteous shall not inherit the kingdom of God? Be not deceived: neither fornicators, nor idolaters, nor adulterers, nor effeminate, nor abusers of themselves with mankind. . . shall inherit the kingdom of God."*

This is God's decree. God's command is still true: "Thou shalt not commit adultery" (Exod. 20:14). "But we are sure that the judgment of God is according to truth against them which commit such things" (Rom. 2:2).

A nation is only as clean as its individuals. Sorokin warned, "The group that tolerates sexual anarchy is endangering its very survival." Our permissive society is paying an awful price for her folly—our very existence is at stake.

Dr. James Dobson, noted expert on family life, believes that "unchecked sexual freedom will lead to the inevitable decay of American society." John D. Unwin, a British anthropologist, after studying the rise and fall of civilizations over a period of 4,000 years, came to the conclusion that no society can long endure widespread promiscuity.

America has lost her sense of guilt. Thus it was with Greece and Rome. Lecky, in his *History of European Morals,* states concerning these two ancient countries: "Remorse was an unknown passion. A penitent's shame was impossible. . . . Men looked on deeds of infamy and were not shocked. . . . Men were naked and not ashamed, not because they were innocent, but because no sense of guilt assailed them."

A nation that cannot repent cannot be saved. Abraham Lincoln warned: "If destruction be our lot, we must live through all time or die by suicide."

## Drinking Our Way Into Oblivion

Strong drink is a destroyer, destroying the greatest nation on the face of the earth—the United States of America. Evangeline Booth stated the truth when she declared:

> Drink has shed more blood, hung more crepe, sold more homes, plunged more people into bankruptcy, armed more villains, slain more children, snapped more wedding rings, defiled more innocence, blinded more eyes, dethroned more reason, wrecked more manhood, dishonored more womanhood, broken more hearts, blasted more lives, driven more to suicide, and dug more graves than any other evil that has cursed the world.

The liquor traffic has been designated thus: "The sum of all villainies, the father of all crime, the mother of all abominations, the curse of all curses." We read that "alcohol has cost more, killed more people, and created more misery than all the wars in the entire history of the human race." "In the course of history," observes one, "more people have died for their drink and their dope than have died for their religion or their country."

William Shakespeare wrote, "O thou invisible spirit of wine, if thou hast no name to be known by, let us call thee—devil!" William Gladstone remarked, "The ravages of drink are greater than those of war, pestilence and famine combined."

Alcohol has been labeled "the world's oldest and most widely used drug." Robert G. Lee wrote these words:

> All that people say in favor of intoxicating liquor is as worthless for pur-chase as counterfeit money, as worthless as painted water for the thirsty. And I can say better things about the rattlesnake and the skunk than I can about liquor. . . .
>
> Search through all histories, delve into all philosophies, look into all tombs, walk through all mad houses, listen to all testimonies, and you cannot find one good thing that can be said about the open traffic in liquor.

Shakespeare spoke the truth when he declared, "Alcohol is a poison men take into the mouth to steal away the brain." Alcoholism has been called by Dr. Morris E. Chafetz, noted authority on liquor abuse, "America's largest untreated illness." But is drunkenness an illness? It has been stated that "it is unfortunate today that some regard alcoholism as a disease like cancer. It may end as a disease, but it begins with an act of will, namely to take a drink."

Peter L. Ream has penned these words:

> "Alcoholism is a disease?" If so, it is the only disease that is contracted by an act of the will. It is the only disease that requires a license to prop-agate it. It is the only disease that is bottled and sold. It is the only disease that promotes crime. It is the only disease that is spread by advertising. It is the only disease that is given for a Christmas present.

The changing of words does not change the evil. God does not classify alcoholism as a disease but as sin. It is a spiritual problem and demands a spiritual solution.

Someone has quipped, "America is well on her way to becoming a nation of 'alcoholics unanimous.' " Another has added, "Eleven million alcoholics in the United States and that's a staggering statistic." Another, "Over 10,000 people are killed each year by liquor while only one is killed by a mad dog; yet we shoot the dogs and license the liquor."

Alcohol is now America's number one drug problem. After heart disease and cancer, alcoholism is the country's biggest health problem. Dr. Karl Mennin-ger, a prominent psychiatrist, remarked, "With this [alcoholic] population, for other illnesses we would call a national emergency."

Consider the tragedy of liquor:

—75 million are harmed directly or indirectly because of alcoholism or problem drinking.

—For every heroin addict in the United States, there are 15 hard-core alcoholics.

—Drunkenness accounts for one-third of all U.S. arrests.

—One-third of all suicides are alcohol-related.

—One-half of all homicides [killings] are alcohol-related.

—On a given Friday night, one out of every 20 persons on the road would not be classified as a safe driver due to the alcoholic content in the driver's blood.

—28,400 of the 50,000 killed in traffic accidents each year had alcohol in their blood at the time of the accident. (50 percent of auto deaths are caused by drunk drivers.)

—One-third of our high school students get drunk at least once a month.

—We are producing five hundred thousand new alcoholics every year, a new crop every 12 months.

—We are producing far more alcoholics than college graduates.

Do not these figures make a case for abstinence? Social drinking is dangerous. One out of ten who take a drink will become an alcoholic. None of us can take up social drinking and be sure he will not become a problem drinker. Social drinking can easily produce alcoholic dependency. And then there is always the power of example: "What you allow in moderation, in your children will be found in excess."

The Bible has much to say on the subject of drinking. There is more Scripture on alcoholic beverages than on lying, adultery, swearing, stealing, cheating, hypocrisy, pride or even blasphemy. Note these verses:

*"Do not drink wine nor strong drink, thou, nor thy sons with thee, when ye go into the tabernacle of the congregation, lest ye die: it shall be a statute for ever throughout your generations."*—Lev. 10:9.

*"Wine is a mocker, strong drink is raging: and whosoever is deceived thereby is not wise."*—Prov. 20:1.

*"Who hath woe? who hath sorrow? who hath contentions? who hath babbling? who hath wounds without cause? who hath redness of eyes?*

*"They that tarry long at the wine; they that go to seek mixed wine.*

*"Look not thou upon the wine when it is red, when it giveth his colour in the cup, when it moveth itself aright.*

*"At the last it biteth like a serpent, and stingeth like an adder."*—Prov. 23:29-32.

*"Woe unto him that giveth his neighbour drink, that puttest thy bottle to him...."*—Hab. 2:15.

John Barleycorn has been no respecter of persons. History teaches us that a nation that has sowed national dissipation has reaped national dissolution. Toynbee has pointed out that alcohol is one of the chief agents of disintegration.

The last three hundred years of the Roman Empire were devoted to "frivolity, pleasure and dissipation." One historian, Ridpath, comments concerning Rome's closing days: "Rome was now effeminated and debauched.... And so high had risen the vices of corruption and dissipation, that the people were no longer capable of any heroic indignation on account of the vices of their sovereigns."

Charles F. Wishart has remarked: "Nineveh drank her hemlock of dissipation and was covered by the sands of the desert. Fifteen hundred years ago, Rome drowned in her wine vats. America may well heed the lessons of the past!" Voiced one: "Alcohol is poison. For a country to legalize the sale of a poison for beverage purposes is one way for it to commit suicide."

Strong drink represents the cup that damns. If no drunkard can get to Heaven (I Cor. 6:10), what about the judgment of a nation? The Prophet Isaiah sounds forth the warning:

*"Woe unto them that rise up early in the morning, that they may follow strong drink; that continue until night, till wine inflame them!*

*"... but they regard not the work of the Lord, neither consider the operation of his hands.*

*"Therefore my people are gone into captivity....*

*"Therefore hell hath enlarged herself...."*—Isa. 5:11-14.

Jesus Christ Himself declared:

*"And take heed to yourselves, lest at any time your hearts be overcharged with surfeiting* [a medical term for nausea after drunkenness], *and drunkenness...so that day come upon you unawares."*—Luke 21:34.

"America cannot be preserved in alcohol." Abraham Lincoln spoke the truth when he asserted, "The liquor traffic has defenders but no defense." It is also true that "those who fondle the serpent shall feel its fangs." An individual can literally drink himself to death—so can a nation!

## The Nightmare of Drugs

"The nurse put one hand under the tiny baby's back and lifted. The infant was stiff as a board. It was two days old and a heroin addict. He was having withdrawal symptoms. His mother was an addict and had passed the addiction to her child through her blood."

"Immediate treatment of addicted infants is difficult. Prone to diarrhea, they can die from dehydration. They constantly vomit and can strangle on their own vomit. Their lungs are weak, and they can contract pneumonia." An estimated 550 such babies were born last year in New York alone.

Senator Strom Thurmond warns:

> Today, a silent and deadly plague stalks our country striking millions of Americans—mostly our young people! This modern disease is known as drug addiction. Unknowingly, students become "hooked" because they are ignorant of the harmful effects of narcotics, and much of this confusion can be directly attributed to the publications of the New Left which loudly proclaim the glory of drug usage.

America is suffering through the nightmare of drug addiction. All stratas of society "seem to be contaminated by this gangrenous epidemic"—especially the young. Never before in the history of our nation have we been confronted with such a phenomenon. Our country has survived many social problems, but it is doubtful if she can survive such a deteriorating influence.

"Unlike their own parents or grandparents, parents with children in school face a different situation that did not exist until recent years" (Public Affairs Pamphlet No. 584, "Children and Drugs," Jules Saltman).

---

## "The liquor traffic has defenders but no defense."

*—Abraham Lincoln*

---

A former U.S. Food and Drug Administrator remarked: "More and more of us are becoming dependent on drugs, hiding from the realities of life—or using them just for thrills. Drug abuse cannot be connected only with narcotic users. The alarming rise in the abuse of stimulant, depressant and hallucinogenic drugs cuts across all strata of society." Thus a seven-year-old was "found dead from an overdose in a Harlem apartment," and thus rock stars are notorious for the same reason.

In an article entitled "Keeping Up With Youth," Pamela Swift remarks:

> Perceptive rock musicians concede that many of their ilk suffer from guilt complexes, that they know they are overpaid, that they drink and drug themselves because they refuse in many cases to face the truth— which is that their music is of little value and that many male stars

are vicarious sex substitutes for many girls.

*—Parade*

Roland H. Berg writes that "Americans hide behind a chemical curtain." Note his words:

America's reliance on drugs is unequalled in the history of mankind. We take pills to pep us up, pills to calm us down, pills to gain pounds, more pills to lose them, pills to avoid conception, other pills to help it. For many of us, life depends on drugs. But all drugs are two-edged swords, capable of saving lives or wrecking them. Today, the abuse of drugs poses a major health and social danger.

*—Look*

It has been noted that approximately 400 tons of barbiturates are manufactured in a single year in our nation. According to statistics compiled by the United States Department of Commerce, "American pharmaceutical companies manufacture enough sedatives, barbiturates and other, to provide every person with from six to eight capsules yearly. It is estimated that the combined total production of both amphetamines [uppers] and barbiturates [downers] exceeds 18 billion per year. That's enough for more than 100 pills per person."

In a short period of years America has become one of the most drug-addicted nations on earth. Tom Monte, in an article entitled, "Is America Going Crazy?" writes these words: "Drugs have become so much a way of life today that there is scarcely a medicine chest or refrigerator in the country that doesn't have some kind of mood-altering medication or beverage within" (*East West Journal*, September, 1980). Is our country going to pot? Consider:

—One out of every six people in the United States takes some type of tranquilizer.
—43,000,000 Americans have experimented with marijuana.
—10,000,000 Americans have tried cocaine.
—There are now over 500,000 heroin addicts in the United States.
—It costs about $28,000 a year to maintain the habit of a drug addict.
—There are about one hundred Americans dying every day because of adverse drug reaction.

Needless to say, God is against the drug traffic. As pointed out in the chapter on Babylon, the Antichrist will perhaps use drugs to subjugate the nations of the world. In Revelation 18:23 we read, ". . . for by thy sorceries were all nations deceived." In other words, '. . . by their enchantment with drugs were all nations deceived.'

"Can Tranquilizers Render a Whole Nation Docile?" is the question asked by John Doig in an article appearing in *Science Digest* magazine for April, 1979. Note his words:

Drugs which modify the psychological state are capable of destroying
the individual's integrity, replacing it with an illusion of freedom and opening the way to tyranny. . . .

Social acceptance of emotion-deadening drugs and consequent casual attitude toward them are the main fears of the anti-tranquilizer vanguard.
Consider the countries. . . where dictatorship has been the form of government for centuries. Could the tranquilizer become North America's coca
leaf or opium?

Paul S. Rees has made this significant statement: "The soul of a nation is
diagnosed by the pills that she swallows and from the titles of the books that
she reads." He adds, "The United States swallows more sedatives, barbiturates,
tranquilizers, and other sleeping tablets than any other nation on the face
of the earth. It is no wonder that the United States has been labeled the most
barbiturate nation in existence today."

Will America end up like the dope addict, crawling the walls and pleading
for a fix? "The wages of sin have never been reduced."

---

## A Nation of Lawbreakers

---

Ezekiel the prophet lamented the fact, ". . . for the land is full of bloody
crimes, and the city is full of violence" (Ezek. 7:23). It has been said that "the
most violent people on the earth are not the savage tribes of Africa. . . no other
nation on earth has a worse record than the United States for certain types
of crimes. There are more killings in Houston, Texas, than in all England.
Some of our larger cities have more crime than many European countries."

The late Noel Smith reported: "Washington, D.C., is one of the most crime-
ridden, dope-ridden, drunken, immoral places on the face of the earth. Murder,
rape and robbery in the shadows of the White House and Department of Justice
are as common and as much taken for granted as tourists" (*Baptist Bible
Tribune*).

A United States Congressman commented: "Safety in our nation's capital
continues to deteriorate so rapidly that it may soon be necessary to assign an
armed guard to every female employee so she can go to the powder room
without being assaulted."

American cities are unsafe. In the book of Lamentations 5:3 we read, "Our
inheritance is turned to strangers, our houses to aliens." A Gallup poll indicates
"that one city-dweller in three has been mugged, robbed, or suffered property
loss. . . nearly half the population is afraid to walk alone at night in
neighborhoods, and one person in six does not feel safe at night even in his
own home."

*U.S. News and World Report* for October 1980 carried an article entitled

"Fear Stalks the Streets." Note these opening paragraphs:

> Serious crime—on the rise again—is casting a pall of fear over the lives of millions of Americans, not only in the nation's biggest cities but in the suburbs as well.
>
> Signs of the alarm that is gripping the public are everywhere—from the sight of citizens on neighborhood anti-crime patrols, to elderly persons whose fear has made them virtual prisoners in their own homes, to women who are packing police whistles and canisters of chemical repellent in their purses.

The same article revealed that

> America is fast becoming a nation living behind dead-bolt locks—with a gun tucked away in a closet.
>
> Four out of every ten Americans feel that they are vulnerable to murder, rape, robbery or assault in their everyday environment....
>
> Today, America is in the ever-tightening grip of fear—fear of criminal victimization, of physical harm and property loss. Americans today have become afraid of one another.

Chapter 1 of the book, *The Law Breakers*, by M. Stanton Evans and Margaret Moore is entitled "We Never Had It So Scared."[4] Alas, how true.

Many of our cities have become veritable jungles. "The fear of crime is so pervasive that it has caused some 40 million Americans to alter their behavior" (Martha Hewson). Crime has increased 50% in the last ten years. In one year in the United States:

A serious crime occurred every 2.6 seconds.

A theft occurred every 4.8 seconds.

A burglary occurred every 10 seconds.

A violent crime occurred every 27 seconds.

A car or truck theft occurred every 29 seconds.

An assault occurred every 51 seconds.

A robbery occurred every 68 seconds.

A forcible rape occurred every 7 minutes.

A murder occurred every 24 minutes.

—Federal Bureau of Investigation

Organized crime is America's biggest business. Crime does pay. "The annual 'take' from crime of all kinds is over $100 billion....Crime is very big business in the United States, currently employing an estimated 500,000 'career criminals.' "[5]

Americans spend more for horse racing than bread. "An overwhelming majority of Americans (more than 80% regard gambling as an acceptable activity." Gambling fever is an increasing calamity on the American scene.

"Atlantic City once lived on golden sun and silver surf. Today it thrives on a new tide: Money—$3,000 a minute, $108,000 an hour, $3,600,000 a day. That is the rate at which cash flows through the six gambling casinos that have opened since 1978" (*U.S. News and World Report*, "Atlantic City's Struggle Against the Mafia," April 13, 1981).

Criminologists are in search as to the source of crime. It extends to all areas of society. For instance, shoplifting has reached epidemic proportions in our country, the cost of stolen goods reaching the billions.

Poverty alone is not the source of crime, for elderly and retired people in dire need seldom resort to illegal activities. The source of crime goes much deeper. Juvenile crime has increased by leaps and bounds, and record number of offenses is being committed at a younger age. Drug addicts resort to criminal activities in order to satisfy their desperate habits. Booze has been called the mother of crime. Today's courts are to be blamed, where crime is explained away rather than punished.

The depravity of man is the source of crime. Change the heart of the man (or youth), and society will not suffer the ravages of crime. Jeremiah asked the question, "Can the Ethiopian change his skin, or the leopard his spots? then may ye also do good, that are accustomed to do evil" (Jer. 13:23). Jesus Christ Himself said, "The things which are impossible with men are possible with God" (Luke 18:27). The Apostle Paul stated a great truth when he declared, "Therefore if any man be in Christ, he is a new creature: old things are passed away; behold, all things are become new" (II Cor. 5:17). Christ can change the lawless.

Someone has asked, "Will crime completely inundate America?" The reply was, "I can't say for sure, but the way things are going now, the floodwaters are building up steadily, and I wonder if there's enough 'righteousness in the land' to reinforce the levies." The rate of crime is increasing faster than our population growth.

Can our nation survive? Juvenile delinquency has been said to be "the ultimate key to America's crime problem." In plain English, it is better to teach them in the high chair than at the electric chair.

The Prophet Amos exclaimed, "For they know not to do right, saith the Lord, who store up violence and robbery in their palaces" (Amos 3:10). Over a hundred years ago a clergyman by the name of William Arnot penned these words:

> Considering our privileges and attainments, I suspect that there is more to make an apostle shudder in Edinburgh and London than there was in Athens and in Rome. Oh, it is pitiful, that nearly a whole cityful of comfortable Christianized inhabitants, so many wretches in human form, should be permitted to torment and destroy themselves and one another by open, organized, wholesale vice and crime.[6]

The prevalence of crime in our country is a symptom of a deadly disease. In the book, *The Law Breakers,* the authors write these discerning words:

> Crime, like pain, has some unpleasant but necessary uses. It is a warning signal which tells us that an organism is diseased or wounded, and that its existence is in some way placed in danger. Physical pain intensifies when the individual life is threatened. Crime intensifies when the community is threatened. In either case, we ignore the symptoms at our peril.[7]

The Prophet Jeremiah cried out, "It is of the Lord's mercies that we are not consumed, because his compassions fail not" (Lam. 3:22). "Today's moral breakdown is at least partially caused by a loss of confidence in the justice of God" (Veulah Dague). Aristotle reminds us: "A country is only as strong as each man in it and its civilization only as great as its dreams." Abraham Lincoln gave this assertion: "I believe in God, the Almighty and Ruler of nations. I believe His eternal truth and justice. I recognize the sublime truth announced in the Holy Scriptures and proven in all history, that those nations only are blessed whose God is the Lord."

---

## Poverty alone is not the source of crime, for elderly and retired people in dire need seldom resort to illegal activities.

---

It is harvesttime in America today. The law of compensation is about to take place. "Shall I not visit them for these things? saith the Lord: shall not my soul be avenged on such a nation as this?" (Jer. 9:9).

In his booklet, *1776-1976, Reflections on America's Past and Future,* Harry Vant Kerkoff remarks that "the basic reason for the crisis facing America today is that we have allowed the foundation upon which our country was built to crumble. We have turned our back upon God and His Word. We have rejected His authority and gone our way."

Crime is but a portent of the coming Tribulation Period when lawlessness shall prevail on the face of the earth. The coming Antichrist will be the personification of lawlessness. "And then shall that Wicked [lawless one] be revealed, whom the Lord shall consume with the spirit of his mouth, and shall destroy with the brightness of his coming" (II Thess. 2:8).

Will Isaiah's prophecy be fulfilled in America—"Your country is desolate,

your cities are burned with fire..." (Isa. 1:7)?
What a tragic way to commit suicide!

## Strangers Devour Your Country

*"... Your land, strangers devour it in your presence, and it is desolate, as overthrown by strangers."*—Isa. 1:7.

America has become a mecca for strange voices. With the breakdown of biblical foundations, evil forces have been let loose in our nation. These voices are based on the reasonings of finite man rather than the dictates of the infinite God. It would be well to heed the warning of Lord Macauley who predicted more than one hundred years ago that our institutions would bring about the downfall of the United States of America.

Our republic has always been interested in the instruction of children and youth. Kate Caffrey writes concerning the early Pilgrims on the *Mayflower*:

> Inevitably they took books, principally, of course, the Bible, English, Dutch and possibly French, and Latin New Testaments. Psalm books...doctrinal tracts...and Bible stories for children, for even then education bulked large in their plans for the future....[8]

It is common knowledge that the early colleges and universities in America taught the precepts of the Bible. David Norris states:

> Education is a beautiful word. It comes from the Latin *educaare,* which means to use up, to take the lowest degrees to the highest spheres of knowledge. America's founding fathers were unwavering advocates of unique and educationally demonstrable principles for man and government. Without them, liberty would have been impossible.[9]

Someone calculated that, "to prepare for lifetime, the public schools instruct over a ten-year period of a child's life 12,000 hours." Teachers help to mold the thinking of our generation.

Walter Lippman declared:

> Professors have become in the modern world the best available source of guidance and authority in the field of knowledge....
> There is no other court to which men can turn and find what they once found in tradition and custom. Because modern man in his search for truth has turned away from kings, priests, commissars and bureaucrats, he is left, for better or worse, with the professor.

The survival of America may depend upon what is being taught in the classroom. One publisher is reported to have said, "Let me publish the textbooks of nations, and I care not who writes its songs or makes its laws"

("Secular Humanism," Homer Duncan, p. 40). An educator declared, "Universities are turning out highly skilled barbarians." U.S. Senator Jesse Helms made this observation:

> It has always dismayed—if not surprised—me to note that the most insidious assaults on our economy have occurred, not in the marketplace, but in the classrooms of colleges and universities. Today we have a generation prepared in effect to repudiate its heritage.[10]

It is reported that the magnificent Parthenon on the Acropolis in Athens is threatened by planes overhead, traffic and "sulfuric acid fumes." The Parthenon was the epitome of learning and culture. What is happening to this beautiful edifice is threatening the educational system of America. As a nation we are permitting our educators to ruin our children.

Note these words by John Q. Citizen:

> What in heaven's name are our kids being taught? I'll tell you what they're being taught. They are being taught that America is a cruel, oppressive country. They are being taught that police brutality is the rule rather than the exception. They are being taught that "hypocrisy" and "middle-class" are synonymous terms. They are being taught that American culture has nothing worth saving and must be destroyed. They are being taught that they have a "right" to break laws. They are being taught "Situation Ethics"—that the degree of honesty and morality to be exercised depends upon the situation.
>
> Isn't it conceivable that some kids turn to drugs to escape from the conflict between the morality they learn at home and what they are being taught in school?[11]

Our children and youth derive their sets of values from their teachers and the textbooks they study. Roy R. Friday has written a pamphlet entitled *My Weekly Brainwash*. Note the opening paragraph:

> Your child is being handed his weekly or biweekly brainwash when he gets his little current events paper in school. For the past two decades I have been watching this insidious propaganda take its toll. In the schools these current events papers are planting the seedlings of socialism, are eating away the foundations of our Constitutional Republic like termites. They are selling our heritage, our children, and our future as a great republic right down the river.

The communists are out to capture the youth of America. What better way than to infiltrate our educational system? Dr. Fred Schwarz, noted authority on communism, states:

"Every time we graduate from high school or college a student who believes: 1) there is no God; 2) human beings are material machines, mere evolutionary animals; and 3) that all human and intellectual and emotional qualities are derived from the environment, we graduate a potential communist recruit" (Christian Anti-Communism Crusade).

Do you realize that "Chou En Lai, Premier of China, went to Paris for his education and was converted to communism? The personal secretary of Chou En Lai was trained at Harvard University; Chu Teh, Commander-in-Chief of the army of Red China, was turned to communism during his Berlin studies. Gunawardens, a government leader of Ceylon, was won to communism at a university in the United States.... According to *Who's Who,* half the top leaders in Red China were educated in the U.S. The universities are proving to be the broadest gateways to our religious and national perdition."

Experts have been defined by Nicholas Murray Butler as people "who know more and more about less and less." Or as someone else has put it, "It ain't so much from not knowin' as it is from knowin' so much that ain't so." That is the case with evolution. In elementary school, high school, colleges and universities, the theory of evolution is taught as a fact of science. According to this theory, "All living forms in the world have arisen from a single source which came from an inorganic form." According to Darwin, man is nothing more than a higher type of an animal. If this is true, Judge Braswell Deen, Jr.'s, remark is appropriate: "If you teach long enough that students are animals, it should be no surprise that they act like animals."

A choice must be made between evolution and the teaching of the Bible. According to Richard B. Bliss, "Evolution... undermines the biblical doctrine of man, the doctrines of the Fall and of original sin, the biblical explanation of death and of sin, and the biblical doctrine of vicarious atonement." In other words, evolution and the Bible are basically incompatible.

John Dewey and his teachings have been a curse to our nation. Tim LaHaye writes, "John Dewey, the most educated of the twentieth century, did more for the humanist takeover of American education than anyone else."[12] LaHaye also makes these significant remarks:

> The only subject upon which I am in agreement with humanists is that "John Dewey was the most influential educator of the twentieth century." He was truly the great high priest of twentieth-century humanism. He and his disciples have taken over the public schools and turned our tax-supported religious shrines that waste the potential of our young.[13]

Wilbur M. Smith gives this evaluation: "The imprint of Dewey's thought is on all our normal schools. It shapes the lives of millions of school children here and overseas, though they may never hear his name."[14]

Dewey was the father of "progressive education." What are the teachings of this influential man? John A. Stormer writes in his book:

What did Dewey believe? In his writings and teaching, Dewey rejected fixed moral laws and eternal truths and principles. He adopted pragmatic, relativistic concepts as his guiding philosophy. Denying God, he held to the Marxist concept that man is without a soul or free will. Man is a biological organism completely molded by his environment. Dewey believed that because man's environment is constantly changing, man also changes constantly. Therefore, Dewey concluded, teaching children any of the absolutes of morals, government, or ethics was a waste of time.[15]

Dewey also taught that "man, because he is man, is forever in quest of certainty, though destined never to find it." In other words, in our permissive society, there are no absolutes. "Children are taught to determine their own values. The theory of educators is that an autocratic teacher who gives right or wrong absolutes will have no success guiding children to formulate their own values."

Much has been written about humanism. What is it all about? Paul Kurtz has edited a book, *The Humanist Alternative: Some Definitions of Humanism.* In the Preface he writes these words:

> The present century has been proclaimed as the humanist century—the century in which anti-humanist illusions inherited from previous ages have been seriously questioned and shattered. Humanism has historic roots in human civilization; yet it is only in recent times that these have begun to bear fruit.[16]

The *Encyclopedia Brittanica* gives this definition: "the attitude of mind which attaches primary importance to man and human values.... Philosophically humanism made man the measure of all things." Fulton Sheen defined it as "the glorification of a man who makes God to his own image and likeness." Tim LaHaye states: "Simply defined, humanism is man's attempt to solve his problems independently of God." In other words, man is deified, and God is humanized.

Where did this malicious doctrine originate? Students of the Scriptures know the answer—in the Garden of Eden. The Devil asked the question, "Yea, hath God said?" The point is, he placed a question mark when God placed a period, and the humanists have been doing it ever since.

"The secular humanists trace their heritage to classical philosophy, the worldly focus of the Enlightenment of the 17th and 18th centuries, and the emergence of the scientific method. Among those who are said to stand in this tradition are Lucretius, Spinoza, Darwin and Einstein." Albert Schweitzer declared, "Humanism in all its simplicity is the only genuine spirituality."

The influence of humanism is enormous. Tim LaHaye remarks: "Most of the evils of the world today can be traced to humanism, which has taken over the government, the U.N., education, TV, and most of the other influential things of life."[17]

It is common knowledge that "humanism works for the establishment of a 'secular society,' a 'socialized order,' world government, military disarmament, and population control by government."

Edward Gibbon was of the persuasion that "[man] can emancipate himself through reason." Kurtz explains the position of humanism:

> If there is a common thread running through this volume, it is the conviction that humanism is committed to the method of reason as the chief means of solving problems and the belief that mankind can survive and humans can enjoy a significant life. This conviction and this belief, however, can be realized only if men continue to have confidence in their own powers and abilities and the courage to use them.[18]

Reason thus demands that God had no part in the creation of the universe; the human race as we know it today evolved over a long period of time; man is an animal with no spiritual nature; man is his own saviour.

Humanism has been called "the most dangerous religion in America." Paul J. Toscano maintains that secular humanism is a religion. Note his words: "It is the egocentric doctrine that morality should be based solely upon man's regard for his own well-being in this present life to the exclusion of all considerations drawn from belief in God, a future state or of a supernatural order."

Humanism is a religion without a Creator, a supernatural theology or morality. Marvin Zimmerman has written a chapter in the book, *The Humanist Alternative,* entitled "Aren't Humanists Really Atheists?" Note his words:

> Nonetheless many humanists disdain use of the term atheist, though their intellectual convictions about God are identical with, and constitute the very foundations of, the convictions of those who call themselves atheists. They have repudiated the belief in a perfect, omnipotent and benevolent creator who performs miracles, responds to prayer and proclaims a fundamental set of eternal moral principles.
>
> There is more than enough wretchedness in the world to justify overwhelmingly the tenet that if there was a deity, he would be either a devil or insane and this view is completely incompatible with any variety of theism that entails the existence of a benevolent and omnipotent God, however limited His characteristics.[19]

Most citizens of our country are totally unaware of the dangers of this doctrine. Dr. W. P. Shofstall has written: "The greatest heresy of all is the confusion between humanism and theism. Here the Devil is most diabolical. If you say to most well-meaning people, 'I am a humanist,' they will without exception say, 'Isn't that beautiful!' "

Humanism is not "beautiful." It is a deadly virus that will bring about the downfall of our nation. Our children in our schools should be inoculated against this deadly disease.

Wilbur M. Smith commented concerning the initial "Humanist Manifesto" (1933): "I do not know of any two-page document in the whole history of American thought that there is such a revelation of amazing apostasy from the faith by men of some importance than a declaration called 'A Humanist Manifesto'"....[20]

Humanism is an adherent of situation ethics (in other words, relativism, no absolutes, no right or wrong). Such a view leads eventually to the collapse of morality.

> When value is annihilated and the standards of unbelief pulled down, why should it surprise us if people begin acting as if there were no such thing as right conduct? When we are instructed by highest authority that everything is relative, why shouldn't we expect augmented crime and a breakdown of morality?[21]

Luther said to Erasmus, "Your thoughts of God are too human." The radicals declare, "God is dead; man is God." Thus the Almighty is removed from the scene, and there remains no standard for moral values. All becomes relevant. It is thus that degeneration in a nation takes place. Mel Gablers makes this observation:

> Between the "old" morality of fixed values and "self-fulfillment," there is the chasm of "self-indulgence"—a mere descent to mere animal gratification. How many immature students can bridge the gap without falling into the chasm, while being taught permissiveness in place of traditional fixed values?

J. Edgar Hoover made this significant statement: "Communism, it is alleged, is not barbarism, but, as originally conceived by Marx, humanism." Homer Duncan, on page 19 of his publication, *Secular Humanism,* gives this contrast:

> Humanism and communism are not identical twins, but they are good bedfellows. A comparison of the Communist Manifesto with Humanist Manifestos I and II reveals that their aims are almost identical. Communism is humanism in political disguise.
> Both deny the supernatural.
> Both deny the Divine revelation.
> Both seek to control the educational system.
> Both seek to destroy all religions, except their own.
> Both promote world government.
> Both seek the alliance of apostate Christendom....

Claude Lanzman, a Marxist, remarks: "There is no end for man higher than

man himself. Man is his own beginning and end, his own Alpha and Omega."
Exit Deity!

The typical humanist attitude is expressed in the creed from the British
Humanist Association:

> I believe in no god and no hereafter. It is immoral to indoctrinate children
> with such beliefs. Schools have no right to do so, nor indeed, have parents.
>
> I believe the religious education and prayers in school should be
> abolished. . . . I believe that children should be taught religion as a mat-
> ter of historical interest, but should be taught about all religions, including
> Humanism, Marxism, Maoism, Communism, and other attitudes of life.
> They must be taught the objections to religion. I believe in a non-religious
> social morality. . . .
>
> Unborn babies are not people. I am as yet unsure whether the grossly
> handicapped are people in the real sense. . . .
>
> I believe there is no such thing as sin to be forgiven and no life beyond
> the grave but death everlasting.
> —*Herald of Freedom,* September 19, 1980

Humanism needs to be exposed for what it is—a fake philosophy from Satan
himself. It ignores the precepts of the Bible, and hence its doctrines are built
on sinking sand. And to think that humanism is the basic philosophy of some
of the leaders of our nation; that it controls the news media, television and
public education. The tragedy is that the liberal churches in America today
have come under its sway.

The criterion of truth is the Word of God. What do the Scriptures say?

*"Beware lest any man spoil you through philosophy and vain deceit, after the
tradition of men, after the rudiments of the world, and not after Christ."*—Col.
2:8.

*"Woe unto them that are wise in their own eyes, and prudent in their own
sight!"*—Isa. 5:21.

*"The wise men are ashamed, they are dismayed and taken: lo, they have re-
jected the word of the Lord; and what wisdom is in them?"*—Jer. 8:9.

The Apostle Paul told the church at Corinth:

*"For it is written, I will destroy the wisdom of the wise, and will bring to
nothing the understanding of the prudent."*—I Cor. 1:19.

*"For the wisdom of this world is foolishness with God. . . .
"Therefore let no man glory in men. . . ."*—I Cor. 3:19,21.

*"O Timothy, keep that which is committed to thy trust, avoiding profane and
vain babblings, and oppositions of science falsely so called:*

*"Which some professing have erred concerning the faith. . . . "*— I Tim. 6:20,21.

Christ Himself warned:

*"Get thee behind me, Satan: for thou savourest not the things that be of God, but the things that be of men."*—Mark 8:33.

*". . . for ye have taken away the key of knowledge: ye entered not in yourselves, and them that were entering in ye hindered."*—Luke 11:52.

Kicking God out of the schools in America was a national tragedy. The Prophet Zephaniah declared, "And I will bring distress upon men, that they shall walk like blind men, because they have sinned against the Lord. . ." (Zeph. 1:17). Without the light of the Bible and prayer, we "walk like blind men"; and, "If the blind lead the blind, both shall fall into the ditch" (Matt. 15:14). A nation needs divine direction.

"To attempt to make man whole again without a blueprint of the whole man and his needs is like driving in a strange city without a map: you soon get lost," remarked James P. Mallory, Jr., and Mark P. Cosgrove.

Robert S. Marlowe of the Council for Educational Freedom in America said "that leaving Christ out of the educational structure is like insisting that students learn about evolution without studying Darwin, science without Galileo, music without Beethoven, literature without Shakespeare." He also added: "Our youngsters can study Plato, Kant, Hitler, Mao, Marx and Keynes, but Christ is a no-no."

---

## Humanism needs to be exposed for what it is—a fake philosophy from Satan himself.

---

A university president admitted that the knowledge explosion hasn't helped us solve our problems. He remarked:

> It is painfully obvious that, despite our new knowledge and all the experts we have prepared, we have not yet solved the complex problems of society. The sad truth of the knowledge explosion is that it has taught us more about the individual parts of society and greatly obscured the total view.

Isaiah declared, "Thy wisdom and thy knowledge, it hath perverted thee" (Isa. 47:10). Christopher Lasch reveals: "In the humanities, demoralization has reached the point of a general admission that humanistic study has nothing to contribute to an understanding of the modern world."[22]

Dr. Edward Bloustein quipped: "Administering a college today is like playing chess on the open deck of the sinking *Titanic*." A religious leader has said that "our youth can pass through our schools with hardly a glimpse of the great heritage of ethical convictions and of. . .religious faiths that have made possible whatever is decent and hopeful in our western culture. As one university graduate summed up the result—'They gave us the spokes, but no hub.' "

William Lyon Phelps once said: "I thoroughly believe in a university education for both men and women; but I believe a knowledge of the Bible without a college course is more valuable than a college course without a knowledge of the Bible."

It has been stated: "All education that is not God- and Christ-centered is the wrong kind of education. Education without the recognition of God makes fools of men; and the more of such education they get, the greater fools they become."

"Education without God produces a nation without freedom," someone said. Theodore Roosevelt spoke words of wisdom when he gave this advice: "To educate a mind in mind and not morals is to educate a menace to society."

When Robert Ingersoll died, the printed notice of his funeral said, "There will be no singing." Infidels have no song in this life or hope in the life to come. In his book, Corliss Lamont explains the humanist view of death: "The Humanist view, stemming from some of the greatest thinkers in history, rejects the idea of personal immortality and death as the final end of the individual conscious personality."[23]

Memory is the only immortality of a humanist believer. No hope beyond the grave! The Apostle Paul affirmed:

*"And if Christ be not raised, your faith is vain; ye are yet in your sins.*
*"Then they also which are fallen asleep in Christ are perished.*
*"If in this life only we have hope in Christ, we are of all men most miserable.*
[margin—'pitiable']"—I Cor. 15:17-19.

The fallacy of humanism and modern education is that it fails to recognize the total depravity of man. "Human nature remains always the same." Man cannot lift himself by his own bootstraps; a higher power is needed. The basic problem is the heart of man; and until that problem is taken care of, all else is secondary. The Pilgrims believed this, and that is why they sought for their children "the glory of the lighted mind." Thus the prominence of the Bible in their instruction.

Thomas Arnold defined *education* as follows: "First, religious and moral principles; secondly, gentlemanly conduct; thirdly, intellectual ability." Russel

Stolp has wisely declared: "Intellectuality without spirituality results in carnality." It might be added that education without God results in chaos.

Christian instruction must first begin in the home. Reverence for authority and moral principles must be taught from infancy on to adolescence. The Bible is the basis for teaching Christian precepts. Next in order is the school. Sidney Smith states the purpose of education: "To give children resources that will endure as long as life endures." But that is not far enough. Man possesses a spiritual nature that goes beyond this life. Here is where Christian schools come in. Children are taught how to live for time and prepare for eternity. Moral values and respect for law and order are taught. Philip M. Crane remarks: " 'Discipline' and 'disciple' have the same root. You can't have one without the other." Christ-centered education is the answer to humanism and modern education.

> **Mock on, mock on; Voltaire, Rousseau;**
> **Mock on, mock on; 'tis all in vain!**
> **You throw the wind against the wind,**
> **And the wind blows it back again.**
> —William Blake

God's truth will prevail but only if it is believed and practiced. America is in danger of committing suicide because of what is being taught in the secular school. B. C. Forbes asserts: "Upon our children—how they are taught—rests the fate of tomorrow's children."

Have we given thought to "tomorrow's children"? Will there be a tomorrow? Noting the utter failure of humanism to provide a solution to a nation's problems, Harold O. J. Brown believes we have been weakened to such a point that the long-term survival of the United States as an independent, sovereign nation is now in question. Merton B. Osborn warns: "Humanism is destined to destroy mankind by the complete dehumanization of society unless we awake to the danger and apply ourselves to the task of reconstruction."

Can a nation survive when the Almighty is ruled out of its courts of learning? Christ declared, ". . . that which is highly esteemed among men is abomination in the sight of God" (Luke 16:15). Earl G. Hunt, Jr., made this statement: ". . . I seriously question whether this nation or Western civilization itself can hope to survive the years just ahead unless education recovers its sense of the sacred" ("Toward a Holiness Beyond the Obvious," *Christianity Today,* February 8, 1980).

The Son of God, while on earth, said, "Man shall not live by bread alone, but by every word that proceedeth out of the mouth of God" (Matt. 4:4). But if that "word" is rejected, what chance does a nation have for survival?

Will the halls of ivy strangle us?

## The Bear and the Eagle

Our generation is witnessing the gigantic spectacle of the bear and the eagle, the bear representing totalitarian *communism* and the eagle glorious liberty. Will our land become "desolate" because we are overthrown by "strangers" (Isa. 1:7)? Communism is the antithesis of Americanism. It is a stranger. The opening sentence of *The Communist Manifesto* reads: "A spectre is haunting Europe—the spectre of communism." That spectre has become a global nightmare, including the United States of America. "What history will think of our times is something that only history will reveal. But, it is a good guess that it will select collectivism as the identifying characteristic of the twentieth century" (Frank Chodorov).

Nikita Kruschev, when Premier of his country, made these significant statements:

> We are the young and aggressive, and you are the decadent civilization. We will wipe the memory of capitalism from the face of the earth!...I can prophesy that your grandchildren in America will live under socialism....The United States will eventually fly the Communist Red Flag...the American people will hoist it themselves.

A naive pastor in Pennsylvania asked his congregation on a Sunday morning, "If the Red Flag flew over our town square, would that be such a calamity?"

"The pendulum of public opinion has swung from the excesses of McCarthyism to no threat at all." Arthur Blumberg remarked:

> By the 1970s the anti-communist hysteria that had gripped the country for generations had pretty much burned itself out and probably could be resurrected only by a major international confrontation with the Soviet Union. Not since the Russian Revolution had America been so unconcerned with the "threat" of domestic communism and so willing to grant communists, socialists, and other radicals their Constitutional rights.[24]

Some liberals in America would absolve communism of any of our woes. Franklin Delano Roosevelt did much to foster the idea that "the communists are men of sincerity, that they are our friends and of no danger to our country."

Back in 1968, Harvey Cox of *The Secular City* fame wrote an article which appeared in *McCall's* magazine entitled "Are We Having a Nervous Breakdown?" In that article he states: "Our paranoid belief that we are somehow still locked in a life-and-death struggle with an organized worldwide conspiracy has become terrible dangerous not just for us but for the whole world....Communism is no longer grimly and tenaciously anti-religious ....The real threat to our well-being is not communism but world poverty."

According to such a view, we are not to oppose those of the Marxist view, but collaborate with them in co-existence. Some seem to have a "blind spot" concerning the Soviet Union. William Randolph Hearst, Jr., in an article entitled "A Peculiar Blindness," gives the other side of the story:

> I say it is just plain foolish when Americans blind their eyes to reality and even go so far as to contend that anti-communism is a "relic" of a now-defunct "cold war."
>
> The cold and often hot war between communism and freedom will never be over so long as communism exists.
>
> The next time somebody tells you that communism is nothing to worry about, you can be sure of one of two things.
>
> Either he hasn't got all his marbles or he is quite far left of center politically and ideologically.
>
> One thing is for sure if he honestly believes that life in some communist state is better, more humane and fairer—he is certainly free to go there.
>
> I, for one, wish he and all of his ilk would go and stay.
>
> —*Hearst Reprint*

Anti-communists have fallen into disrepute these days. Some Christian leaders contend that, since the communists ultimately will be defeated according to Scripture, why manifest such a concern over them? They have much to say for their viewpoint. However, we must be realists. Madame Chiang Kai-shek declared: "I would rather die fighting communism than to live under it." Fred Schwarz, of the Christian Anti-Communism Crusade, declares: "There are diseases which are painful but which do not threaten life; there are others so deadly that there is no alternative but to defeat them or die. Communism is in this latter category. Communism is a disease because it has destroyed the health and life of uncounted millions" (Letter, October 15, 1980).

Whether you know it or not, freedom has become a very fragile commodity in this world, particularly in the United States. Alexander I. Solzhenitsyn in a speech put it this way:

> It can happen. It is possible. As a Russian proverb says: "When it happens to you, you'll know it's true."
>
> But do we really have to wait for the moment when the knife is at our throats? Couldn't it be possible, ahead of time, soberly to assess the worldwide menace that threatens to swallow the whole world? I was swallowed myself. I have been in the dragon's belly, in the red burning belly of the dragon. He wasn't able to digest me. He threw me up. I have come to you as a witness to what it's like there, in the dragon's belly.

It has been said that first we are kids, then we kid ourselves. We should be careful not to kid ourselves about the deadly threat of communism. The stakes are too high.

Remember the story about the little boy who cried "wolf"? He would go into the hills to play; and he soon discovered that he could scream and cry "wolf" and all the townspeople would rush to his aid, believing, of course, that a wolf was after the little boy—only to find there wasn't any wolf at all. The little boy got a big kick out of seeing all those people running to help him.

After having done this a considerable number of times, one day the little boy went into the hills again to play, only this time a real wolf was after him. He screamed and cried "wolf" again, but not one single person paid any attention to him. They thought he was up to his old tricks again, and they completely ignored him.

The followers of Lenin consider human life cheap; for man, after all, is but a higher type of an animal. Lenin himself remarked: "What would it matter if two-thirds of this earth were destroyed if one-third remains communist?" Joseph Stalin showed his utter contempt for human life when he asserted: "The death of one man is a tragedy; the death of a million is a statistic." What a horrible wreckage of mankind suffering and heartache for the victims of red communism!

> None knows their exact number, except God, and attempts to arrive at a figure for them are fated to be no better than informed estimates. One thing we do know: the total number of the dead is an awesome and awful number. It is probable that more than 100 million souls have been dispatched by purges, murders, intolerable conditions of imprisonment and labor, famine, in transit to prisons, civil war, and such like. Numbers, however, are but abstractions; they can convey but little of the anguish, heartbreak, disorientation, fear, and misery that have surrounded all this.
> —*Notes From Fee*, March 1980.

J. Edgar Hoover (whose name is in the process of being discredited) gave this evaluation:

> We are face to face with a tyranny more monstrous, more devious, less understood and more deadly than any which has threatened civilization heretofore. . . . They [the communists] have infiltrated every conceivable sphere of activity: youth groups; radio, television, and motion picture industries; school, educational and cultural groups; the press; national minority groups and civil and political units.

Their numbers may be insignificant; it is not how many they are but where they are. The Reds are masters at propaganda. Eugene Lyons remarks: "Whatever else the Kremlin may or may not have accomplished, everyone agrees that it has perfected a global propaganda machine without precedent for size and penetrative power."[25] Since morality has no part in the thinking of the communists, their propaganda is not to be believed. They are notorious liars. "The world by now has received ample proof that nothing emanating from a Red source can be believed. The ideology of the Communist Party—by teaching that truth is what conforms to its changing political line and that good is what helps the party—excuses any lie, atrocity, or aggression so long as it is pro-Red in intent."[26]

Communism has been called a "substitute for religion." David Benson defines it thus: "Communism is a religion, if by religion we mean a collective cult which excites the adoration and motivates the actions of a people." Arnold Toynbee gives this definition: "The worship of the collective power of man in place of the worship of God." This is pure humanism. Henry M. Morris writes:

> The real nature of communism can be understood only by recognizing it as a powerful religious system. Its god is evolution, which has supposedly originated and developed all things into their present forms. Its heaven is the future utopian state of perfect communism at the end of history. Its prophets are Marx, Lenin, Mao, and others of like kind, and its sacred Scriptures are their writings. Its devil is Christian civilization, destined for final destruction in the fires of global revolution. Its local church is the commune, or in non-converted cultures, the underground cell.[27]

If there is no God, then there is no morality or spiritual values. It follows there is therefore no respect for freedom or law and order. "Communism denies the dignity of the individual, his transcendence before the collectivity. The person has no private, human rights; he is merely a cog on a wheel serving the machine of the collectivity." Joseph Stalin was guilty of killing millions of fellow Russians in the name of collectivism. It is well known that Karl Marx preached hate—"the reckless criticism of all that exists." Anatole Lunacharsky is vehement in his denunciation of Christianity:

> We hate Christianity and Christians; even the best of them must be regarded as our worst enemies. They preach love of one's neighbor and mercy, which is contrary to our principles.
>
> Christian love is an obstacle to the development of the revolution. Down with love of one's neighbors. What is needed is hatred. . . . Only thus shall we conquer the universe.[28]

Disarmament is not the answer. The only thing the Soviets understand is "brute strength." Our nation can only survive if we are adequately secure. The Reds talk peace and prepare for war. Gangsters cannot be trusted with their treaties. Lenin himself declared, "Peace treaties are like pie crusts, made to be broken." Joseph Stalin remarked, "Sincere diplomacy is no more possible than dry water or iron wood."

It is to be remembered—"The bee that hath honey in her mouth hath a sting in her tail." J. Kesner Kahn has put it this way: "The communists don't want racial peace in the United States; they want the United States. The communists don't want peace in the world; they want the world. The only place the communists want peace is in their captive nations."

It is a sad fact that we have helped to make communism succeed. Without our provisions of food and technological aid and financial assistance, the Soviet experiment would have proven an utter failure. Lenin said that communism would be built by its enemies. Sun Tzu boasted: "The supreme excellence is not to win a hundred victories in a hundred battles. The supreme excellence is to subdue the armies of your enemies without even having to fight them." Back in 1919 Lenin remarked that the Bolsheviks would "hang the bourgeoisie." One of his associates replied, "But, Comrade Lenin, there is not enough rope." "Don't worry," answered Lenin, "they will sell it to us."

A high ranking government official has stated, "The danger facing the West is that the Western world could find itself confronted with a choice between surrender or suicide." The late General Douglas MacArthur gave these words of wisdom:

> The history in war can be summed up in two words: too late. Too late in comprehending the deadly purpose of a potential enemy; too late in realizing the mortal danger; too late in preparedness; too late in uniting all possible forces for resistance; too late in standing with one's friends.[29]

Perhaps the admonition of a patriot in the early days of America should be heeded—"Pray and keep your powder dry!"

The stakes are high—for being Red is like being dead. Life under a communist dictator is intolerable and unthinkable. We have never had it so good when we consider the plight of those behind the Iron Curtain. America has nothing to hide; all is open for the inspection of the world. Someone has quipped, "If the Russians were really proud of their communist experiment, instead of an Iron Curtain, they would put in a Plate Glass Window." America has more to offer to the world.

> With all the shortcomings and errors of our government, we still have the finest country, the best form of government, the richest and most prosperous nation in the world. You students and other persons who are trying to destroy our government should get down on your knees each day and thank the Lord that you live in the United States. To exchange our form of government for communism would be sheer madness. If men will jump into the ocean to escape communism, you know it must be bad.
> —Lt. General Sumter L. Lowry

The answer to the problem of communism is not socialism. A communist speaker, addressing a university audience, declared: "And when socialism comes onto the agenda, I am convinced that the majority of you in this hall tonight will not only be for it but will be advocating it—and helping it work."[30] Socialism is the next step to communism. As Tom Anderson has put it simply, "Socialism is communism without the firing squad."

The closing sentences of *The Communist Manifesto* are significant: "Let the ruling classes tremble at a communist revolution. The proletarians have nothing to lose but their chains. They have a world to win. . . ."

But no political theory has brought more victims into chains. Talk about liberation—there is nothing more liberating than the message of Jesus Christ: "If the Son therefore shall make you free, ye shall be free indeed" (John 8:36). We too have "a world to win" in obedience to the Great Commission (Matt. 28:18-20).

In Solzhenitsyn's Harvard address, he declared that "neither diplomacy nor military strength could abolish the danger posed by the Soviet Union, and that only a reinvigoration of moral and spiritual character would be effective in the struggle with communism." The Soviet Union knows this, and that is why Christianity and the church are attacked so vigorously.

Note the words of the late J. Edgar Hoover:

> Why does the Church—which has no military forces—merit the most explosive of communist rockets, the most venomous of communist hate, the most vituperative of communist scorn? Because religion, of all facets of Western civilization, represents the eternal "thorn in the flesh" of communism, that jagged rock which is constantly puncturing, exposing and unmasking communist claims, performances and hopes. The communists realize that unless the Christian pulpit—that mighty fortress of God—is liquidated, pitilessly, mercilessly, finally, the very existence of communism itself stands in jeopardy. The spiritual firepower of the Christian Church—based on the love of God—is sufficient to destroy all the Soviet man-made missiles and rockets and extirpate this twentieth century aberration.
>
> And the communists know it—and fear it.[31]

Communism is an attack on God, the Bible and everything that is sacred in the Christian faith. It is satanic. Whittaker Chambers makes this observation:

> Communism is what happens when, in the name of Mind, men free themselves from God. . . . There has never been a society or a nation without God. But history is cluttered with the wreckage of nations that became indifferent to God, and died. The crisis of communism exists to the degree in which it has failed to free the peoples that it rules from God.
>
> Economics is not the central problem of this century. . . . Faith is the central problem of this age. The Western world does not know it, but it already possesses the answer to this problem—but only provided that its

faith in God and the freedom He enjoins is as great as communism's faith in Man.[32]

Americans cannot afford to be complacent. This is no time for neutrality. Someone has written: "Usurpers are ignoring our Constitution and making a mockery of our American heritage. The American people have been drugged into insensibility. Paul Revere today would probably be laughed at or ignored as the people went back to sleep."

Our dedication must match that of the communists. Lenin said, "If you are not willing to crawl in the mud for communism, you are not a good communist." Listen to the challenge of two ex-communists: "And so, if the cause of freedom is to win, we must have people who are dedicated to it, people who are prepared to go anywhere, do anything for the principles of freedom in which they believe."[33]

Will the communists take over America? I don't know. Opinion is divided. Remember the words of Solzhenitsyn: "I wouldn't be surprised at the sudden and imminent fall of the West" [and of course that includes the United States of America]. United States Senator Jesse Helms sounds this warning:

> Considering the might of our enemy, delaying action is not a reasonable option. Our forebears had the sense to heed the words of Paul Revere: "The British are coming!" Unless we heed the words of his counterparts to-day...we are going to be invaded: "The Russians are coming!" The possibility we refused to admit will come to pass, and we will be powerless to respond to it.
>
> The moment of truth will have come upon us, and the agony and upheaval and desolation which we observed in the fall of Vietnam will be simply a foreshadowing of what to expect when the United States becomes the last of the falling dominoes.[34]

I repeat: I don't know if the communists are going to take over America, but I do know that "a forest takes a century to grow; it burns down in a night"; and also that "the communists can never conquer a nation that really puts its trust in God." The answer is in the sovereign will of the Almighty.

But as for Russia, her future is bleak. As Malraux exclaimed, "In a universe without God, life is absurd." The judgment of God is upon the Soviet Union. The demise of the communists is certain because the Word of God declares it. Russia will be defeated because she is anti-God.

In Psalm 14:1 we read, "The fool hath said in his heart, There is no God." Russia's military might will be as nothing in the presence of deity. "He that sitteth in the heavens shall laugh: the Lord shall have them in derision" (Ps. 2:4). Russia's defeat is foretold in the Word of God because of her blasphemy: "So will I make my holy name known in the midst of my people

Israel; and I will not let them pollute my holy name any more" (Ezek. 39:7).

Russia will be defeated because of her ill-treatment of God's people, the Jews and the Christians. The Prophet Zechariah declared: ". . . for he that toucheth you toucheth the apple of his eye" (2:8). "Vengeance is mine; I will repay, saith the Lord" (Rom. 12:19).

Russia will be defeated because she is guilty of murder. Hitler killed six million Jews, but Stalin's "purges" far exceeded that. "Since 1945, the communists have murdered in one country alone enough people to wipe out the entire population of over fifteen of our states." God will demand an accountability: "What hast thou done? the voice of thy brother's blood crieth unto me from the ground" (Gen. 4:10).

Russia will be defeated because of her hypocrisy. She talks peace and prepares for war. The Word of God declares, "The hypocrite's hope shall perish" (Job 8:13). "For when they shall say, Peace and safety; then sudden destruction cometh upon them" (I Thess. 5:3).

Russia will be defeated because the Bible predicts it. Ezekiel 38 and 39 give the complete details:

*"Son of man, set thy face against Gog, the land of Magog, the chief prince of Meshech and Tubal, and prophesy against him,*

*"And say, Thus saith the Lord God; Behold, I am against thee, O Gog, the chief prince of Meshech and Tubal."*—Ezek. 38:2,3.

Most evangelical teachers believe that these verses refer to Russia and in verses 5 and 6 to her latter-day confederation. Note that God is announcing His judgment upon them.

Where will communism end? When Russia attacks Israel in the end time, her doom is sealed.

*"And it shall come to pass in that day, that I will give unto Gog a place there of graves in Israel, the valley of the passengers on the east of the sea: and it shall stop the noses of the passengers: and there shall they bury Gog and all his multitude: and they shall call it The valley of Hamon-gog.*

*"And seven months shall the house of Israel be burying of them, that they may cleanse the land."*—Ezek. 39:11, 12.

Here is the graveyard of communism. That which was propagated by Engels and Marx and all the followers will find its final doom when God meets them in Israel! This is the bitter end of communism. Russia's days are numbered.

What about America? Will the ponderous bear of the North defeat the mighty eagle of the heavens? Not if the eagle remembers her high and lofty habitat—the freedom of the skies. As it has been said, "Our attitude will determine our altitude."

To forget that we are eagles is to commit suicide.

## Religious but Lost

America, like the ancient Athenians, is suffering from a plethora of religion. However, there is a difference between religion and Christianity. Religion is what you do for God; Christianity is what God in Christ has already done for you. In that sense, Christianity is not one of the great religions of the world, but a life. That is what it means to be "born again" (John 3:3)—to receive a supernatural life within you.

In spite of favorable statistics toward religion (the term we will use for clarity's sake), all is not well on the religious scene. The picture is not as bright as the pollsters claim. In fact, Isaiah's prognosis is more applicable to our nation. Note the spiritual conditions found in Isaiah 1:9-15.

• There was a small remnant that believed. "Except the Lord of hosts had left unto us a very small remnant, we should have been as Sodom, and we should have been like unto Gomorrah" (vs. 9).

• "The word of the Lord" was to be their guide. "Hear the word of the Lord, ye rulers of Sodom; give ear unto the law of our God, ye people of Gomorrah" (vs. 10).

• God is displeased with their offerings.

*"To what purpose is the multitude of your sacrifices unto me? saith the Lord: I am full of the burnt-offerings of rams, and the fat of fed beasts; and I delight not in the blood of bullocks, or of lambs, or of he goats.*

*"When ye come to appear before me, who hath required this at your hand, to tread my courts?*

*"Bring no more vain oblations; incense is an abomination unto me; the new moons and sabbaths, the calling of assemblies, I cannot away with; it is iniquity, even the solemn meeting.*

*"Your new moons and your appointed feasts my soul hateth: they are a trouble unto me; I am weary to bear them."*—Vss. 11-14.

• God will no longer hear their prayers. "And when ye spread forth your hands, I will hide mine eyes from you: yea, when ye make many prayers, I will not hear: your hands are full of blood" (vs. 15).

God looks at things differently from man. The words of Christ should be considered. Note Matthew 7:13, 14:

*"Enter ye in at the strait gate: for wide is the gate, and broad is the way, that leadeth to destruction, and many there be which go in thereat:*

*"Because strait is the gate, and narrow is the way, which leadeth unto*

*life, and few there be that find it."*

Luke 18:8 is a verse for this generation to consider: "I tell you that he will avenge them speedily. Nevertheless when the Son of man cometh, shall he find faith on the earth?"

It is admitted that this verse will have its fulfillment during the Tribulation Period, but surely the coming apostasy is found in our day.

Note the description that the Son of God gives concerning the Laodicean church (the church of our day) in Revelation 3:17: "Because thou sayest, I am rich, and increased with goods, and have need of nothing; and knowest not that thou art wretched, and miserable, and poor, and blind, and naked."

Apostasy brought the downfall of Israel. They followed other gods and rejected the Lord God Jehovah. Because of apostasy, Israel was led into captivity and has suffered ever since. The Bible teaches that there is no remedy for apostasy but judgment. Apostasy is the deliberate rejection of revealed truth. America is guilty of that. Herman J. Otten writes:

> The Christian church today faces the greatest crisis it has ever confronted. For centuries the church has had to defend various doctrines when they were denied. But today the very foundation of the historic faith is under attack. It is no longer a matter of one or another doctrine. Direct revelation and the very concept of truth and doctrine are being rejected within the established churches of our day. The very thought that God revealed Himself or any truths to man in certain propositions recorded in Holy Scripture is rejected.[35]

The religious scene in America is a disaster. A fitting description would be when Paul faced the Ephesian mob: "Some therefore cried one thing, and some another: for the assembly was confused; and the more part knew not wherefore they were come together" (Acts 19:32).

Confusion reigns supreme in the American ecclesiastical world. The myriad of siren voices leaves the average church member in a quandary as to which way to go. In the meantime, the moral fiber of our nation has been drastically lowered. The foundations are crumbling.

The late Fred J. Meldau analyzed our nation thus: "More knowledge, less wisdom; more religion, less Christianity." Dr. J. Vernon McGee observed: "Confusion, compromise and comfort—these three words seem to characterize the Christian community."

Someone has said that the church "has lowered its sights and become preoccupied with the here and now." Thus the social gospel is again being emphasized.

> The decline of the influence of religion has meant that the promise of
> a better life in the beyond no longer has the same hold on man's imagina-

tion as in the past, and where religious belief is still strong, the feeling has grown that man has a right to the good life here and now, quite independently of the happiness of the soul in the hereafter.[36]

There has been a definite departure from "the faith which was once delivered unto the saints" (Jude 3). Several theologians suggest "the twilight of the church." Sherman Williams remarks: "The permissive view of many evangelicals today corresponds to the liberal's stance of fifty years ago." And even fundamentalists are being moved. Eternal truths of God's Word have been forsaken in the quest to establish social justice on earth. With the departure from the Faith has come a spirit of materialism. Paul Blumberg writes this interesting paragraph:

> Some years ago Buick ran an expensive advertising campaign: "Buick— something to believe in." And why not? If God is dead, then why not an automobile? The rise of Sunday store openings in America is also no accident; for Sunday, after all, is the day of worship; and what better place to worship than in the shopping center? Worship or therapy? As Arthur Miller observed, shopping is now the great American psychotherapy— something to do when depressed, to lift the spirits and give meaning.[37]

G. K. Chesterton's remark is appropriate here: "If a man won't believe in God, he will believe in anything." All of this caused a disgusted individual to comment: "The old-time religion, the faith of our fathers, is sometimes so up-to-date, so inoculated and improved, so analyzed, purified, educated and hypnotized that the apostles and their Lord would never recognize it as the faith for which they gave their lives!"

The problem of the church today is religion without revelation. Baudelaire has put it thus: "Race of Cain mounts to the sky; while God lies on the ground." God had become a god of neutrality; He doesn't take sides.

The Prophet Zephaniah wrote, "...that say in their heart, The Lord will not do good, neither will he do evil" (Zeph. 1:12).

Malachi, the last of the Old Testament prophets, rebuked Israel for lack of moral standards (although professing devotion to Jehovah): "Ye have wearied the Lord with your words. Yet ye say, Wherein have we wearied him? When ye say, Every one that doeth evil is good in the sight of the Lord, and he delighteth in them; or, Where is the God of judgment?" (Mal. 2:17).

Thus pseudo-theologians are having a field day deriding the Almighty.

One "Reverend Dr." states: "The struggle between good and evil is Sunday school stuff." "Sunday school morals," he implies, are not only puerile but reprehensible—in fact, evil. He wants men and women to be set free from "rigid, archaic rules and codes like the Ten Commandments."

The gullibility of the average church member is amazing. No wonder Lenin remarked: "We will find our most fertile field for the infiltration of Marxism within the field of religion, because religious people are the most gullible and will accept most everything if it is couched in religious testimony."

"The Devil once lived in Heaven, and those who have not met him are unlikely to recognize an angel when they see one." Bible students know that the Devil does not deceive by appearing as a demon with horns on his head and a long, ugly tail, but he appears as "an angel of light." The apostle warned the church at Corinth about him:

*"For such are false apostles, deceitful workers, transforming themselves into the apostles of Christ.*

*"And no marvel; for Satan himself is transformed into an angel of light.*

*"Therefore it is no great thing if his ministers also be transformed as the ministers of righteousness; whose end shall be according to their works."*—II Cor. 11:13-15.

It is therefore possible to be aiding the work of the Devil through a form of religion. The old adage is true, "If you can't beat them, join them."

In the later years of Mr. Robert Ingersoll's life, a friend inquired one day why he did not go out on the lecture platform, as in former years, to deliver his popular lectures on the "Errors and Inconsistencies of the Bible." The famous unbeliever replied, "There is no need for me to do that anymore as many preachers in the pulpits are denying the truths of the Bible in the churches of our land and are accomplishing more to destroy faith in the Bible than I could by taking to the lecture platform." One has written these discerning words: "A butcher who advocated vegetarianism would be a rarity; but clergymen with strong atheist proclivities are as common as blackberries."

The Prophet Jeremiah asks the question: "The prophets prophesy falsely, and the priests bear rule by their means; and my people love to have it so: and what will ye do in the end thereof?" (Jer. 5:31). Jeremiah also notes the calamity of following false prophets: "My people hath been lost sheep: their shepherds have caused them to go astray, they have turned them away on the mountains: they have gone from mountain to hill, they have forgotten their restingplace" (Jer. 50:6).

Apostasy is conceived in the liberal seminaries of our country and filtered down to the pulpit and eventually the pew. Ministers must bear much of the blame. Lamentations 2:9 asserts: ". . .the law is no more; her prophets also find no vision from the Lord." Zephaniah 3:4 adds: "Her prophets are light and treacherous persons: her priests have polluted the sanctuary. . . ."

James Steward said, "A patronizing enemy is more dangerous than a persecuting enemy." The late Dr. A. W. Tozer spoke words of wisdom when he said, "There isn't anything quite as chilling, quite so disheartening as a man without the Holy Spirit preaching about the Holy Spirit."

Liberal preachers have played into the hands of the Devil. In his book, *Only America,* Harry Golden comments:

> There is nothing to offend me in the modern church. The minister gives a sermon on juvenile delinquency one week, reviews a movie next week, then everyone goes downstairs and plays bingo. The first part of a church they build nowadays is the kitchen. Five hundred years from now people will dig up these churches, find the steam tables and wonder what kind of sacrifices we performed.

Paul C. Konnor explains the pathos of the modern pulpit: "We are telling the people what they want to hear—telling a sick and dying world that all is well. We are afraid to preach judgment, sin, damnation—such preaching has never been popular."

In their pursuit of popularity, some preachers have not been true to their high and holy calling. Today the emphasis has been placed on happiness. The pew has been made very comfortable. Leonard Ravenhill gives this evaluation:

> Our present-day effete evangelism with its emphasis on happiness would have shocked John the Baptist. We try to induce happiness on a heart diseased with sin. We offer Band-Aids to folks who need radical spiritual surgery for the cancer of carnality in the breast.[38]

The church offers a religion of convenience—"short sermons and a sunny theology." The Gospel has been made palatable with a huge dose of "saccharin Christianity."

The church has gone into the entertainment business. The emphasis is on bigness. If it is big, it is good. If it is big, surely it must be of God. One is reminded of Mark 9:34, "...for by the way they had disputed among themselves, who should be the greatest." God judges the motive. It seems that some ministers are better promoters than they are preachers.

Norman H. Wells has written an article worthy of note, entitled "Ecclesiastical Entertainment." Note these paragraphs:

> If what we want is entertainment, let's be honest enough to call it that and quit trying to disguise it as religion.
>
> In general, religion has become a big business with hallelujah hucksters peddling packaged piety and bargain blessings. Our ministers have become merchants of morality who spend their time promoting instead of preaching. The latest selling methods are employed and religion finds itself commercialized and dispensed in convenient, easy-to-take capsules.
>
> —*Baptist Publications*

A. W. Tozer makes this discerning prediction: "It is our belief that the evangelical movement will continue to drift further and further from the New Testament position until its leadership passes from the self-effacing saint to the modern religious star."

We live in a day of open rebellion against the church. Renan, the French philosopher who lost his faith, declared, "It is possible that the collapse of supernatural belief will be followed by the collapse of moral convictions and that the moment when humanity sees the reality of things will mark a moral decline."

> ## " . . . The evangelical movement will continue to drift further and further from the New Testament position until its leadership passes from the self-effacing saint to the modern religious star."
>
> —A. W. Tozer

Ernest T. Campbell comments: "Many of today's young people have little difficulty believing that God was in Christ. What they find it hard to accept is that Christ is in the church." That is why some speak and write of "the Post-Christian Era." Because hungry hearts are not being fed, the cults are having a field day. Note these facts:

—Forty to sixty million Americans are involved in the occult.

—912 men and women and children died in the Jonestown massacre.

—It is said that forty million individuals in the U.S. check the signs of the zodiac each day.

—According to recent reports, the First Church of Satan in San Francisco claims a membership of 20,000 members. It is reported that the satanic bible outsells the Holy Bible on many university campuses across the nation.

Mel White gives the background of the Jonestown tragedy:

> Jones used psychological coercion as part of a mind-programming campaign aimed at destroying family ties, discrediting belief in God and causing contempt for the United States of America. . . . Jones' followers were murdered by the man who promised to give them life.[39]

A noted denominational leader asks the question: "Can you deny that there is a correlation between the disintegration of the American way of life and the disintegration of the major denominations and their attitudes toward the Word of God?"

The church is the last bulwark against anarchy and the dissolution of a nation. It is imperative, therefore, that Jesus Christ should have His rightful place in the church and hence in the nation.

A. W. Pink wrote these words back in 1967, but they are still appropriate today:

> While some of our national leaders still give thanks to "God" and own our dependence upon "the Almighty," that is no more than any Orthodox Jew or Muhammedan would do. There is a studied avoidance of any reference to the Lord Jesus Christ and to the Holy Spirit. Though that is said, it is not to be wondered at; it is simply the shadowing forth in the civil realm of what has been obtained in the religious.[40]

As Tozer has said, "It is becoming harder and harder in our churches to tell which brother is Abel and which is Cain."

Pastors and Christian workers must bear much of the blame for the condition of the average church in our country. First of all, some should not be in the pulpit; Jeremiah describes them as unsent prophets. "I have not sent these prophets, yet they ran: I have not spoken to them, yet they prophesied" (Jer. 23:21). These unsent prophets have no message from God to deliver but "speak a vision of their own heart, and not out of the mouth of the Lord" (Jer. 23:16). Pastors should forget about pleasing their congregations. If God called, don't spend time looking over your shoulder to see who is following.

Preachers are to preach the Word. Paul's admonition to Timothy is specific: "Preach the word; be instant in season, out of season; reprove, rebuke, exhort with all longsuffering and doctrine" (II Tim. 4:2).

Listen to the words of Oswald Chambers: "There is far more wrought by the Word of God than we will ever understand; and if I substitute anything for it—fine thinking, eloquent speech—the Devil's victory is enormous, but I am of no more use than a puff of wind." Martin Lloyd-Jones, in his book on *Preaching and Preachers,* likens the pulpit to a place of surgery: "When you go away, you ought to have felt not pleasure but pain; for when you come in, something is wrong with you."

A survey of the religious section of a public library will reveal a pitifully small number of books on Bible doctrine. The Apostle Paul's prediction has come true: "For the time will come when they will not endure sound doctrine; but after their own lusts shall they heap to themselves teachers, having itching ears" (II Tim. 4:3). Thus the average pulpit has become a "religious smorgasbord" (pick out what you like and leave the rest).

Harold O. J. Brown writes:

> A characteristic of the church in our day—of the whole church and of each individual—is the avoidance of doctrine. In churches and in church-related schools (both Sunday schools and the regular schools and colleges maintained by the churches), there is a growing reluctance to teach anything specific and definite about the Christian faith....
>
> The major problem with doctrine in Christian churches today is that it is virtually nonexistent. This represents a fundamental and ultimately fatal apostasy. The Christian and the church are morally bound to have a clear idea of the Christian faith and to proclaim it clearly to the world. The present confused babble of the theologians is not only irresponsible; it is a betrayal of this obligation.[41]

Jim Reapsome states that, "according to the best statistics, four out of five American churches are still not growing." Biblical illiteracy is high even among those who attend church. August Bang has commented that "denominations are God's little kindergartens." The tragedy is, the kindergarten is where most of them remain spiritually.

John R. W. Scott remarks: "Nothing troubles me more in church today than our Christian superficiality. So few are 'mature in Christ.'" Martin Lloyd-Jones also declares: "But today we have a pseudo-intellectualism that is theologically shallow."

The need of the hour is expository preaching and Bible doctrine.

There is a need for ministers of the Gospel to be more militant in their defense of the Faith. Henry Parsons Crowell of Moody Bible Institute fame stated that the basic problem in the churches today is the attitude that allows us "to be tolerant of believers who are tolerant of unbelievers."

Wilbur M. Smith is very dogmatic when he writes:

> What I am now going to say will probably shock many people; it is so contrary to everything that is being expressed in this age of an anemic toleration of every conceivable kind of heresy, in this age when people are so glibly advocating a spineless universal religion, and fearful of offending anyone by our own religious convictions.
>
> Let me put it frankly in one brief sentence: what we need today is some downright, manly, courageous intolerance in the Christian church of all those tendencies and humanistically-derived theories which, while they may encourage the pride of man, are wholly destructive of anything bearing a resemblance to New Testament Christianity.[42]

Peter Muhlenberg in 1766 spoke these words in a farewell sermon to his congregation: "There is a time to preach and a time to fight, and that time has come." William Arthur Ward wrote, "When we should speak out against evil, our silent assent is as self-damaging, as destructive, and as cowardly as verbal consent." Dr. J. Gresham Machen was a stalwart for the Faith. Note his comments:

> Paul was a great fighter. Read the Epistles with care, and you will see Paul always in conflict. At one time he fights paganism in life. At another time he fights paganism in thought. Everywhere we see the great apostle in conflict for the preservation of the church.
>
> If you have the peace of God in your hearts, you will never shrink from controversy; you will never be afraid to earnestly contend for the Faith.

Martin Luther was an angry man. Note his words: "I never work better than when I am inspired of anger; when I am angry, I can write, pray, preach well, for then my whole temperament is quickened, my understanding sharpened, and my mundane vexations and temptations depart." So wrote the last angry man of the Middle Ages.

Peter declared, "For the time is come that judgment must begin at the house of God. . ." (I Pet. 4:17). The pastor's primary concern should be "the house of God." In other words, revival must begin in the pulpit. Ezekiel in holy desperation cried out, "Begin at my sanctuary" (Ezek. 9:6). There must be repentance in the pulpit if there is to be repentance in the pew. Joel, the prophet of Judah, shows the way:

*"Gird yourselves, and lament, ye priests: howl, ye ministers of the altar: come, lie all night in sackcloth, ye ministers of my God: for the meat-offering and the drink-offering is withholden from the house of your God."*—Joel 1:13.

*"Let the priests, the ministers of the Lord, weep between the porch and the altar, and let them say, Spare thy people, O Lord, and give not thine heritage to reproach, that the heathen should rule over them: wherefore should they say among the people, Where is their God?"*—Joel 2:17.

In spite of theological confusion and ecclesiastical chaos in the religious world, it is going to turn out all right. Did not Jesus Christ Himself assert that the gates of Hell would not prevail against His church (Matt. 16:18)?

Divine providence was evident when the Apostle Paul was shipwrecked. The object was to make it safely to the shore. Acts 27:43,44 describes the scene:

*". . . and commanded that they which could swim should cast themselves first into the sea, and get to land:*

*"And the rest, some on boards, and some on broken pieces of the ship. And so it came to pass, that they escaped all safe to land."*

Those who are born again are going to swim through the turbulent theological waters and make it to shore!

Our nation may not fare so well. Apostasy is always a forerunner of judgment. God plays no favorites. America is sinning against light. No nation has more light than our nation. It is said that "some 47 percent of Americans see at least one religious program a week on TV." Sin against light brings darkness.

Isaiah's prognosis is strikingly true of America: "the whole head is sick, and the whole heart faint." Our "wounds, and bruises, and putrifying sores. . . have not been closed, neither bound up, neither mollified with ointment." A patient who does not accept the diagnosis of a doctor and refuses the remedy for his ills must suffer the consequences. Such folly could cost him his life.

Is America committing suicide?

## ENDNOTES:

[1]W. E. Vine, *Isaiah*, 13.

[2]Francis A. Schaeffer, *How Should We Then Live?* 190.

[3]Richard Hanser, *Putsch*, 227.

[4]M. Stanton Evans and Margaret Moore, *The Law Breakers*, 21.

[5]David Harrop, *America's Paychecks: Who Pays Them?* 223, 224.

[6]William Arnot, *Church in the House* , 377.

[7]Evans and Moore, 13.

[8]Kate Caffrey, *The Mayflower*, 71.

[9]David A. Norris, *Before You Lose It All*, 31.

[10]Jessie Helms, *When Free Men Shall Stand,* 30.

[11]John Q. Citizen, *The Angry American*, 24.

[12]Tim LaHaye, *The Battle for the Mind*, 43, 44.

[13]*Ibid.*, 137.

[14]Wilbur M. Smith, *Therefore Stand*, 527.

[15]John A. Stormer, *None Dare Call It Treason*, 99, 100.

[16]Paul Kurtz, ed., *The Humanist Alternative: Some Definitions of Humanism*, 5.

[17]LaHaye, 9.

[18]Kurtz, 7.

[19]*Ibid.*, 83.

[20]Smith, 67.

[21]Evans and Moore, 89.

[22]Christopher Lasch, *The Culture of Narcissism*, 19.

[23]Corliss Lamont, *A Humanist Funeral Service*, 8.

[24]Paul Blumberg, *Inequality in an Age of Decline*, 239.

[25]Eugene Lyons, *Workers' Paradise Lost*, 13.

[26]Edward Hunter, *Brainwashing*, 281.

[27]Henry M. Morris, *The Bible Has the Answer*, 235.

[28]Charles M. Crowe, *In This Free Land*, 61, 62.

[29]Richard Nixon, *The Real War*, 1.

[30]J. Edgar Hoover, *On Communism*, 13.

[31]*Ibid.*, 92.

[32]Chambers, 16, 17.

[33]Phillip Abbott Luce and Douglas Hyde, *The Intelligent Student's Guide to Survival*, 52.

[34]Helms, 98.

[35]Herman J. Otten, *Baal or God*, 1.

[36]William Ebenstein, *Great Political Thinkers*, 811.

[37]Blumberg, 235.

[38]Leonard Ravenhill, *America Is Too Young to Die*, 62, 63.

[39]Mel White, *Deceived*, 144, 149.

[40]A. W. Pink, *Gleanings from Paul*, 86.

[41]Harold O. J. Brown, *The Protest of a Troubled Protestant*, 101, 103, 104.

[42]Smith, 485.

# 10       Is My Rome Burning?

*"And turning the cities of Sodom and Gomorrha into ashes condemned them with an overthrow, making them an ensample unto those that after should live ungodly."*—II Pet. 2:6.

*"Behold, your house is left unto you desolate."*—Matt. 23:38.

Paul L. Maier informs us that "probably the most popular misinterpretation in history is that 'Nero fiddled while Rome burned.' The violin, of course, was not invented until fourteen centuries after the fire."[1] However, the fact remains that wicked Nero witnessed its conflagration. It is reported that, when the fall of Paris marked the doom of France, Hitler was so ecstatic that he danced a jig.

Will "Old Glory" ever be pulled down from the flagpole in Washington, D.C., and another flag be unfurled in its place? That which at one time was considered inconceivable could become a grim reality.

The pages of history are strewn with the debris of ancient cities and nations. The greatest civilizations lie buried in ruins. The most magnificent of ancient buildings are either utterly oblivious in ashes or the fragments of a departed glory. Where is Solomon's Temple? Gone. Where are the Seven Wonders of the Ancient World? Gone. Gone the city of Babylon, gone the Acropolis, gone the Forum of Rome. Going and gone—Washington, D.C.?

Benedetto Croce, the Italian idealist philosopher, reached the conclusion that "all history is contemporary" and that, "in the end, philosophy and history are one." J. A. Froude, the historian, said that "history is a voice sounding across the centuries that in the end it is well for the righteous and ill for the wicked."

Could it be that the American dream is over? A corporation executive warned against over optimism with these words: "We should not be misled by the

appearance of a light at the end of the tunnel. It is probably an oncoming train."
Will Durant compares the United States to ancient Rome: "We have reached
our zenith, and are beginning to crumble and share with Second Century Rome
great wealth, great freedom, loss of religious faith, and have overextended
ourselves in the world with wide avenues of commitment."

Lucretius wrote, "How sweet it is to behold from shore another's shipwreck!"
Americans should visit the ruins of ancient Pompeii. They were secure in their
smugness. Bulwer-Lytton's classic, *The Last Days of Pompeii,* is worth reading.
Note this description of what took place on the fatal day of 79 A.D.:

> The period was the beginning of the Christian era. Pompeii, nestled
> almost within the shadow of Vesuvius, was a careless, dreaming city,
> devoted to luxurious living. Life was centered in the amphitheater and
> the forum, the shops and the baths, the lavishly ornate palaces and the
> gladiatorial combats; it was one long round of pleasure.
>
> But one day Vesuvius erupted. Pompeii was attending the circus at the
> time. The terror-stricken people saw "a fire that shifted and wavered in
> its hues with every moment, now fiercely luminous, now of a dull and dy-
> ing red that blazed forth terrifically with intolerable glare. Then there
> arose on high the universal shrieks of women. The men stared at one
> another, but were dumb. They felt the earth shake beneath their feet, the
> crash of falling roofs; an instant more and the mountain-cloud seemed to
> roll toward them, dark and rapid, like a torrent; it cast forth from its bosom
> a shower of ashes mixed with vast fragments of burning stone! Over the
> crushing vines, over the desolate streets, over the amphitheater itself, far
> and wide with many a mighty splash in the agitated sea, fell that
> shower. . . . Each turned to flee—dashing, pressing, crushing against the
> other. It was save-himself-who-could in that night of horrors.
>
> —Adapted

There are those who laugh at the prospect of such a calamity happening in
Washington, D.C., New York City, Los Angeles, Hollywood; but the words of
Mark Twain are significant: "There is no humor in Heaven."

> If the American vision is to be sustained, the American people must
> guard against the easy rationalization that anything can be excused in
> defense of the American way of life. Otherwise, we may one day wake
> up to discover that the face in the mirror is no longer our own.[2]

In his book, *Doomsday 1999 A.D.,* Charles Berlitz is quoted in the Dedication of the book thus: "To the world of the future—if there is one. . . . " Students
of the Bible know that God in His sovereignty is going to take care of this
world, but the question that confronts our nation is, will there be a tomorrow?

When the ancient city of Carthage was going up in flames in 146 B.C., the
Roman commander Scipio the Younger exclaimed: "A glorious moment . . . but

have a dread foreboding that the same doom will be pronounced upon my own country."

The wise acknowledge that "the future is only the past again, entered through another gate." A Chinese proverb states, "All the flowers of all the tomorrows lie in the seeds of today." It has been said that, "when all the past is lost, the future remains." But what if there is no future? Ezekiel the prophet warned, "...the time is come, the day of trouble is near" (Ezek. 7:7).

History records that Rome burned in 64 A.D., ten of its fourteen precincts consumed by flames. An observer remarked: "Nero was holding holiday while Rome burned." There are some who believe that the plight of America is more hopeless than that of ancient Rome. Said Harold O'Chester, "Our nation is burning.... Our impotence as Christians rules supreme. As a nation we have quit hearing the notes of the drummer we once heard, and we are marching to familiar tunes."

Is "the last citadel of freedom on earth being ignited by the fires of revolution"?

Propped up in front of his TV set, the average American has little thought of the future of his country. The successful typical TV show is one that produces laughs. Others prefer the fun of the glamorous nightclubs. Everybody seems to be having fun.

Leo C. Rosten comments:

> I know of nothing more demeaning than the frantic pursuit of "fun." No people are more miserable than those who seek desperate escapes from the self, and none are more impoverished, psychologically, than those who plunge into the strenuous frivolity of night clubs, which I find a form of communal lunacy. The word "fun" comes from the medieval English "fon," meaning fool.

In the parable of the rich young fool, the Lord Jesus portrays also a nation. Note the account in Luke 12:19-21:

> *"And I will say to my soul, Soul, thou hast much goods laid up for many years; take thine ease, eat, drink, and be merry.*
>
> *"But God said unto him, Thou fool, this night thy soul shall be required of thee: then whose shall those things be, which thou hast provided?*
>
> *"So is he that layeth up treasure for himself, and is not rich toward God."*

The rich young fool did not have a tomorrow: "This night thy soul shall be required of thee."

Is the United States in prophecy? Bible scholars believe that Russia plays a role in the end time (Ezek. 38 and 39). What about America? S. Franklin

Logsdon in his booklet, *Is the United States in Prophecy?* writes: "Actually, it is unthinkable that the God who knows the end from the beginning would pinpoint such small nations as Libya, Egypt, Ethiopia and Syria in the prophetic declaration and completely overlook the wealthiest and the most powerful nation on the earth" (p. 9). On the secular scene, note this evaluation by Paul Blumberg, sociologist:

> The 1970s were not kind to the United States. At the beginning of that decade, only a handful of prophets foresaw that the structure of postwar American international hegemony was going to crumble. By the end of the decade, even the most casual viewer of the television news realized that American power was no longer what it once was and that if America was still first, it was more and more first among equals.[3]

Does the United States have a place in the future among the nations of the world? What does the Bible say?

There is a variance of opinion. Some prophetic scholars quote chapters and verses. It is not our purpose to enter into that discussion. Ezekiel 38:13 mentions "the merchants of Tarshish, with all the young lions." There are those who interpret "Tarshish" to mean Spain and "the young lions" to be a reference to Great Britain and the U.S.A. Armstrong follows the Anglo-Israel theory [British Israelism] "that the United States and Great Britain are the two tribes of Ephraim and Manasseh," hence the promises of Israel can be applied to them.

But it cannot be proved by Scripture that the United States is Manasseh. There is an abundance of material to refute this heresy.

The late Noel Smith declared categorically: "I know of no prophecy that specifically mentions North and South America. I know of none that specifically mentions the United States." Dr. Robert L. Moyer writes in his booklet, *The United States in Prophecy,* page 13:

> Is the United States in prophecy? No! Is the United States symbolized in prophecy? No! The United States is neither named or symbolized in prophecy, but the United States is in prophecy.... When we say that the United States is neither named or symbolized but involved in prophecy, we mean that there are certain prophecies made of the world which must include us.

Howard E. Estep pointed out that "the only time a country or nation is mentioned in the Scripture between the 12th chapter of Genesis and the second chapter of Acts is that that country has any dealings with Israel."

Are we witnessing the decline of America as a major world power? Noel Smith remarks: "The bitter truth is that the United States no longer believes that she has a destiny." He then quotes Professor Hacker, professor of government at Cornell University: "There is a growing suspicion that the American nation has lost its credentials as a teacher of moral lessons; that our presence abroad is evidence only of a power, carrying no enlightenment in its wake" (*Baptist Bible Tribune,* April 28, 1972).

The two authors, John F. Walvoord and John E. Walvoord, make this observation in their book, *Armageddon, Oil and the Middle East Crisis*:

> While the United States and Russia are the two greatest powers in the present world international scene, prophecy does not indicate that either will figure largely in end-time events. No specific prophecy whatever is found concerning the role of the United States, indicating that its contribution will be a secondary one as the world moves on to Armageddon. Russia, too, according to prophetic Scripture, is destined for declining power and influence. Instead, there will arise in the Middle East a new center of political and economic power, a new dramatic leader, and a new rapid sequence of events for which the present situation serves as a well-equipped stage.[4]

What is the future of America according to the Bible? *The Nations in Prophecy* is the title of a book by Dr. John F. Walvoord. The last chapter deals with the United States in prophecy. Note his words:

> Although the Scriptures do not give any clear word concerning the role of the United States in relationship to the revived Roman Empire and the later development of the world empire, it is probable that the United States will be in some form of alliance with the Roman ruler. . . .
>
> If the end-time events include a destruction of Russia and her allies prior to the final period of the great tribulation, this may trigger an unbalance in the world situation that will permit the Roman ruler to become a world ruler. In this event, it should be clear that the United States will be in a subordinate role and no longer the great international power that it is today.[5]

He also adds:

> It is evident, however, that if Christ came for His church. . . America then would be reduced to the same situation as other countries. . . . It may well be that the United States, like Babylon of old, will lose its place of leadership in the world, and this will be a major cause in the shift of power to the Mediterranean scene.[6]

Dr. Herman A. Hoyt has a valuable booklet on the subject of the United States in prophecy which gives the following summary:

1. The Prophetic Diagram of the Age Makes No Provision for the United States as a World Power;

2. The Phenomenal Development Within Recent Years Does Not

Guarantee the Continuation of the United States as a World Power;
    3. The Perilous Deterioration Now in Progress Is Preparing the Way
for the Passing of the United States as a World Power;
    4. The Possible Disappearance of the United States as a World Power
Will Not Take Place Until God Has Fulfilled His Purpose in This Nation.

There is a limit to the mercy of God. The psalmist wrote:

*"Forty years long was I grieved with this generation, and said, It is a people
that do err in their heart, and they have not known my ways:*

*"Unto whom I sware in my wrath that they should not enter into my rest."—*
Ps. 95:10, 11.

America had more than forty years to repent of her sins. God has shown
remarkable grace and mercy toward our nation. Whether the United States
will play a prominent role in the future remains to be seen.

Let us face the facts: God gives up nations as He does individuals. When
a nation rejects God, God rejects that nation. Note the warning of His Word:

*"I am the Lord thy God, which brought thee out of the land of Egypt: open
thy mouth wide, and I will fill it.*

*"But my people would not hearken to my voice; and Israel would none of me.*

*"So I gave them up unto their own hearts' lust: and they walked in their own
counsels."—*Ps. 81:10-12.

*"And even as they did not like to retain God in their knowledge, God gave
them over to a reprobate mind, to do those things which are not convenient."—*
Rom. 1:28.

["A 'reprobate' mind is a mind void of sound judgment. The judgment of a
'reprobate' mind is unapproved by God; it is rejected, worthless."]

Rudyard Kipling in his *Recessional* wrote:

> **If, drunk with sight of power, we loose**
> **Wild tongues that have not Thee in awe...**
> **Lord God of Hosts, be with us yet,**
> **Lest we forget—lest we forget!**

This is a time for soul-searching. Some are optimistic. One educator put it
this way: "There is yet left in our nation enough moral integrity and intelligence for a desperate and victorious effort." Perry C. Cotham gives this
view:

> Lest we despair, recall from both biblical and secular history that the
> character of a nation is not necessarily determined by the majority of its
> people—a deeply committed minority is quite sufficient....

If God spared an entire nation because of the dedication of one woman named Esther, if He spared multitudes because of the prayers of one man named Moses, if God would have spared Sodom for ten righteous people in Sodom, then will not the Almighty spare this great nation because of the leavening influence of some truly converted people?"

In his Harvard address, Solzhenitzyn warned his listeners: "You are being softened by inflated luxury and permitted luxury and permitted lawlessness. No modern weapon, however powerful, can help you if you have lost national willpower." This willpower must be spiritually motivated. Melvin Munn, former radio news commentator, has guarded optimism:

> *U.S. Minus Character Equals Rome:* There is no longer any question about the fall of the United States. The only remaining question is how far.
>
> As a nation, we decline by leading in the wrong things. We suffer from the loss of the most important element in national power. The United States minus character equals Rome....
>
> Over a decade ago the late Roger Babson, noted economist, wrote in his syndicated newspaper column: "The test of a nation is the growth of its people, physically, intellectually and spiritually. Money and so-called prosperity are of very little account!
>
> "Babylon, Persia, Greece, Rome, Spain and France all had their turn in being the richest in the world. Our nation is now the richest, but it could easily become a second-class nation and head downward. Money will not save us. Only a sane, spiritual revival which changes the desires of our people will save us! We must be filled with the desire to render service, to seek strength rather than security, to put character ahead of profit."
>
> Mr. Babson has said it. Let me sum up: *The United States Minus Character Equals Rome.*

In the perilous days of Elijah, 7,000 had not bowed the knee to Baal. The hope for America is found in its remnant. The millions of Bible-believing citizens who comprise the population of our country are a potent force. They are not only "the salt of the earth" but represent that which is preserving the United States from moral putrefaction.

This remnant of grace believe that the Bible is the Word of God; that prayer is a mighty spiritual force, that their children should be taught moral and spiritual principles; that Israel (according to the Scriptures) is to be treated as God's people; that "righteousness exalteth a nation."

The hope of America is found in the proclamation of the Gospel of the grace of God. This holy proclamation must be accompanied by united prayer. Of course prayer and repentance must go together. The Bible is replete with examples of God's delaying judgment because of the prayers of His people. While the Almighty is sovereign in His actions, He definitely hears the supplication of His own ("And the Lord repented of the evil which he thought to do unto his people."—Exod. 32:14). The only remedy for sin is the blood of Christ applied in forgiveness to an individual or a nation.

In II Timothy 3 the Apostle Paul outlines the characteristics of the age in which we live. It reads like a daily newspaper. In the closing verses he shows the believer's resource in times of apostasy. These resources represent a hope for an individual and a nation. In verse 14 Paul writes: "But continue thou in the things which thou hast learned and hast been assured of, knowing of whom thou hast learned them."

Paul explains we have the Faith. "Faith of our Fathers"—the torch which was lit by the early martyrs and handed on to the heroes of the Reformation and placed in our hands today—is our godly heritage. It is to be taught to our children and proclaimed to a world. This Faith may involve persecution, for in this same chapter, in verse 12, the apostle declared, "Yea, and all that will live godly in Christ Jesus shall suffer persecution." This is the high cost of godly living.

In verse 15 we read, "And that from a child thou hast known the holy scriptures, which are able to make thee wise unto salvation...." We have the Faith and the Book—the precious Word of God. This is the Book that helped to establish America. This is the Book to which we must return. This Book has the answer to all the sordid problems of our nation. This Book meets the need of the human soul.

Then in the same verse, Paul adds, "...through faith which is in Christ Jesus." The Faith, the Book, the Name. It is necessary for an individual or a nation to believe not only in God: salvation is in a person, Christ Jesus. The hope of a nation is found in that name: "Neither is there salvation in any other: for there is none other name under heaven given among men, whereby we must be saved" (Acts 4:12).

When the Lord Jesus was on earth, He declared, "I am the way, the truth, and the life: no man cometh unto the Father, but by me" (John 14:6).

Paul closes this chapter to Timothy by saying, "That the man of God may be perfect, throughly furnished unto all good works" (II Tim. 3:17). In other words, that a believer may be "complete," "adequate," "well-fitted," a mature child of God in an evil world.

When David sinned in numbering his people, the Prophet Gad came to him and offered him the choice of judgments that the Lord would send on him and his people. In II Samuel 24:14 we read, "And David said unto Gad, I am in a great strait: let us fall now into the hand of the Lord; for his mercies are great: and let me not fall into the hand of man."

America is being offered God's options today. Upon our choice depends our destiny.

Does America have a place in the sun? What are our options? Thomas Jefferson exclaimed, "I like the dreams of the future better than the history of the past." However, the "dreams of the future" are dependent upon our adherence to scriptural principles. Robert R. Hoyt said, "History has not abandoned America; on the contrary, Americans have abandoned their place in history."

United States Congressman Lawrence P. McDonald has written these words: "The great use of history is to recognize in it recurring patterns which, read rightly, may serve as guideposts for action. History does not have to repeat itself if persons who understand it take proper precautions."

Author James Michener in an interview commented, "America is not immortal—but her strengths can yet again overcome her weaknesses." Her strengths are found in the realm of the spiritual.

Professor Lawrence W. Reed commented, "A nation that can put a man on the moon can resolve to mold a better future." "A better future" for America is only available if that nation chooses the right direction.

Baron Opperheim wrote, "To every people there comes one terrible and inevitable final hour, when it must choose between those things by which men live, or those things by which they die." The option before America is plain: "Except ye repent, ye shall all likewise perish."

Herbert J. Muller, in the Preface of his book, *The Uses of the Past*, comments on Arnold Toynbee's *A Study of History*:

> Our one hope of salvation, Toynbee asserts, is a return to the "one true God" from whom we have fallen away... "we may and must pray" that God will grant our society a reprieve if we ask for it "in a contrite spirit and with a broken heart." In effect, he seems to be saying that only a miracle can save us.
>
> I think he may be right. But I think we had better not live on this assumption. Toynbee's own study offers no evidence that prayer will save a society any more than it saved the Roman world after its conversion to Christianity. If we want to save our world, not merely our private souls, we might try to keep and use our heads.[8]

Muller perhaps should have substituted the word *hearts* for *heads*. Prayer alone is not enough; it must be accompanied by repentance. It is true that "the Pentecostal revival of A.D. 33 did not save Jerusalem or prevent its total destruction by the Romans in A.D. 70, but it saved thousands of souls and lit a fire that has not yet gone out."

President Dwight D. Eisenhower declared in his Inaugural Address, January 20, 1953, "Whatever America hopes to bring to pass in the world must first come to pass in the hearts of America." A Washington correspondent wrote:

"Unless there is a change, deep down, in the American people, a genuine crusade against self-indulgence, immorality public and private, then we are witnesses to the decline and fall of the American Republic."

The Prophet Jeremiah cried out to Jehovah, "Turn thou us unto thee, O Lord, and we shall be turned; renew our days as of old" (Lam. 5:21). He also declared, "If that nation, against whom I have pronounced, turn from their evil, I will repent of the evil that I thought to do unto them" (Jer. 18:8).

Second Chronicles 7:14 is often quoted in connection with the revival in America. Although it has been pointed out that "we Americans are not God's covenant people," surely it has an application to our nation: "If my people, which are called by my name, shall humble themselves, and pray, and seek my face, and turn from their wicked ways; then will I hear from heaven, and will forgive their sin, and will heal their land." And surely our beloved land needs healing.

Revival begins with believers. "As go the believers, so goes the nation." A nation can only be reached by those who have the light. Back in the '40s a leaflet appeared in England by Allister W. Smith entitled "Our Last Chance (An Appeal to Christians)." Note this paragraph:

> Conditions may be bad in the U.S.A. and in our Empire. They may be worse in some nations. But if we have had more light than other nations, our sin is greater; just as Capernaum was greater than that of Sodom (Matt. 11:23). Sodom had no church, no Bible, no crucified Christ. The British Empire and the U.S.A. enjoy more Gospel light and liberty and privileges than most nations, and should lead the world in revival.

Hosea 10:12 states, "Sow to yourselves in righteousness, reap in mercy; break up your fallow ground: for it is time to seek the Lord, till he come and rain righteousness upon you." Rejection of divine light brings eternal darkness.

Nations, like men, can be saved because they are given an extension of time. Although with the Almighty the time is always "now," He is sometimes merciful and gives another opportunity. Joel asked the question, "Who knoweth if he will return and repent...?" (Joel 2:14).

In chapter 20 of II Kings, Hezekiah was told to set his house in order, for he was going to die. Hezekiah prayed and wept before the Lord. Note how God wonderfully answered his prayer: "I have heard thy prayer, I have seen thy tears: behold, I will heal thee.... And I will add unto thy days fifteen years" (vss. 5,6). God gave Hezekiah a respite of fifteen years because of a contrite heart.

The city of Nineveh was under the judgment of God because of her wickedness. The command of the Lord to Jonah was, "Arise, go to Nineveh, that great city, and cry against it; for their wickedness is come up before me"

(Jonah 1:2). Under the apocalyptic preaching of the fiery prophet, great revival broke out in the city. Note Jonah 3:9,10 as the prophet cries out:

*"Who can tell if God will turn and repent, and turn away from his fierce anger, that we perish not?*

*"And God saw their works, that they turned from their evil way; and God repented of the evil, that he had said that he would do unto them; and he did it not."*

Nineveh, the doomed city of despair, was spared because of the repentance of the people.

America has a chance if she will accept the prognosis of Isaiah as to her spiritual condition and apply the remedy for her wretched condition as found in Isaiah 1:16-20:

*"Wash you, make you clean; put away the evil of your doings from before mine eyes; cease to do evil;*

*"Learn to do well; seek judgment, relieve the oppressed, judge the fatherless, plead for the widow.*

*"Come now, and let us reason together, saith the Lord: though your sins be as scarlet, they shall be as white as snow; though they be red like crimson, they shall be as wool.*

*"If ye be willing and obedient, ye shall eat the good of the land:*

*"But if ye refuse and rebel, ye shall be devoured with the sword: for the mouth of the Lord hath spoken it."*

There it is in plain language—if America is going to survive, she must "be willing and obedient"; otherwise, Isaiah declares, she shall be "devoured." The Almighty has laid down the conditions. Will we meet them?

> **Once to every man and nation**
> **Comes the moment to decide,**
> **In the strife of truth with falsehood**
> **For the good or evil side.**
>
> —James Russell Lowell

There is a cure for sin; it is found in the blood of the Lamb. The Prophet Jeremiah asked, "Is there no balm in Gilead; is there no physician there? why then is not the health of the daughter of my people recovered?" (Jer. 8:22). Yes, the Great Physician declares, "There is a balm in Gilead that can heal the sinsick soul."

For a nation to refuse that wonderful cure is to commit suicide!

## ENDNOTES:

[1]Paul L. Maier, *The Flames of Rome*, 433, 434.

[2]David Wise and Thomas B. Ross, *The Espionage Establishment*, 294.

[3]Paul Blumberg, *Inequality in an Age of Decline*, 3.

[4]John F. Walvoord and John E. Walvoord, *Armageddon, Oil and the Middle East Crisis*, 55.

[5]John F. Walvoord, *Nations in Prophecy*, 173.

[6]*Ibid.*, 175.

[7]Perry C. Cotham, *Politics, Americanism, and Christianity*, 234.

[8]Herbert J. Muller, *The Uses of the Past*, x.

# Epilogue

All suicide is tragic. Life is that valuable entity given to man from his Creator. To definitely forfeit it is to face the judgment of God. Suicide among nations is the same. If a nation turns its back on God, ultimately God has no choice but to bring judgment.

Over sixty years ago *The Bible Champion* was the name of a monthly periodical devoted "to maintain the historic faith of the church in the divine inspiration and authority of the Bible as the Word of God." In the July issue of 1928 there appeared an article by Dr. George Boddis entitled "The Hand of God in Human History." The author states three lessons every nation should learn:

1. God alone is the true protection of a country;
2. Neither nations nor individuals can sin without impunity;
3. In every national crisis God is the only safe Guide of a people.

It is our privilege and sacred responsibility to live in these perilous days—"and who knoweth whether [we are] come to the kingdom for such a time as this?" (Esther 4:14).

Nate Saint, missionary martyr of South America, wrote in his diary: "I would rather die than live a life of oblivious ease in so sick a world." Our task as believers is to be faithful where the Lord has placed us.

> When Pompeii was destroyed, there were very many buried in the ruins of it who were afterwards found in very different situations. There were some found who were in the streets, as if they had been attempting to make their escape. There were some found in deep vaults, as if they had gone thither for security. There were some found in lofty chambers; but where did they find the Roman sentinel? They found him standing at the city gate with his hand still grasping the war weapon, where he had been placed by his captain; and there, while the heavens threatened him; there,

while the earth shook beneath him; there, while the lava stream rolled, he had stood at his post; and there, after a thousand years had passed away, was he found. So let Christians stand to their duty, in the post at which their Captain has placed them.

—Author Unknown

The words of Amy Carmichael are appropriate: "We have all eternity to celebrate the victories, but only a few hours before sunset to win them."

Eventually we all bow to the sovereignty of God. The future of nations and individuals is in the hands of our Maker. Dr. Graham Scroggie declared that it was better to have a sane pessimism than a blind optimism—which pessimism, after all, is a sane realism. "The clearer sight we have of the sovereignty and power of God, the less we shall fear the calamities of this earth."

The psalmist offers to the redeemed and to the nations of the world the promise: "Our God shall come, and shall not keep silence" (50:3). I like how someone stated it: "How glorious to know that God is not sitting off in some distant corner of Heaven with His finger in His mouth pouting because Satan and sin have taken over His world. No! God is still sovereign! He is reigning over His creation; and in His own time, He will redeem it from the curse of Satan and sin."

The immutable God is our refuge. "Thou art the same, and thy years shall not fail" (Heb. 1:12). The splendor and glory of Babylon, Greece and Rome faded with time. Their ancient stones and ruins confirm the eternal verity of the Word of God. "For ever, O Lord, thy word is settled in heaven" (Ps. 119:89). With the passing of these empires, the most magnificent city of all the ages and Christ's literal kingdom are yet to appear.

"And I saw a new heaven and a new earth: for the first heaven and the first earth were passed away; and there was no more sea.

"And I John saw the holy city, new Jerusalem, coming down from God out of heaven. . . .

"And I heard a great voice out of heaven saying, Behold, the tabernacle of God is with men, and he will dwell with them, and they shall be his people. . . . "—Rev. 21:1-3.

# addendum

## Sodom and Gomorrah Revisited

The awful curse of AIDS has descended upon America like a plague. Isaac Asimov in his book, *A Choice of Catastrophes,* describes the Black Death of the 14th century as "devastating cities, countryside, whole nations, killing a third of the population of Europe and Asia 'convincing those that had not died that the end of the world was effectively at hand.'" In today's language "a full-scale nuclear war might not equal it." Another plague threatens us today. "As many as 100 million could die of AIDS worldwide before the end of the century—about one in every 500 people on earth."

"The United States is threatened by a plague which is sweeping through the sodomite and drug addict communities. It is expanding with geometric progression." "AIDS will kill more Americans than Korea and Vietnam." "Daily 10,000 are infected with the dreaded killer." "There is an AIDS death every 12 minutes." "We now spend more on AIDS than any other ailment, more than cancer and heart disease which claim 12 to 15 times as many victims." "The typical AIDS patient can run up hospital tabs of $2,000 every day and total bills of more than $200,000." "In many areas the number of persons affected with AIDS is at least 100 times greater than the cases reported."

The awful scourge is not to be taken lightly. Moody Adams in his book, *AIDS—You Just Think You Are Safe,* warns: "The Statue of Liberty will become the most expensive tombstone in history. . . . AIDS is the torture racks of Inquisition, the bone-crushing lions in Rome's amphitheater, and Hitler's Auchwitz, all rolled in one. AIDS is pain, pain, horrible pain, unrelenting pain. . . . There is no end to the catastrophic chronicle of pain."

As Christians our hearts should show deep, tender compassion for these unfortunate ones. We should minister to them with a warm spirit of empathy. It is tragic that innocent ones are also victims. We must be understanding.

Some assert that this dreaded disease has nothing to do with God's judgment. In fact, they go out of their way to defend almost the homosexuals. One dying AIDS victim declared, "God is too good to punish me for what I've done." This seems to be the reasoning of many. It is true that God will forgive the sins of the homosexual, but there is a penalty to be paid for its perversion. There is ample evidence in medical science.

The AIDS crisis is a spiritual problem. Of course it is true that, "If God is dead, everything is permitted." The floodgates of sexual perversion have been let down, and our nation is drowning in its awful consequence. Moody Adams explains, "The success of the AIDS epidemic is largely a result of demon slavery. Men become helpless to their passions." Such lewd conduct is the result of "walking in the gutters" of life. "When the genie of unclouded lust is out of the battle, the results are too horrible to contemplate." Human life then becomes very cheap.

Rus Walton asks: "Is AIDS a plague from God? His holy Word would indicate that it is, as are syphilis, gonorrhea, genital herpes, and a host of other diseases that are basically transmitted by sinful acts which are so rampant throughout the world in these days. . . . God's laws for sex cannot be broken any more than His laws of gravity. . . . So the innocent suffer with the guilty? In some cases, yes. . . . Is our nation—indeed the whole world—in danger? Yes. For the Lord does indeed hold a society responsible for allowing such immoralities to take hold and proliferate" (*Biblical Solutions to Contemporary Problems: a Handbook*). America must confront the plague of AIDS.

The Bible is plain in its warning against sexual perversion. In the Old Testament the penalty was death (Lev. 20:13). In the New Testament the Apostle Paul wrote, "For this cause God gave them up unto vile affections. . . And likewise also the men, leaving the natural use of the woman, burned in their lust one toward another; men with men working that which is unseemly, and receiving in themselves that recompence of their error which was meet" (Rom. 1:26, 27).

San Francisco and Sodom and Gomorrah have much in common. It is reported that the Bay City has "the highest concentration of gay people with no parallel in history." It should be noted Sodom and Gomorrah did not have a tomorrow, for "the time of their visitation" was over. They were utterly destroyed by fire and brimstone (Gen. 19:24). Such a catastrophe should be an object lesson to the Hollywood crowd, the radical left, the liberal talk show hosts, yes, even those in high places in our government!

Mark it down: America will be judged by the Almighty for its sexual perversions.

## Has the Ferocious Bear Become a Harmless Cub?

There is much rejoicing that our generation has been privileged to witness the apparent fall of communism. Christians are pleased that the barriers have been broken down and the gospel message is now proclaimed in countries and areas that have long been closed.

However, such good fortune should be greeted with guarded optimism. "There are those who believe that the Russian bear can be turned into a harmless pet."

We are confronted with a dilemma: A barking and snarling dog with its tail wagging encircled a frightened boy. He was admonished, "Don't be afraid; can't you see his tail is wagging?"

To which the boy replied, "Yes, but I don't know which end to believe." Kruschev once exclaimed, "Do not believe that we have forgotten Marx, Engels and Lenin. They will not be forgotten until shrimp learn to sing."

An Hungarian novelist warned, "Communism is dead, but communists are still alive. Nothing is more dangerous than people who cease to believe the idea but are still defending the spoils." Years ago Lenin predicted: "The capitalists of the world and their governments, in pursuit of conquest of the Soviet market, will close their eyes to the indicated higher reality and thus will turn into deaf-mute blindness. They will extend credits, which will strengthen us for the Communist Party in their countries and, giving us the materials and technology we lack, they will restore our military industry, indispensable for our future attack on our supplies. In other words, they will labor for the preparations of their own suicide." This prediction has come true.

America has experienced a gigantic period of brainwashing. We have been conditioned to a liberal point of view. Writing in his book, *In the Arena*, former President Richard Nixon explains: "It is a result of the influence of commentators, columnists, and other opinion leaders who always took the line that the Soviet threat was overstated. . . . In larger part it is a result of the fact that it is more pleasant to imagine living in a world that is calm and safe rather than one that is fraught with tension and danger."

The Soviet Union has been described as "a nation of illusion, delusion, and collusion." The communist camel under the guise of socialism has been sneaking its head into the government of our land with the determined intention of taking it over. We are in the process of becoming a socialized state. Charles Burnham once stated that "the only difference between a communist and a liberal is the communist knows what he is doing." It has been said, "Socialism is workable only in Heaven where it is not needed and in Hell where they've already got it." "A communist is a socialist with a gun in his hand." "Communism is the same as socialism with a happy face." But face the facts:

"Socialism has provided the world with nothing more than famine, fear and chronic backwardness."

Dr. D. James Kennedy sounds out a warning, "These goals for attaining a communist state are frightening when one recognizes how close our nation has drifted toward the same social and economic philosophies that are practiced in communist-controlled countries."

Discernment is needed. Divine wisdom should be the portion of every Christian. Someone has observed, "If you pretend that the avalanche is not there, you may die happily convinced that the boulders that bury you are only little pebbles dropped by passing birds." The Russian newspaper, *Pravda,* boldly declared, "The purpose of the Soviet Union is the complete and final victory of communism on a world scale."

In the interest of peace we should be ready for war. Remember Lenin boasted, "Peace treaties are like pie crusts—made to be broken." The Red Bear has always considered the weakness of the enemy as its greatest ally. Our naive generation should heed the words of Solzhenitsyn, "There has never been on this entire planet and in all history a regime more cruel, more bloody and at times more clever.... Only force can soften or make the Soviet system. The entire system rests on brutal force and thus it recognizes only brutal force." "For when they shall say, Peace and safety; then sudden destruction cometh upon them..." (I Thess. 5:3).

The prophetic Word reveals that Russia has yet a rendezvous with the Almighty!

## Lord, Have Mercy!

America needs to cry out for the mercy of God. Jeremiah, the weeping prophet, stated the condition of our country: "It is of the Lord's mercies that we are not consumed..." (Lam. 3:22).

It is time to face reality. A leading columnist asks, "Is this the Eagle's last scream?" A noted clergyman has responded, "The scream of the Eagle has become the twittering of the frightened sparrow."

Our nation demands strong, courageous spiritual leaders. Instead we have "little men riding horses that go nowhere." Paul Harvey writes, "When small men cast long shadows, the sun is about to set." The Greeks have an expression, "The fish rots from the head down." We desperately need the type of leaders who governed America in its early days. King David stated a divine principle, "He that ruleth over men must be just, ruling in the fear of God" (II Sam. 23:3).

"There seem to be two forces at work in the present destruction of America, ignorance and immorality" (Charley Reese). Someone has quipped (and rightly so), "The man in the moon has to hold his nose when passing over America." We are suffering from "constipation of the mind" and "spiritual leprosy of the soul." Our music reveals a decadent ulceration. George Wills described modern rock music as "America's slide into the sewer." Dr. Joyce Brothers claims that "50% of all congressmen visit a brothel or have call girls." No wonder some insist that our country is rapidly becoming a second-rate nation.

It is noteworthy that this generation has experienced "the eclipse of God." The famous Billy Sunday would "turn over in his grave" if he were to witness our spiritual decline. He once thundered from the pulpit, "The rivers of America will run with blood before we submit to them taking the Bible out of our schools." And what has happened in our day? A national syndicated columnist has pointed out: "There can be no manger scene at city hall, no prayer at public high school graduations, no posting of the Ten Commandments on a public school bulletin board, no prayers to open the school day—not even a 'moment of silence' if the intent is to allow kids to pray." To be consistent we should stop minting on our coins "In God We Trust." We don't want God; we've given Him the boot! And thus we are on a collision course with the Sovereign of the universe!

Demonic forces seem to have taken control of our great nation. McCandlish Phillips in his book, *The Spirit World,* comments: "Satan is, at the moment, having a kind of heyday in America. . . . For a very long time Satan softened up the nation for the present moral and spiritual attack by drawing the Bible and its powerful words further and further away from the center of American life. . . . The tide of idolatry, immorality, impurity, lawlessness, perversion, and false supernaturalism comes upon a people after they have been persuaded to trade the truth of God for a lie, and that is happening in America today."

A. W. Tozer penned, "Future historians will record that we of the 20th century had intelligence to create a great civilization but not the moral wisdom to preserve it." Solzhenitsyn, with years of experience in a Siberian Gulag, wrote, "To destroy a country you must first cut its roots. America's roots have, in a large measure, been severed." A nation that doesn't fear God doesn't have a chance (Rom. 3:18). "The deadliest of sins is the consciousness of no sin" (Thomas Carlyle). How can we be so blind!

While the Ship of State is sinking, we are as busy as beavers arranging the chairs on deck. The ecclesiastical leaders of our day warn against being "negative" and with syrup-like demeanor insist that "everything is wonderful." This is no time for naivety or neutrality. Tragically, "There are some who are so neutral that they don't even have a blood type." Chiang Kai-Shek remarked, "No nation can ruin us, unless we ruin ourselves." We have traveled far down that precarious road. "Responsibility involves accountability." Will we be remembered as a nation that sold its soul for a saturnalia of "wine, women and song"? What have we done with our greatness? John Dryden wrote, "Beware the fury of a patient man." God's patience is about to come to an end. He is about to lay bare His arm in terrible judgment!

"No man loves his alarm clock," but the alarm clock is ringing in our nation. This could be our final hour. Our survival depends upon whether or not we wake up in time. Abraham Lincoln challenged a divided country with these historic words of hope: ". . . that this nation, under God, shall have a new birth of freedom, and that government of the people, by the people, and for the people, shall not perish from the earth."

"History is largely a spiritual story." The great historian Will Durant concluded, "The greatest question of our times is not communism versus individualism, not Europe versus America, not even the East versus the West; it is whether men can live without God."

"This is a day when man is judging and God is silent," but "Our God shall come, and shall not keep silence" (Ps. 50:3).

*Maranatha!*

*"O Israel, thou hast destroyed thyself; but in me is thine help."*—Hosea 13:9.

Austin L. Sorenson

For a complete list of books available from the Sword of the Lord, write to Sword of the Lord Publishers, P. O. Box 1099, Murfreesboro, Tennessee 37133.